K2

THE 1939 TRAGEDY

K2

THE 1939 TRAGEDY

Andrew J. Kauffman
and
William L. Putnam

THE MOUNTAINEERS
DIADEM BOOKS

5 4 3 2
5 4 3 2 1

Published in the U.S. by The Mountaineers, 1011 SW Klickitat Way, Seattle, Washington 98134.

Published simultaneously in Great Britain by Diadem Books, London. All trade enquires U.K., Europe and Commonwealth (except Canada) to Hodder and Stoughton, Mill Road, Dunton Green, Sevenoaks, Kent TN132YA

Manufactured in the United States of America

Edited by Linda Gunnarson
Maps by Dee Molenaar; typography by The Typeworks
Cover design by Elizabeth Watson; book design by Barbara Bash

Cover photograph: K2 from the south (© Greg Child). Inset: Official photo of the K2 1939 expedition members, from *left* to *right*, standing: George Sheldon, Chappell Cranmer, Jack Durrance, George "Joe" Trench; seated: Eaton O. (Tony) Cromwell, Fritz Wiessner, Dudley Wolfe. (Durrance collection)
Frontispiece: Summit of K2 by Dee Molenaar

Library of Congress Cataloging in Publication Data
Kauffman, Andrew J.
    K2: the 1939 tragedy / Andrew J. Kauffman and William L. Putnam.
    p. cm.
    Includes bibliographical references and index
    ISBN 0-89886-323-6 (U.S. and Canada)
    1. Mountaineering – Pakistan – K2 (Mountain) – History.   2. K2 (Pakistan: Mountain) – Description and travel. 3. American Karakoram Expedition (2nd : 1939) I. Putnam, William Lowell.   II. Title.
GV199.44.P182K18268   1992
796.5'22'095491 – dc20   92 – 19176
                                                                    CIP

British Library Cataloguing in Publication Data
Kauffman, Andrew
    K2: 1939 Tragedy--The Full Story of the
    Ill-fated Wiessner Expedition
    I. Title II. Putnam, William L.
    915.46
    ISBN 0-906371-69-4 (U.K.)

To our friends and teachers,
Bob and Miriam Underhill,
and Ken Henderson

ACKNOWLEDGMENTS

THE AUTHORS WISH TO EXPRESS THEIR GRATITUDE to several persons, all of whom contributed materially to the creation of this book and without whose assistance this story could never have been fully told:

Robert Hicks Bates, for correcting certain factual errors and for suggestions that have helped improve the text's readability.

Henry Welty Coulter, for early and ongoing interest in this project and for successfully persuading his brother-in-law, John Randall Durrance, to make available his diary to the authors.

Chappell Cranmer, for providing access to his photograph collection.

John Randall Durrance, for entrusting us with the original text of his diary, without which certain critical events that took place during the 1939 American Karakoram Expedition to K2 would remain unclear and incorrectly interpreted.

Linda Gunnarson, for her hard work as manuscript editor.

Kenneth Atwood Henderson, for supplying the authors with material and comments about the American Alpine Club's reactions to the outcome of the expedition and for his recollections of the spirit of the times.

William Pendleton House, for an interview with one of the authors and for his penetrating observations about the expedition leader's personality.

Charles Snead Houston, for his advice and suggestions concerning the medical aspects of high-altitude mountaineering.

Dudley Francis Rochester, for genealogical comments about the Wolfe family and for furnishing a motion-picture film taken on the expedition by his uncle, Dudley Francis Wolfe.

Jean Sheldon, for providing access to George Sheldon's photograph collection.

Andrew Wiessner, for his reading and critique of an early manuscript of this undertaking and for furnishing further comments and quotations from his father's original diary of the expedition.

Fritz Hermann Ernst Wiessner, our friend and teacher, an honorary member of almost every alpine society of consequence in the world, now deceased but inscribed in the authors' memories, who gave us typescript copies of his expedition diary, correspondence in the field among various members of the expedition, himself included, a typescript English-language translation of his German book on the venture, numerous post-expedition statements and documents by officials and members of the American Alpine Club, several taped interviews, and additional material both written and oral for our use in an undertaking that was in its embryonic stage during his lifetime.

CONTENTS

PREFACE

THERE ARE A NUMBER OF CELEBRATED MYSTERIES in the history of alpinism: Was the rope cut on the first descent of the Matterhorn on July 14, 1865? Did George Mallory and Andrew Irvine complete their ascent of Mount Everest on June 8, 1924? And exactly what went wrong on the 1939 American Karakoram Expedition to K2, the world's second-highest summit?

People behave strangely under the stress of high altitude, and as in military conflict, detached reflection is seldom to be expected when crisis after crisis bears down with the suddenness of an avalanche. The 1939 American K2 expedition was a serious tragedy even by the standards of a later generation hardened to war and more willing to accept the risks of high-altitude combat against nature.

But in the context of the day, and with the seeming reticence of the key players to be candid and completely forthcoming with all available evidence, uncertainties inevitably arose as to who did what and who could be held accountable for the death of one American climber and three heroic Sherpas in a tragic outcome to what came so close to being a shining hour in mountaineering history.

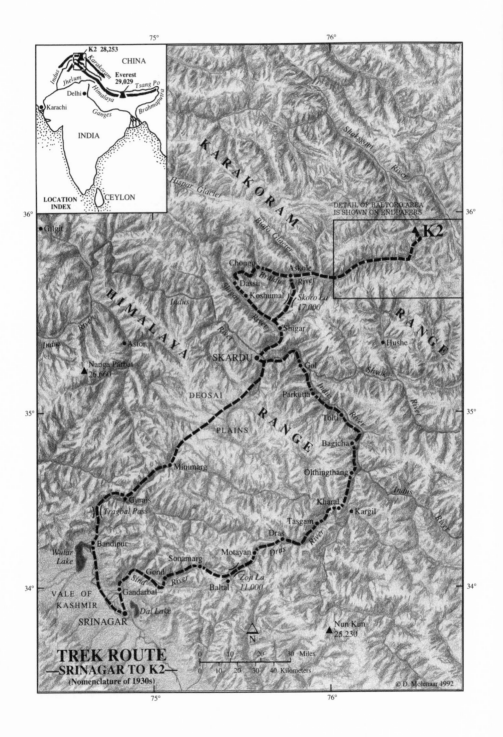

TREK ROUTE
—**SRINAGAR TO K2**—
(Nomenclature of 1930s)

© D. Molenaar 1992

INTRODUCTION

THIS IS THE TRUE STORY of a mountaineering expedition that took place more than half a century ago, so far in the past of a rapidly evolving sport that one might almost begin with the words "Once upon a time." Parts of the story have been recounted so often that this narrative may seem redundant. But recently revealed primary source material has clarified many questions raised by earlier accounts and proves that certain matters once accepted as fact are at least dubious and in some cases simply wrong.

Indeed, there has long been an aura of mystery surrounding the catastrophe that terminated the 1939 American Karakoram Expedition to K2. As long after the event as 1961, the great Italian mountaineer, journalist, and Tibetologist Fosco Maraini described the story as "one of the worst tragedies in the climbing history of the Himalaya, and it is one on which no full light has ever been shed."[1]

By one interpretation, the expedition anticipates modern mountaineering, wherein the players take big risks to achieve big goals. But since it took place in an era when the prevailing alpine philosophy emphasized safety more than success, the venture should be judged in accordance with the spirit of those times, for most of its participants espoused that belief. Yet one, the expedition leader, foresaw the future. Those who disregard traditional safety rules or, more especially, the weaknesses of their comrades, would do well to study the story; even those of less daring persuasion who wish to lead a party into the world's wild places can learn object lessons from the narrative. Finally, the expedition remains to this day one of the most complex, dramatic, and gripping mountain adventures of all time.

A fascinating aspect of this expedition, one that sets it apart from most others, is that the grim tragedy in which it ended did not result from a single event, but rather from a chain of circumstances, all of which contributed first to the expedition's failure and then to the subsequent tragedy. Some events, of course, had more importance than others, but all played a role.

Side by side with the first chain of events there developed another, which led to the bitter quarrel that arose after the expedition members returned. These two chains became so intricately intertwined that they could never be fully unraveled.

Older climbers – and some young ones as well – know the general facts, even if not the details. Until recently, most of us accepted with few doubts what has become the conventional interpretation of events – the parts told again and again by sundry mountaineering historians. We also came to know and hold in admiration the leader – Fritz Wiessner – a man who, we felt, had received more than his share of unfair criticism after the expedition, taking a bum rap for its failure and for his, at the time, unpopular national background. A generation later, after the events recounted herein and because of Wiessner's other great mountaineering achievements, the authors of this book campaigned vigorously and, in the end, successfully for his election to honorary membership in the American Alpine Club. Almost two decades after that, we embarked for a while on a project to write his biography, focusing attention on the 1939 K2 expedition and its unhappy consequences. Our project was altered in midstream when we found that some elements of Wiessner's account of events on K2 were simply not in accord with reality. And when we were denied access to some of his original sources of documentation, our desire for truth overrode our desire to memorialize our old friend.

Somewhat simplified, the conventionally accepted story runs as follows. Fritz Wiessner, leader of the 1939 expedition to K2, a man who is a superb climber and an inspiring leader, together with a Sherpa porter and another expedition member, Dudley Wolfe, attempt to climb the final slopes of the world's second-highest mountain, and, next to Everest, the highest unclimbed summit. On the first try Wiessner reaches a point less than 800 feet (250 meters) below his goal, but then finds he must turn back to carry up additional supplies. Upon descending to the lower camps the three men discover them deserted, with all valuables gone. Wiessner has been betrayed by young climber Jack Durrance and a Sherpa porter, who, for unexplained reasons and on their own authority, have stripped the camps. This action not only causes the venture to fail, but initiates catastrophe – specifically, the deaths of Dudley Wolfe and three Sherpas.

So goes the commonly believed story. The truth, it turns out, is somewhat different.

The more that inquisitive, skeptical, but knowledgeable persons studied the story, the more they ran into missing pieces. The expedition had ended with the loss of four lives and numerous other casualties – frostbite, concussion from stonefall, broken ribs, and more. However, unlike most other mountain tragedies, where catastrophe results from a single event, this expedition's unhappy outcome depended on a long and sometimes loosely related sequence of events. After studying the facts of this celebrated venture, interested parties found that much of the accepted version didn't fit; there were just too many inconsistencies, omissions, unanswered questions, and sheer mystery involved. Some questions were mired in confusion, while the resolution of others depended on interpretation. The principal source for latter-day historians consisted of material, supplied by Fritz Wiessner, that could not always be checked against other testimony. Much of the written data he furnished had been reworked in the years after the event; even those portions of his diary released to the authors of this book were typed copies of the original, handwritten text. No one doubted Wiessner's good faith, but any serious researcher prefers access to original data. Other survivors of the adventure seemed reluctant to talk because they did not wish to rekindle the controversy that arose from the expedition's failure, or, at least in one case, to protect a friend. On top of this, more than a few influential and concerned older members of the climbing community expressed the opinion the subject was best left where it lay and not revived.

For our part, we, as writers, could not forget the story. It burned in our minds. One day, unexpectedly, one of us received a long, handwritten document: a diary. One look at it and the identity of the sender – Jack Durrance – were all that was needed. Here was primary source material, new evidence. We began to read, and the pieces of the puzzle fell, one after another, into place. Put together with previously collected material, this document enabled us to confirm or refute many allegations. We then turned to another unrealized source of fact.

ROUGHLY SPEAKING, TWO VERSIONS OF EVENTS leading to the 1939 K2 tragedy have at one time or another enjoyed acceptance. Early on, the bulk of the criticism descended on the leader. People charged that Fritz Wiessner violated the norms of accepted mountaineering conduct. Then, with the emergence of more liberal climbing attitudes, the blame shifted to Jack Durrance, who was accused of having acted thoughtlessly and negligently. In time Wiessner obtained almost complete absolution from historians, as well as acclaim for his excellence as a climber and his contribution to mountain sports. Captivated by his climbing skill, writers tended to overlook his leadership record. Then, with only the flimsiest of evidence, they directed their accusations toward Durrance, a subordinate on K2 who had no role in the administration of the venture and very little as a decision-maker. Like some of the accusations leveled at Wiessner immediately after the expedition, these charges, in the absence of proof, were also unfair.

Where did the truth lie?

Back in 1940, the American Alpine Club's committee of inquiry into the conduct of the expedition faced a dilemma. If it took a stand for or against leader Wiessner, however justified, it would exacerbate what had become a divisive and vicious controversy. In the interests of peace, the committee issued a bland, noncommittal statement. The action had the desired effect; slowly the quarrel died down. Not so the bitterness. Nor did the committee's action represent justice.

Would it be of interest, would it serve any purpose, to revive the story? Much can be done with any tale that combines mystery, tragedy, human frailties, courage, leadership, hardship, peril, and death in one of the most magnificent and inhospitable settings on Earth. And this tale is an especially dramatic one: a leader, in all apparent ways a giant of a mountaineer, towering over inadequate companions, so committed to his quest that he makes no allowance for their weaknesses, while those same companions, all men of good will, lack the right stuff to meet the challenge and literally fall by the wayside. Then, at the moment of truth, a stranded participant and three loyal and dedicated servants who go to his rescue disappear forever among the mountain's storms and precipices.

But why bother to rehash a story whose broad outlines are known? Why set out to correct the innumerable factual errors found in virtually every available account? For two important reasons: truth and justice. They are the reasons this book was written. Surely a man who has endured unfair accusations for half a century and has never recriminated deserves to be heard. And, more important, now that additional source materials have been released for review and analysis, a fuller and more accurate account of the expedition is possible.

The story that follows is that of the 1939 American Karakoram Expedition to K2, its team members, and its leader, Fritz Wiessner, in large part as witnessed at the time on a day-to-day basis by John Randall Durrance and corroborated in critical areas by the firsthand and dispassionate analysis of the American Consul in Calcutta, Edward Miller Groth.

Authors' Caveat to the Reader

In the following text the reader may find a few instances where place and proper names vary or do not correspond with those on modern maps. In many cases both proper and place names are based on local languages with alphabets different from the Roman and therefore subject to translator interpretation. We have tried to be as consistent as possible, but there may be some minor transgressions. The matter is further complicated by the fact that in 1939 the area where the events we relate took place was under British rule; therefore, certain terms of Asian origin were Anglicized.

The same applies to altitudes. In our case we have adhered to those provided by Fritz Wiessner in his official report to the American Alpine Club, which appears as an Appendix to this work. Later visitors to the Baltoro, notably Ardito Desio, have made some modifications. Most important of the divergences is that the 1938 Camp I was situated on the Godwin-Austen Glacier, whereas the 1939 Camp I was located some 500 feet higher, at the site of the Italian 1909 camp.

K2
28,253

Highest point reached
(27,500)

West Ridge

South Ridge

East Ridge

IX 26,050

Shoulder 25,600

VIII 25,300

VII 24,700

VI 23,400

V 22,000

House Chimney 21,600

IV 21,500

SOUTH

SOUTHEAST

FACE

III 20,700

R I D G E

IIa 20,000

II 19,300

A B R U Z Z I

FACE

I 18,000

K2 FROM SOUTHEAST

To Base Camp
(16,500)

© D. Molenaar 1992

1

THE CHALLENGE

I N THE 1939 ISSUE of the *American Alpine Journal,* somewhat belatedly, there appeared the following notice:

> Second American Karakoram Expedition. *In continuance of the excellent work of last year's American Alpine Club Expedition to K2, a second party will leave for Kashmir, sailing from New York on March 17th. The members of the party are: Chappell Cranmer, Denver, Colorado; Eaton Cromwell, New York City; Bestor Robinson, Oakland, Calif.; Dudley F. Wolfe, Boston, Mass.; Fritz H. Wiessner, New York City, leader. As a sixth member the party hopes to include either John Durrance, Hanover, N.H., or George Sheldon, Hanover, N.H. A British Army Officer who is stationed in Kashmir will accompany the Expedition as Transport Officer.*
>
> *The members will arrive in Bombay on April 10th and proceed immediately to Srinagar. After their arrival in Srinagar, the group plans to ski and climb in the lower Himalayan ranges around Srinagar for a period of about three weeks and then proceed to the foot of K2 during May, arriving on the mountain by the end of May. Nine Sherpa coolies[1] from the Darjeeling district have been engaged to help the party in the high altitude work on the mountain and local Kashmir porters will be used for the transport work during the march to the mountain.[2]*

Short, terse, not particularly informative, and containing several minor errors, the American Alpine Club notice limited itself to the bare essentials. It gave no description of the mountain and a cursory introduction of the men who would step upon it—hardly anything, in fact, about the expedition's leader, Fritz Wiessner. Nor was there any update that, by the time of publication, Bestor Robinson had decided not to go and that George Sheldon and Jack Durrance had definitely been invited–the first by Wiessner and the second by officers of the American Alpine Club–to come aboard.

Who, then, were these men intent on embarking on an uncertain and perilous adventure? What, too, was K2, and what was its history? Why did its ascent seem important enough to persuade six men to journey halfway around the world, abandon normal occupations, and sacrifice half a year of their lives in so distant and difficult a quest?

To understand these things it is necessary to go back to the beginning.

THERE EXIST FOURTEEN MOUNTAINS in the world whose altitudes surpass 8000 meters (26,247 feet), a magic and arbitrary figure devised by mountaineers in a somewhat vain effort to separate the adults from the children. Without exception, these lofty summits belong to the Himalayan chain (ten) and to its northwestern extension, the Karakoram (four), the two ranges being separated only by the deep gap formed by the Indus River, which over the ages has carved a gorge through the mountains.

As most people know, Mount Everest (called Sagarmatha by the Nepalese and Chomolungma by the Tibetans) in the east-central Himalaya on the border of Nepal and Tibet is the world's highest summit at 29,029 feet (8848 meters). Less well known, though increasingly notorious in recent years, is Everest's giant Karakoram rival, K2, only 776 feet lower at 28,253 feet (8611 meters). Indeed there was a brief period in 1988 when some geographers contended the topography of much of the Karakoram had been miscalculated and that, in fact, K2 was actually some 500 feet (152 meters) higher than Everest. More recent and careful studies revealed, however, that the original triangulations of the two mountains had been close to correct, with possible variations of only a dozen or so feet.

Whatever the true altitudes, most alpinists consider K2, more than any other 8000er, the "mountain of mountains" and, for those who know both, a greater challenge than Everest in all respects except altitude. If Everest is Asia's Mont Blanc (and almost twice as high), then K2 is its Matterhorn.[3]

Whoever wishes to glimpse K2 from the ground must have some mountaineering experience, or at least the benefit of experienced companions. Its summit towers over what is today the China-Pakistan border, far out of reach in the wild Karakoram, surrounded by a galaxy of protective satellites, and lost in a bleak wilderness that some explorers and cartographers have felt to be the end of the world.

In recent years jeep roads have slowly replaced footpaths on the approaches, and unlucky travelers who fall ill or are injured can, with minor delay, be hoisted out by helicopter. But in the 1930s things were more primitive. The jeep had not been invented; air service into the provincial town of Skardu, a flight that today cuts the approach time in half, was unheard of. The closest roadhead was Srinagar, capital of Kashmir, 330 miles (550 kilometers) and a month's walk from K2. Between lay the Deosai Desert of Baltistan, with canyons of mud, broken rock, falling stones, thundering torrents, and snow-blocked passes that formed the mountain's outer defenses. On the inner periphery were huge, hostile valley glaciers with toilsome moraines, hidden crevasses, giant water maelstroms, and other pitfalls. Add to this the normal perils of most arid, semitropical regions, esoteric diseases with strange names such as amoebiasis, filaria, salmonella, hepatitis, dengue fever, trachoma, and, of course, the more common plagues of cholera and tuberculosis, most of them still present if not so lethal.[4]

K2 had strong defenses.

As far as Askole, the last village, situated at 10,000 feet (3048 meters), some scarce local supplies were available–always, however, at the expense of the inhabitants' winter reserves. Beyond, for the final 60 miles (100 kilometers), there was–and still is–nothing. From Askole onward a party was totally dependent on its internal resources until it returned. It existed, as it were, in an isolated little world, one might even say a cocoon of its own. The countryside became ever more savage, like a vista on the moon, its twisted, tortured landscape an external manifestation of cataclysmic struggles deep beneath the earth's surface. All elements combined in hostility to life, and most of all to humans. Even today it is no country for the weak of heart.

Such is the countryside on the approaches to the Baltoro Glacier, the great river of ice, 40 miles long, that takes its source among Earth's highest snows and slowly bears them in frozen form to its terminus, where they emerge as churning, rushing, muddy waters to form a raging torrent called the Braldu.

The harshest of forces have their beauty. The Baltoro country is no exception, but the beauty is stark and severe. Even that jewel among mountains, K2, at the head of the Godwin-Austen Glacier, one of the Baltoro's remotest tributaries, is from every side more like a huge, uncut diamond than a polished stone. The facets, the cleavage, like those of the Matterhorn, are classic. But the structure, rather than gracefully slender, is massive, elemental, barely touched by the chisel of its Promethean creator.

What of the mountain's notoriety among people? As far as can be determined, it did not begin until after the mid-nineteenth century. In 1856 a Topographical Survey of India party, led by the Scots Lieutenant (later Colonel) T. G. Montgomerie, sighted the mountain, measured its altitude, and noted its coordinates. It was the second high point to be triangulated during Montgomerie's visit. He asked around but could find no local appellation. Accordingly, in conformance with the pattern of his studies, he labeled the mountain K (for Karakoram) and 2 (for the second summit measured): logical, practical, and unimaginative.[5]

In later years Europeans learned of local names – Chogori, Dapsang, Shinmang, Chiring, Laufafahad, and Lamba Pahar – and there were foreign proposals, some in what would today be considered in some quarters as bad taste, such as Godwin-Austen, Prince Albert, Montgomerie, and even the hard-to-pronounce Waugh. None stuck. What did was Montgomerie's original K2. Today, transliterated into local Balti as "Ketu," it stands, better than all the others, as a tribute to the mountain's stoic grandeur.

Decades passed. Few people knew of K2; fewer still saw it, even from great distances. It was just too far away. Rare, intrepid explorers came and went: Surveyor-Lieutenant Henry Godwin-Austen in 1861; Sir Francis Younghusband on an epic journey from Peking to Rawalpindi in 1887, the first Westerner to view K2 from the north; Sir William Martin Conway in 1892; and finally, on repeated occasions, those extraordinary Americans, Dr. William Workman and Fanny Bullock Workman. No sightseers.

From its first sighting by Europeans until 1939 only three attempts had been made to climb K2. Meanwhile there were eight expeditions to Everest and at least four to Kangchenjunga, the world's third-highest summit, north of, and visible from, Darjeeling.

The first effort, if it can be so called, was in 1902. The party was organized by Aleister Crowley, of British nationality (and later known most commonly for his occult activities), and included Guy J. F. Knowles and Oscar Eckenstein, both British; Dr. Jules Jacot-Guillarmod, a Swiss; and a pair of thirty-two-year-old Austrians, Heinrich Pfannl and his frequent climbing partner, Victor Wessely. The group employed no professional guides, something unusual for the times; but most members of the team, notably Crowley and the Austrians, were competent amateurs, with a number of startling ascents to their credit in the Alps. The party, like many of its successors, was delayed for political reasons – Eckenstein, in particular, being held up for weeks allegedly because of anti-Semitism on the part of highly placed members of the Alpine Club in London. The expedition also suffered from poor coordination, a frequent complication in international efforts; was unable to find a practical route; experienced personality disputes; and, above all, endured the unpredictable and thoroughly unbalanced character of Crowley. The group managed to get up the lower part of K2's Northeast Ridge, but not beyond.

The first serious attempt to climb K2 came seven years later, in 1909, and included more than one person whom Fritz Wiessner was to meet in later years. This was an elaborate Italian expedition, organized and led by the eminent alpinist and explorer Luigi Amadeo di Savoia, Duke of the Abruzzi, a member of Italy's royal family and a direct descendant of the dukes of Savoy, who for centuries had governed the areas surrounding the Graian and Pennine Alps. The duke espoused the principles of the post-Garibaldi and Mazzini generation, whose objective was to export the best that Italy had to offer and thereby contribute to the welfare and advancement of all humankind.

The duke was no greenhorn. He had conducted successful climbing ventures to Alaska's Mount St. Elias and to Africa's mysterious Mountains of the Moon.[6] He had organized and led an outstanding, pre-Peary effort to reach the North Pole. Like its predecessors, the 1909 expedition would be executed in princely style.

The duke brought along veteran companions as well as new ones. There was his deputy, Marquis Federico di Negrotto; the geographic writer Filippo de Filippi; four Courmayeur guides, Giuseppe and Lorenzo Petigax and Alessio and Enrico Brocherel; three apprentice guides from the same area; a Britisher and resident of Kashmir, A. C. Baines; a photographic assistant, Erminio Botta; and, as the party's crown jewel, Vittorio Sella, to this day regarded as the finest mountain photographer-artist of all time.

After a month's march from Srinagar, the expedition set up its base camp near the junction of the Sovia and Godwin-Austen glaciers (see map) at an elevation of about 16,500 feet (5028 meters). The duke scouted around a bit here and there. Then, together with the Courmayeur contingent and some cargo bearers, the party reconnoitered the Southeast (nowadays Abruzzi) Ridge, where, after several false starts, the guides reached about 20,340 feet (6199 meters). They disliked what they saw; the ridge was climbable, but it was far too long and steep for inexperienced Balti porters, and there seemed to be no decent campsites. Not practical, they said. It was, in short, beyond the era's "state of the art." The duke called off the effort.

What the duke could not know was that he and his guides had, in fact, pioneered what would one day become the favorite approach for mountaineers. Forty-five years later, by that very route, another gallant Italian team would be the first to tread the summit of K2.

Further reconnaissance took place. One party scaled the dangerous Savoia Glacier to the Savoia Saddle, at 21,871 feet (6666 meters). Another studied the Northeast Ridge. Reports from both were pessimistic. Clearly the ascent of K2 would be no picnic.

The duke turned south, toward more promising territory. There he personally reached 24,500 feet (7500 meters) on Bride Peak, now Chogolisa (25,122 feet; 7636 meters), only some 600 feet from the summit, before being turned back by fog and bad weather. This was the highest point on Earth yet reached by humans. The altitude record set by the duke would not be surpassed for thirteen years.

The expedition had done good work. Negrotto's photogrammetrically produced 1:100,000 map became the model for future cartography of the Karakoram. De Filippi's account of the journey is a classic of its kind.[7] Sella's photographs of K2, Broad Peak, wedge-shaped Gasherbrum IV, and the awesome Mustagh Tower are to this day treasured in the world's alpine museums.

Then came World War I, and a curtain descended over the Baltoro. Afterward, in the early 1920s, attention focused on the epic British struggles on the north side of Everest,[8] later on one international and two German efforts to climb Kangchenjunga,[9] and, finally, on the recurrent and ever more poignant catastrophes on Nanga Parbat.[10]

A few parties did visit the Baltoro. But the British then ruling India quite rightly discouraged those incursions because of the drain they caused on meager local resources. In 1929 there was a further scientific expedition, again Italian, under the Duke of Spoleto, this one following up on the 1914 study led by de Filippi. Then, in 1934, an international expedition under Austrian professor G. O. Dyhrenfurth reconnoitered the Upper Baltoro south of K2 and, including the leader's wife, Hettie,[11] climbed the various summits of Sia Kangri (24,350 feet; 7422 meters)[12] and reconnoitered Hidden Peak.[13] Finally, in 1936, a strong but unlucky French expedition to Hidden Peak was stopped by what was believed to be the early arrival of the monsoon.[14] That was all.

K2 was untouched. The duke's party had given it a mighty reputation; at a lecture in Milan in 1910, the duke had said, "If ever man sets foot on that crystalline head of K2, it won't be a climber, it will be an aviator." Those rare climbers who later laid eyes on it tended to agree. K2 would be a hard nut to crack.

MEANTIME, HALFWAY AROUND THE WORLD, in the United States, there was growing interest in expeditionary mountaineering. Behind it, of course, were traditional American influences–those of the pioneer spirit and the lure of the unknown, which could no longer be satisfied by "opening the West." There had been Mount McKinley (now again called Denali) with its frustrations, its triumphs, its tragedies, and even its imposters.[15] Then, in 1925, came an epic first ascent of the Yukon's Mount Logan, the second-highest summit of North America. It was, therefore, no surprise in 1930 to find a small nucleus of adventurous, amateur American climbers, mostly clustered around Harvard University. Best known in later years was the tenacious Bradford Washburn, who, with his tireless cohorts, kept leading trip after trip to the debatably named Fairweather Range above Alaska's Lituya Bay.[16] He learned much, often the hard way, but after 1933, Washburn and his friends were among the most experienced mountain expeditionaries in the world.

In early 1933, Terris Moore, Arthur Emmons, Richard Burdsall, and J. T. Young returned, somewhat battered, from a fantastic adventure into Szechwan, then a little-known part of southwestern China. Two of them had reached the summit of what was at the time China's highest peak, the second-highest mountain ever climbed, Minya Konka (24,891 feet; 7587 meters), now Gonga Shan. The trip had its casualty–Emmons lost his toes to frostbite–but the story of the odyssey stirred the blood of the small, enthusiastic band of young American climbers.[17]

The first major American participation in a Himalayan climbing venture took place in 1936. Adams Carter, Arthur Emmons (shorn of his toes but back on his feet), Charles Houston, and Farnsworth Loomis invited Britishers T. Graham Brown, Peter Lloyd, Noel Odell, and H. W. Tilman to attempt the first ascent of Nanda Devi (25,645 feet; 7816 meters). This was the highest mountain wholly within the British Empire, and its successful ascent by the Anglo-American party made it the loftiest summit scaled to that time. That record stood until Maurice Herzog and Louis Lachenal raised the French flag on Annapurna (26,545 feet; 8091 meters) on June 3, 1950, fourteen years later.

On January 23, 1937, the American Alpine Club (AAC) held its annual meeting in Boston. There were two main speakers. First was Charlie Houston, who, on an initial attempt, had been to less than 1000 feet (300 meters) below Nanda Devi's summit, only to succumb in camp that night to food poisoning from a punctured tin of corned beef. He held his audience spellbound for more than an hour with a description of the previous summer's exploits.

The other speaker was Fritz Wiessner, a respected member of the AAC. He gave a vivid account of his ascent of Mount Waddington, hitherto the highest (and no doubt most difficult) unclimbed major peak in provincial Canada.

FRITZ WIESSNER SEEMS TO HAVE BEEN THE ORIGINATOR of the plan for an American expedition to K2. There may have been other progenitors, but it does appear from conversations with him that he first approached Terris Moore and, more seriously, Dick Burdsall, then later the Harvard expeditionary crowd, notably Charlie Houston, by that time a medical student at Columbia University's College of Physicians and Surgeons. There was, of course, immediate enthusiasm, dampened only by the realities of fund-raising. Next, Wiessner went to the American Alpine

Club's president (later treasurer), Joel Ellis Fisher, who showed equal excitement. Sitting down together, the two, according to Wiessner, hammered out a formal application, filed through U.S. authorities, to attempt K2. The Department of State duly forwarded the request to British authorities in India and semi-independent Kashmir.[18]

In 1937, communications were slow. Most mail traveled by surface. Too, British colonial administrators in India, albeit highly competent, invariably exercised caution and therefore moved even more slowly than their modern subcontinent successors. Any application for a foreign expedition to visit a remote and sensitive frontier country was treated with skepticism. Months passed with no reply.

Finally, in November 1937, word came. To everyone's delight the application had been granted–for 1938, and with the understanding that if a first attempt were to fail, the permit would be renewed for 1939.

It had been expected that Wiessner would lead the 1938 party. Unfortunately he had important and urgent business commitments that year, and he did not like the prospect of organizing a party too hurriedly, which would have been the case since the permit arrived only in November 1937. Furthermore, over the years he had developed a habit of letting others make a first try at anything he had in mind; then, if they failed, he made his own attempt, all the more likely to succeed because he could take advantage of the experience of others. He had done it in Europe and on Canada's Mount Waddington; why not on K2?

As leader in his stead, Fritz suggested Charlie Houston, the American who had climbed highest on Nanda Devi. Not only an experienced expeditionary, Houston had already proven his leadership qualities when, as a very young man, he had organized a superb first ascent of Alaska's 17,400-foot (5300-meter) Mount Foraker. He was twenty-eight years old and well along in medical school, a real advantage for the expedition.

Fisher gave Houston his marching orders: he was "to complete the [duke's] reconnaissance of the mountain's ridges and, weather permitting, to make an attack on the summit."[19] In case of failure, Wiessner stood in the wings to take over in 1939.

Houston knew how to move fast. He recognized that in those depression years good men with time and money would be hard to find. But he had a nucleus: Robert H. Bates, twenty-eight, a teacher and veteran of several Alaskan trips–one of them particularly hair-raising–and Dick Burdsall, forty-two, who had climbed Minya Konka. He also enlisted India-based Captain Norman Streatfield as transport officer. Streatfield, a Scot and member of the Bengal Mountain Battery, possessed considerable experience at altitude.[20] Better yet, he had accompanied the 1936 French expedition up the Baltoro to Hidden Peak. Through Nanda Devi expedition member Farnsworth Loomis, who could not go, Houston recruited Paul Petzoldt, a sometime Teton mountain guide. But he needed at least one more man.

Houston called Bill House, who, at twenty-five, was past president of the Yale Mountaineering Club and had been Wiessner's sturdy companion on Devil's Tower, Waddington, and elsewhere. Reluctant at first, House yielded to persuasion.

Houston also recruited a team of six Sherpas, five of whom would return to K2 in 1939. They proved of immense help, even though only one, their sirdar, Pasang Kikuli, was allowed to climb high on the mountain.

Money proved a major problem. Most of the funds had to be raised from within. The rest appear to have come out of the pockets of two or three of the American Alpine Club's most affluent officials.[21]

Like all Himalayan expeditions before the era of global transport, Houston's party was gone a long time. It did more than had been expected, but less than some had secretly hoped. It was a highly competent, small, mobile, close-knit group; its members were cautious and meticulous. Few parties on any mountain have been more homogeneous: all except Petzoldt were already personal friends; they had had similar expedition experience; and all knew their mountaineering jobs.

After reaching the base of K2, the first problem was to follow the American Alpine Club's instructions and find a route. The men shuttled back and forth around the mountain's base in the duke's footsteps. First they tried the south and west flanks toward the Savoia Saddle (see map), where they were blocked by steep ice and avalanche danger. Then they explored the Northeast Ridge, only to deem it long and treacherous. Finally, they trudged 1500 feet (450 meters) up the Southeast, or Abruzzi, Ridge, more properly a shoulder of the mountain. As the duke's guides had indicated, it was climbable. The rock was loose everywhere and there were frequent stonefalls; the downward-sloping strata imparted a constant feeling of insecurity. Worse still, the ridge rose without a break for 7000 steep feet (2130 meters) above its beginnings on the glacier. In that entire distance there was no sign of a suitable campsite. So the climbers went back to the Northeast Ridge and the Savoia Saddle area, only to confirm their earlier apprehensions. It would, after all, have to be the Abruzzi Ridge.

Time had been lost. Supplies had begun to run low. One three-gallon tin of gasoline, essential to fuel stoves, had been crushed by a boulder and its precious contents lost. Nevertheless, the entire party marched bravely up the Godwin-Austen Glacier and, on July 1, 1938, established Camp I at 18,600 feet (5670 meters) at the foot of the ridge.[22] From here on, Houston's group once more moved fast and efficiently.

In teams of two that relayed one another, the men pushed up the ridge, here and there rigging the difficult passages with fixed ropes to assist the laden Sherpas, and ever looking for elusive campsites. They found a cozy snow pocket for Camp II at 19,300 feet (5882 meters); but for Camp III, at 20,700 feet (5300 meters), there was nothing but an outward sloping platform, exposed to high winds, where the unlucky residents were under constant stone bombardment whenever anyone was moving up above. Camp IV, at 21,500 feet (6705 meters), was placed just beneath an evil-looking, ice-choked chimney. This last turned out to be the toughest part of the ridge. Though it was only 80 feet high, Bill House, the party's best rock climber, spent four hours climbing it. Camp V, therefore, had to be pitched at 22,000 feet (6710 meters), barely a stone's drop above its lower neighbor. The chimney could never be climbed with heavy loads, so the party hauled its freight up on climbing ropes.[23]

The weather turned bad and then cleared; the men climbed on. At 23,400 feet (7140 meters) they literally carved a rock platform out of the precipitous terrain for Camp VI. At 24,700 feet (7530 meters) they reached the top of the Abruzzi Ridge. Here they emerged on a steep ice and snow field descending from beneath K2's summit. At this point, just beyond an icy traverse, they would pitch Camp VII.

It was July 19. The party was extended over long and fragile lines of communication. Up at Camp VI only four of the team (Bates, House, Houston, and Petzoldt) and one Sherpa (Pasang Kikuli) were available. Everyone else was far below; the other Sherpas never climbed above Camp III.

Supplies, already short, were growing shorter still, especially matches. The monsoon clouds gathering in the distance looked increasingly ominous. Yet with one more camp and three days of good weather, the summit could be theirs. Was it worth the risk?

The team members held council. To dare or not to dare? They were young and had not yet overcome their sense of awe for the vastness and majesty of their surroundings. Their good fortune and rapid success in the preceding three weeks surprised and elated them. But they knew they were ahead of the law of averages, and they had been trained in the school of caution. Only one of the four present had previously climbed in Asia.[24] Why tempt fate?

Caution prevailed. They reached a compromise. Petzoldt and Houston, presumably the two strongest, would be established at Camp VII with help from the others, who would return to Camp VI. The next day the pair would push as high as they safely could, try to outline a route to the summit, and then return. Thereafter, salvaging its equipment, the party would commence an orderly retreat.[25]

And so it was. In still gorgeous weather, at noon on July 21, Houston and Petzoldt reached a shoulder on the crest at 25,600 feet (7800 meters), then proceeded a few hundred feet higher to about 26,000 feet (7920 meters), only 2250 feet (700 meters) below the summit. There Houston sat down to rest and admire the landscape. Petzoldt, alone, scrambled a few feet higher. There was, he noted, room for a camp, and the route above seemed clear.

The two climbers turned and headed down into the gathering shadows whence they had come. For the next two months, by foot, horse, truck, rail, and, finally, by ship, the men of the expedition slowly made their way home.[26]

The expedition's achievements were widely acclaimed, with only two criticisms. The first, that too much time had been spent reexamining known ground, can be dismissed. That was part of Houston's mandate, a specific instruction he had to follow. Besides, the expedition itself wished to leave no stone unturned before making an irrevocable commitment. Since the duke's era, the state of the art had improved, and what had been judged impossible in 1909 might well be practical a generation later. There was also the fact that, on peaks large and small, snow and ice conditions sometimes change dramatically from year to year, and certainly from decade to decade.

There is only slightly more justification for the second criticism that the party, though short of resources, should have failed to make a final, all-out attempt on the summit. Modern expeditions would fly in the face of calculated risk and go for the prize. But this was 1938, when attitudes were different. In addition, since then, equipment has been perfected, knowledge expanded, and techniques improved. For better or worse, attitudes have changed. In hindsight, the Houston party's decision to turn back was cautious, but it was certainly not unwise.

Some of the accomplishments were unparalleled. The expedition had found a practicable route up the world's second-highest mountain. It had laboriously determined a string of campsites, most of which later parties would use. In barely three weeks it had overcome the mountain's chief difficulties—something many subsequent teams, including that of 1939, would fail to achieve in so short a time. It had engaged, notably in the House Chimney, in some of the finest rock climbing yet undertaken above 20,000 feet (6100 meters). It had demonstrated the advantage of light, mobile expeditions on even the highest peaks, and it had placed two men within striking distance of the summit. Moreover, Charlie Houston and Paul Petzoldt were now the world's only two persons to have attained an altitude of 26,000 feet (7925 meters) on any mountain other than Everest.[27]

Slowly the applause died. One by one the participants resumed the day-to-day work they had interrupted. Once more the Baltoro was deserted with unclimbed K2, giant among giants, towering above everything else.

2

The Leader

K2 FIRST CAST ITS SPELL on the man who led the 1939 expedition long before the germ of that ill-fated venture entered the minds of those who later accompanied him. It was in 1932, at his high point of 23,000 feet (7010 meters) on Nanga Parbat. There he first saw from a distance of 130 miles (210 kilometers) the great mountain that would become the obsession of his lifetime. Who was this man and what were his qualifications?

His name was Fritz Hermann Ernst Wiessner. He was born in Dresden, Empire of Germany, on February 26, 1900, the first child of four. Not rich, but well-to-do, Fritz's family derived their income principally from real-estate rentals, but their chief passion was art and architecture. Fritz's father, Hermann Ernst, considered his professorship of painting and his ability as an artist to represent his true occupation, while Fritz's Uncle Max, an architect, had achieved the exalted status of *Baumeister* (master builder). Dresden, dubbed the "Florence of the Elbe," had long been famed as a center of art, culture, science, and education. Its artisans had originated the European version of porcelain, which previously had been a Chinese monopoly, and had turned their discovery into a unique craft. Almost from birth, Fritz Wiessner found himself immersed in a world of quality and beauty, the pursuit of which occupied him all his life.

Even more important was his parents' – chiefly his father's – love of nature and outdoor sports. When Fritz was still a toddler, Hermann Ernst took him into the nearby countryside on ever longer hikes into the wooded hills known as the Ertz and Lausiter mountains and along the Elbe River towards what was then the Austro-Hungarian frontier. Along the way, they viewed the spectacular cliffs known as the Elbesand-steingebirge (sandstone mountains of the Elbe), but locally also referred to as Saxon Switzerland, albeit the area bears no resemblance to anything Helvetian. His love of the beauties and wonders of nature, instilled by his parents, became Fritz's lifetime passion – even more than his interest in art.

Fritz's earliest awareness of the allure of alpinism came from books in his father's library. At the age of eight he was already fascinated by their contents, which he shared with his cousin Otto, son of his Uncle Max. Then, when he was twelve, Fritz received his first taste of alpinism when his father took him, as a special treat, to the top of the Zugspitze, Germany's highest summit. The introduction to mountaineering had been gentle.

Very soon Fritz and cousin Otto developed a raging interest in rock climbing. This sport was now popular among Dresden outdoorsmen thanks largely to the proximity of the Saxon Switzerland pinnacles. To be sure, there were a few of the escapades and narrow escapes commonly experienced by all unsupervised neophytes. At first the outings were conducted secretly so as not to alarm protective parents. But soon enough Fritz's father found out. Rather than disapprove, he encouraged the boys, but advised formal schooling under experienced teachers. He also asked them not to reveal their new activity to Fritz's mother, Bertha, who learned about it only after Fritz turned sixteen. Thus did Fritz's activities as a rock gymnast begin.

Saxon Switzerland represented an ideal training ground for would-be mountaineers. It contained a multitude of possible routes of every description and difficulty, mostly on cliffs that rarely surpassed 300 feet (about 100 meters). The quality of the rock was excellent. There existed plenty of good teachers: local enthusiasts in the preceding twenty-five years had achieved the highest standards for rock climbing anywhere in the world.

Fritz learned fast and well. By the time he reached fifteen he had led Saxon Switzerland's most demanding routes; by seventeen he had begun to wander elsewhere, into the minor but difficult unglaciated ranges east of the Bodensee and south of Bavaria known as the Allgauer, the Lechtal, and the Fernwalls. The high Alps were out of reach for Germans because of World War I.

The war at first had little impact on the Wiessner family. Fritz's class was not called up until well into 1918. When drafted, Fritz, against the advice of parents, friends, and teachers, volunteered for the shock troops, or *Schützen*. By 1918, German shock troops rarely survived two weeks of combat. The war ended just before Fritz was scheduled to enter the trenches near Verdun.

Once more a civilian and now a university student in chemistry, Fritz sought out new peaks to conquer. On weekend visits he blazed routes on ever more demanding ground in Saxon Switzerland; on brief vacations he visited the Adamello and Presanella Alps near the lakes of the Italian Piedmont. In the Dolomites he made a difficult ascent, solo, of the Crozzon di Brenta's north face, then led the third ascent of the spectacular Guglia di Brenta. In 1920 he ventured farther yet, to the Pennine Alps, where he scaled the famous Dent du Géant, technically the most difficult, but not the highest, of the alpine peaks that surpass 4000 meters (13,124 feet). Then his interest in rock climbing for a time replaced his brief encounters with ice and snow, and he shifted his attention to the Kaisergebirge (Emperor Mountains) of the Austrian Tyrol.

Though the Kaisers rarely exceed 2300 meters (7550 feet), their steep limestone faces offer excellent rock climbing on solid rock. By the early 1920s they had become a popular sporting ground for German and Austrian climbers alike, particularly because of numerous opportunities to forge new routes. The British mountaineer Frank Smythe wrote of them as follows: "This is a famous rock-climbing ground and of evil reputation. Many lives are lost annually on its limestone precipices, a large portion as a result of competitive climbing... It is probably safe to say that on no other range of similar size are so many lives lost annually."[1]

Fritz never got so much as scratched in the Kaisers. He was extremely safety conscious for all his life,[2] and, whether accurately or no, he at least described himself as noncompetitive. In the Kaisers Fritz made an enormous number of climbs, most of the highest order of difficulty. These included a solo ascent of the Tito Piaz Route on the west face of the Totenkirchl, the Dülfer Direct Route on the same face, the Dülfer Couloir on the Fleischbank, and the Fichtl-Weinberger and Schüle-Diem routes on the Predigstuhl.[3] Finally, with Roland Rossi, Fritz made the first ascent of what climbers considered at the time as the range's outstanding unsolved problem, the southeast face of the Fleischbank. A week later, with Emil Solleder, Fritz solved the similar problem of the Dolomites, the first ascent of the north face of the Furchetta. These two feats established him as one of Europe's outstanding rock climbers.

From 1925 through 1928 Fritz added to his laurels, first in the Dolomites and later in the Pennine Alps, where his last season culminated with the thirteenth ascent of Mont Blanc's famed and demanding Peuterey Ridge.

HARD HIT BY THE GERMAN INFLATION OF 1923, which for a time ruined the Wiessner family, Fritz was obliged to end his chemistry studies and seek employment. A good businessman, he first opened a small chain of pharmacies in the Dresden area, then moved to the import-export trade in Hamburg. The latter involved procurement of resins from America in exchange for waxes, dyes, and polishes. In 1929 business considerations drew Fritz to visit the United States. The sojourn was to have been temporary, but it became permanent, and, except for biennial visits to Germany, Fritz remained in America thereafter. After breaking off from his Hamburg partnership, he worked for a time with various American chemical firms, notably Squibb, and saved enough money to buy a partnership in Ultra Chemical. When his partners wanted no part of the idea, Fritz also founded a small firm of his own that made ski waxes. He slowly established himself and in 1935 applied for and obtained American citizenship.[4]

Meanwhile, in 1932, Fritz participated in his first and, until K2, only major mountaineering expedition, this to Nanga Parbat,[5] the world's ninth-highest peak (but then believed to be the seventh-highest), located in what was then Northwest India and never before seriously attempted. Thanks to Fritz, it was a combined German-Austrian-American undertaking. The party, not counting its British transport officer, consisted of nine in all: five Germans, one German expatriate (Fritz), two Americans, and one Austrian. Generally speaking, the Germans supplied the climbers, all first rate, including the leader, Willi Merkl; the Americans furnished the money. Fritz had managed to acquire a few rich, or still rich, friends in the United Sates, notably Rand Herron, also an excellent climber; and, despite some protests from the male-chauvinistic Germans, he brought along Elizabeth Knowlton, somewhat of a mountaineer, a good journalist, an excellent money raiser, and an intense feminist.

No one in the party had previous Himalayan experience; but the team was strong and determined and had a good, if somewhat gruff, leader in Willi Merkl. The expedition did not reach the top, but it found a practicable route over previously unmapped territory. Three men, including leader Merkl and Fritz Wiessner, reached 23,000 feet (7010 meters), 3653 feet (1115 meters) below the summit. Though delayed by porter strikes and plagued toward the end by illness, no lives were lost. Not bad for a first try.

Back in the United States, Fritz settled in. He joined the New York chapter of the Appalachian Mountain Club, the Ski Club, and, in 1932, the American Alpine Club. During winters he skied with friends, mostly affluent, in upper New York and New England. In spring and autumn he led others on difficult rock climbs he pioneered in the East. Among his major contributions to eastern rock climbing was his discovery and early development of the Shawangunk Cliffs above New Paltz, New York. This area has since become the most important training ground for rock climbers in the eastern United States. In summer, when he could manage, he visited the mountains of western North America.

Fritz had brought with him from Europe climbing techniques almost unknown in North America. Both as a skier and climber his presence and tutelage were much in demand, the more so because, having never acted as a professional guide or used guide services, he seemed particularly well fitted to haul people around and show them new tricks in amateur-oriented America.

Invariably his companions consisted of people seriously interested in outdoor activities–notably rock climbers and skiers who wanted to perfect techniques–people with time on their hands and, preferably, money in their pockets. In those days the pickings were lean, but those who came to Fritz's attention justified the time investment. Some, such as Bob Underhill, could almost match Fritz's climbing skills; others, including Dudley Wolfe and Tony Cromwell, could finance major expeditions, while a few more had enough to afford long vacations. As time passed, Fritz became recognized as one of the foremost authorities in North America on the technical aspects of mountaineering.

New conquests added to his reputation. In 1936 he led a small, four-person expedition to British Columbia, where he and companion Bill House made the first ascent of Mount Waddington (13,177 feet; 4016 meters), the "Mystery Mountain," discovered only in 1922. The peak had already earned a bad reputation. After sixteen attempts, in one of which a life was lost, Waddington defied conquest until Wiessner arrived. The ascent did for Fritz in North America what Fleischbank and Furchetta had done for him in Europe. Among the rare American and Canadian climbers of those days, he became an overnight celebrity.

Other achievements followed: various first ascents in the Tetons, in the Saxon-Switzerland-like Needle country of South Dakota, and elsewhere. He was the first to climb Wyoming's Devil's Tower without direct aid. There was also an unproductive, rain-soaked sortie into Alaska's wet panhandle. Then, in 1938, with Dartmouth student Chappell Cranmer, he visited Alberta and British Columbia and met defeat on the Bugaboos' Snowpatch Spire,[6] success on Mount Columbia, North Twin, and Twin Towers (a first ascent), and triumph (and almost tragedy) on Mount Robson, the Canadian Rockies' crowning jewel.[7] Thus, with North Twin, Columbia, and Robson, he had climbed in a single season three of the four summits of the Canadian Rockies that surpass 12,000 feet (3660 meters). He returned to New York to discover that Charlie Houston's K2 expedition had finally discovered a route up the mountain and nearly climbed it. The permit for that first expedition had been obtained thanks to Fritz and was renewable for one year. Thus it came as no surprise when the American Alpine Club turned to Fritz and asked him to lead the next expedition. Without hesitation, he accepted the challenge.

What kind of man, one may ask, was Fritz Wiessner, one of the world's most famous mountaineers, acclaimed in climbing circles throughout Europe and North America? Was he just an exceedingly strong rock climber, or also an accomplished mountaineer? Did he have the right stuff to lead a major expedition? Clearly, Fritz's record, as outlined above, answers the first two questions. His performance as an expedition leader on K2, as described in later chapters, attempts to reply to the third.

SQUAT, BALD-HEADED, WITH A MOON-SHAPED VISAGE that earned him the name of "baby-face," relatively short (five feet, six inches) in stature, with powerful, bulging muscles and enormous physical strength, Fritz Wiessner at first appearance seemed a simple, rough-hewn man, modestly educated and perhaps a bit naive – an impression enhanced by his strong German accent. But appearances are deceptive.

When one knew him better, one learned to appreciate him as a highly talented, well-educated, and sophisticated man of strong, almost inflexible will and opinions with a personality that, for many people, seemed oppressive, sometimes overwhelming. Being tenacious to the point of obstinacy, he had little respect for the weak or for those he believed not to be doing their best. He saw the world in black and white – for him grey areas did not exist. Once decided, he headed straight for his objective, pretty much ignoring advice or suggestions. Tunnel vision, some people might say.

German by birth and upbringing, Fritz had been reared in the school of absolute obedience to authority that characterizes much of the Teutonic ethos: the leader leads, and the troops obey, whatever the situation. He may have been ideally suited to command a German venture, but his background did not lend itself to directing Americans, whose informal and democratic practices, even on expeditions with a formal commander, require decisions to be based on mutual discussion and debate.

Though interested in the humanities, Fritz was no humanist. Rather he preached Darwinian naturalism with its emphasis on survival of the fittest. The weak must perish so the strong may live – such was his philosophy – one, however, that he tended occasionally to shelve, particularly when family or old friends were involved. Despite some of the hardships of his early years, he had a soft and generous side.

Fritz literally seethed with the paradoxes and contradictions of most brilliant minds. The resulting inconsistencies tended to confuse those whom he met until they became close to him. Those who knew him well and were not compelled to remain too long in his company just kept quiet, let him have his way, and watched what happened. Action followed soon enough, and what occurred was often remarkable. He had an enormous number of worthwhile lessons to impart. Accordingly, exposure to him contributed to one's education. He could be good company, especially for people he liked, which in the 1930s meant the rich and the influential–"the good people," he called them. He could ooze with central European charm and knew precisely how to do "the proper things in proper situations" with grace and courtesy, but he could be brutally curt with those he disliked or who meant little to him. His presence was best absorbed in small doses. To be in his company, especially when serving under his command, for a period of months, must at the very least have been trying.

Fritz detested those he considered vain and boastful or lacking in solid accomplishments. Publicly he displayed great modesty; whether he observed it privately no one can be sure. There is, however, no question that from the start he wanted to get ahead in life. For a person like Fritz, transplanted to a foreign land, it was imperative to exploit whatever promising opportunities crossed his path. Whether inherent in his character or, more likely, acquired out of necessity, Fritz was a bit of an opportunist.

Because of his background and education, Fritz observed conservative conventions all his life, but he also kept an eye on the future. Within the boundaries of accepted rules, he pushed for progress and innovation. Never a radical, he nonetheless was always ready to accept a good and novel idea, provided he first satisfied himself that it had merit.

Fritz may not have been the world's greatest technical rock climber; in his time he had worthy rivals, including Hans Dülfer, Emilio Comici, and Pierre Alain. But in 1939 he was already an outstanding mountaineering figure on two continents, and throughout his life he preached an evangel whose basic philosophy, sometimes modified as time passed, ran roughly as follows: (l) The world is dominated by nature; therefore nature must be respected. (2) Mountaineering should be an amateur occupation for most of us and restricted to our leisure time. (3) Climbing is not properly a sport, but a means of traveling on foot over difficult terrain from one place to another. (4) Climbing is a personal and private experience. (5) Every safety precaution should be observed, except in those instances where the prize justifies risk-taking. (6) In the outdoors we should behave as naturally and simply as possible; it is unrewarding to employ machinery or special devices except in the interests of safety. (7) Mountaineering is a cult of beauty; the mountains lose their charm under competitive pressures. Competition shifts the focus to human beings. In the mountains the focus should be nature.

IT IS IMPORTANT FOR THE PURPOSES OF THIS CHRONICLE to stress that in all his life Fritz Wiessner never climbed professionally, and until after World War II he never availed himself of guides. Guides have a different viewpoint about climbing from that of amateurs. Generally speaking, the amateur has little moral or legal responsibility for his companions. Not so the guide, who also must be constantly on the lookout for the actions of incompetent clients. A good amateur is forever at liberty to try to set new standards of difficulty and excellence. The guide, on the other hand, must evaluate the limitations of his clients and devote himself to their needs and welfare. On K2, Fritz's approach would represent that of the best of amateurs, but this attitude would not necessarily meet with the approval of some of his guide-oriented companions.

Hard in body, Spartan (but not invariably), stoic in outlook, ready for sacrifice, and dedicated to the achievement of what became his life's ambition, Fritz Wiessner had the blessing of the prestigious American Alpine Club to lead the 1939 American Karakoram Expedition to K2. And thus, at the age of thirty-nine, he embarked on his mighty quest with flags flying, spirits high, and, in his own words, "in the best physical condition of [my] life."[8]

3

THE TEAM

I N LATE 1938, following the 1937 relapse into depression, most Americans found themselves once more short of cash, or short of time, or both. Too, the climbing community was tiny, and tinier still the number of people who possessed the qualifications to tackle a Himalayan monster such as K2. There was so little interest in mountaineering that, depression or no, neither public nor private funds could be raised from outside sources. Participants had to finance their share of the venture and also have the leisure time to absent themselves for a voyage that, in those days, required five or six months. With one possible exception, no one from the 1938 expedition to K2 was in a position to engage so soon in a second attempt. If he was to proceed at all, Fritz Wiessner would have to seek right and left and still be obliged to make do with a second-rate team.

Fritz approached a number of people. He selected his candidates with as much care as circumstances allowed. In the end, not including himself, he had nine potential companions, with almost all of whom he had either climbed or skied at one time or another: Chappell Cranmer, twenty; Eaton O. (Tony) Cromwell, forty-two; Sterling B. Hendricks, thirty-six; William P. House, twenty-six; Alfred Lindley, thirty-five; Bestor Robinson, forty-one; George Sheldon, twenty; Roger Whitney, thirty-four; and Dudley Francis Wolfe, forty-four.

And what of them and their qualifications?

Chappell Cranmer, quiet and introspective, had been Fritz's climbing partner during the 1938 Canadian tour that began with the abortive attempt on Snowpatch Spire and terminated in triumph on Mount Robson.

This aside, his mountaineering experience was limited to outings in the Colorado Rockies and to weekends on the cliffs of New England – a modest record that today would doubtless be unacceptable for a party headed for so formidable a mountain as K2, even by the easiest route. Chappell did, however, show promise, and he had performed well and faithfully in Canada. Nor had Fritz failed to note that Chap, as he was called, belonged to one of the most socially prominent families in Colorado. When approached, Cranmer was a student at Dartmouth College, where he was a classmate of George Sheldon.

EATON O. (TONY) CROMWELL WAS THE SECOND-OLDEST CANDIDATE. A New Yorker with Philadelphia ties, he belonged to an old and even more patrician family than Cranmer. Tony was sufficiently rich to be classed among the affluent unemployed. Not, however, a playboy, he handled his own financial affairs reasonably well for many years, after which one or more ill-fated marriages ended in law courts in such a way as to deplete his bank account. The circles in which Cromwell moved are best described by alluding to his brother James. After serving honorably as a captain in the U.S. Marines during World War I, and after a divorce from his first wife, Jimmy became the husband of tobacco heiress Doris Duke and would briefly serve in 1940 as American minister to Canada under Franklin Roosevelt. A later bid for the governorship of New Jersey would fail.

Tony's chief interest was mountaineering. His main climbing qualification for candidacy on the 1939 expedition consisted of the longest, but not most distinguished, list of mountain ascents of any member of the American Alpine Club; and there is some reason to believe that no one has ever attempted to surpass this record, much less to boast of it. Aside from a few of his easier Canadian excursions, Tony had always employed the services of guides. Thus, except for choosing his objective, he developed the habit of leaving the decision-making process to professionals, a practice that made him more of a follower in the mountains than a leader. Almost always courteous and accustomed to being treated as a gentleman, a delightful companion and a superb gourmet cook, Tony had a tendency toward irresoluteness and vacillation, characteristics that serve to undermine anyone who must make hard decisions. Nor did he seem particularly committed to the task of reaching the summit of K2. When he first accepted Fritz's invitation he stipulated that he would not climb high. Yet on more than one occasion thereafter he underwent a change of heart. During his climbing career he had no doubt experienced his share of bad weather, but it had invariably occurred within easy marching distance of luxury hotels or well-catered camping grounds.

Modern alpinists would label Tony a "fair-weather climber" and direct him away from big mountain projects.

Fritz did feel, however, that Tony's record and availability made him as good a candidate as any. If nothing else, Tony had a lot more experience in the mountains than any of the others except Fritz. Fritz appointed Tony his deputy and also his treasurer. Tony served somewhat hesitantly in the first of these positions, and with considerably more confidence in the second, until the expedition's return.

STERLING B. HENDRICKS WAS A MOST EXTRAORDINARY MAN and one of the outstanding American alpinists of the era. He had a modest background with roots in Arkansas and northern Texas. His father (later a country doctor), upon being accepted as a freshman at Princeton, and unable to pay train fare, walked the distance from home to gain a college education. Sterling himself earned his way through Cal Tech largely due to his ability as a bridge player, a game in which he seldom indulged thereafter. As a young chemist he turned down several lucrative job offers. The reason? A concern about waste disposal, this in an age when people believed the primitive methods then in use would suffice forever. In time Sterling gravitated toward biochemistry. He made a career in the Department of Agriculture's Bureau of Plant Industries and conducted major research into the then mysterious process of photoperiodism, work that almost won him a Nobel prize. Notwithstanding his many achievements, Sterling was extremely modest and unassuming and, even on long, difficult trips, a consistently pleasant and outstanding companion.

As a mountaineer, Hendricks, an excellent athlete, was largely self-taught. He performed most of his climbs guideless, often in the company of Canadian Rex Gibson. Usually his activities, most of them in Canada, took place in the form of mini-expeditions to difficult mountains that could be reached only through the hard work of long approach marches across territory then unmapped and in fair weather and foul. He had met Fritz Wiessner and Chappell Cranmer in the Bugaboos of British Columbia in 1938 and, despite the fact that he was not rich, had made a strong and favorable impression on Fritz.

WILLIAM P. HOUSE, A FORESTER, was the only member of the 1938 expedition to K2 who might have been able to stage a repeat performance. From an affluent Pittsburgh family, he could at least obtain the money, but perhaps not the time. A 1935 Yale graduate, House had created and for some years activated a short-lived Yale Mountaineering Club, which, under his leadership, briefly threatened to eclipse its older and more entrenched Harvard counterpart. Partly on his own and partly thanks to Fritz Wiessner, House had become one of North America's outstanding rock climbers and was passably good on ice and snow. He had climbed extensively with Wiessner, following in his footsteps to the top of Mount Waddington, to the Tetons, and to Devil's Tower. House now had behind him the invaluable experience of the 1938 expedition to K2, on which he had personally led the critical section of the Abruzzi Ridge route. No doubt about it, Fritz very much wanted Bill House aboard.

ALFRED LINDLEY, A NATIVE MINNESOTAN, was born not only with a silver spoon in his mouth, but was endowed with even more valuable hereditary assets, among them a healthy body and a fine mind. Like House he was a graduate of Yale, where he stroked the 1924 crew that won that year's Olympic races in Paris. In time Lindley became an attorney, turned to politics, and repeatedly endorsed the political ambitions of Harold Stassen. By 1939 he had also become one of the nation's outstanding sportsmen. Sailor, boxer, horseman, polo player, you name it – Lindley always managed to excel. From the age of sixteen he climbed extensively in the Alps, Canadian Rockies, Tetons, and Wind Rivers. But he was best known as a skier and ski-mountaineering enthusiast. In 1930 Lindley and others made the first return-trip ski tour from Jasper to the Columbia Icefield, a round-trip distance of 250 prehighway miles in the course of which he made the first winter ascent of 10,100-foot Mount Castleguard above the Saskatchewan Glacier. In 1932, the year he and Wiessner joined the American Alpine Club, Lindley and Erling Strom executed a superbly successful winter ski ascent of Mount McKinley's twin summits. Lindley would be a real trump card for Fritz's team.

BESTOR ROBINSON WAS ANOTHER STRONG CANDIDATE. Highly innovative, he was one of the earliest persons to develop rock climbing in California, chiefly in Yosemite. Robinson and others devised specialized techniques of direct-aid climbing with the use of expansion bolts not used elsewhere that became known in California as "rock engineering." Today the practice has lost much of its popularity, but at one time it had a large following. Wiessner, a purist, never employed the technology, but he had no objection to its use by others. In addition to his Yosemite activities, Robinson, also a strong skier, led several small expeditions to the British Columbia Coast Range, notably in 1935 and 1936. It was in this last year that he met Wiessner at the base of Mount Waddington. Fritz gave Bestor first try at the mountain; then, when Bestor failed, Fritz climbed the peak by a route of his own. Robinson was a particularly good organizer and clear thinker. Fritz was delighted when he accepted the K2 invitation. His presence would beef up a growing team.

GEORGE SHELDON, A DARTMOUTH CLASSMATE and an old friend of Chappell Cranmer's, probably joined at Chap's request. He had only two seasons' experience, all in Wyoming's Tetons, where he had made a number of climbs with Jack Durrance. The son of a small-town doctor, Sheldon was young, strong, and enthusiastic and bubbled with energy. He wrote passably well and would serve as the expedition's chronicler. He also had a delightful way of getting the best out of everything that came across his path. Just how he would perform on K2 was uncertain, but Fritz seems to have thought it would be good enough.

ROGER WHITNEY, TOGETHER WITH HIS BROTHER HASSLER, was one of the few Americans who had seriously studied mountaineering techniques in Europe under qualified specialists, yet who, on major ascents, never employed guides. The Swiss Alps had been his training ground, but by 1938 he had climbed in Alaska, British Columbia, Alberta, and the Tetons. Like Lindley and House, Whitney had done his undergraduate work at Yale. He graduated from Harvard Medical School in 1932 and then, after internships and residencies in the East, moved to Colorado Springs. He, too, was a strong candidate, with the added advantage that he could serve in a dual capacity, both as a climber and as expedition physician.

DUDLEY FRANCIS WOLFE MERITS SPECIAL ATTENTION because his presence high on K2 at a critical moment late in the expedition precipitated the great tragedy that was to overwhelm many of the participants.

Wolfe was rich. His father had been a wealthy British coffee merchant who had moved to the United States, where he married Mabel Smith, daughter of Benjamin Franklin Smith, one of Colorado's great silver barons. Partly because of his father's early death, Dudley, two brothers (Grafton and Clifford), and one sister were largely brought up by their maternal grandmother, whose surname Clifford opted to assume. Young Dudley, always a bit behind on his education, attended Pomfret School in Connecticut, then Andover Academy (Class of 1918), but never graduated owing to his decision to participate in World War I. The U.S. Army turned him down because of poor eyesight. Undaunted, he joined the French Mallet Reserve Transport Service, then drove an ambulance on the Italian front. Finally, he obtained a spot in the French Foreign Legion, but too late in the war to see action and, in all likelihood, like most other Legionnaires (counterparts of the German Schützen, which Wiessner had joined), get killed. Wandering around here and there after the end of hostilities, he eventually resumed his studies and graduated from Harvard in 1929 at the age of thirty-three.

Dudley owned a large estate on the Maine coast, described by his nephew, Dudley Rochester, as being like something out of Scott Fitzgerald's *The Great Gatsby,* with immaculate grounds, chauffeured limousines, Rolls-Royces, large power racing boats, and his favorite vessels – the schooner *Mohawk* and the racing cutter *Highland Light.* In the *Mohawk* Wolfe placed second in the 1931 trans-Atlantic race to Santander, Spain, and later competed in the Fastnet race to England. In the *Highland Light* he joined several races and won the Findlay Trophy in 1938 for the Bermuda race; this boat later became the property of the U.S. Naval Academy and may still be seen at Annapolis.

Dudley meantime developed an interest in skiing and, although a very heavy, somewhat clumsy man with myopic vision, managed in time and under the guidance of St. Anton's Hannes Schneider, to perform creditably on the slopes. Guide Otto Führer next persuaded him to take up climbing. By 1939 Dudley had three seasons' mountaineering behind him, but it frequently required more than one guide to haul his large bulk to the summits. Like his friend Tony Cromwell, though far less agile, he was not accustomed to making decisions in the mountains and could move over difficult terrain only with the guidance and help of others. On the other hand, he was physically strong, highly motivated, and, according to Cromwell, "apparently felt the rigors of life at high altitude as little as any of us."[1] In addition, Dudley was a splendid, gregarious companion who was also patient, kind, and compliant. And he had one thing all mountaineers need, but some do not have: a sense of humor.

There seems little doubt that Fritz selected Dudley more because of his money than his other qualifications, whatever those might have been. But on K2, though completely out of his element, Dudley displayed greater stamina, enthusiasm, and determination to reach the expedition's objective than anyone save Wiessner. As the expedition progressed, Wiessner and Wolfe became increasingly attached to each other. The two almost invariably climbed on the same rope. In fact, there came a point when other expedition members, notably Cromwell and Durrance, began to believe there existed, or certainly grew to exist, a special guide-client relationship between the two. But Dudley, as client, was heavy and clumsy to handle, while Fritz had never trained as a guide.

HOUSE, HENDRICKS, LINDLEY, ROBINSON, Whitney, Cromwell, Cranmer, Sheldon, Wolfe, and leader Wiessner–a somewhat unbalanced mixture. But with the first five a strong team emerged. Unfortunately that's not the way the dice fell. From the start, the best yarn began to unravel and the strongest men dropped out. Fritz was forced to accept whomever was left or abandon the project.

Hendricks and House turned down the invitation early on. Sterling told Fritz that he did not have the money and could not easily arrange a long leave of absence; also his wife, Edith, had misgivings. Privately he indicated, then and later, that he was disturbed by what he had seen of Fritz the previous summer in the Bugaboos. He felt the weight of Wiessner's personality would represent a hard cross to bear during a stressful adventure destined to last half a year.

House, who had climbed with Fritz many times before, had similar reservations. On Waddington and elsewhere Fritz had become and remained a close friend. But Bill felt the friendship was best preserved from a distance, so he cited various priorities that, in fact, did represent valid underlying reasons for his refusal.

With Hendricks and House out, new misfortunes descended to shake the recruitment process, as though the gods were warning of trouble to come. First, Lindley's wife, the former Olympic skier Grace Carter, suffered a miscarriage, and Al felt obliged to stay behind. Roger Whitney broke a leg skiing, and this accident deprived the expedition of a physician and also a strong climber. Then, after Wiessner had sailed for Europe, Bestor Robinson announced he would be unable to go. These losses dealt the expedition a hard blow even as it set out.

The team had dwindled from ten, of whom five were proven expeditionary mountaineers, to five, four of whom were relative neophytes. Only one, Fritz Wiessner, had the requisite qualifications to climb K2. And with the exception of Wolfe and Wiessner, no one seemed really dedicated to what this expedition really was–a life or death undertaking, not a summer pleasure trip to the Alps.

When the last expedition lynchpin, Bestor Robinson, dropped out, the venture was already so well in motion that it could hardly have been stopped. Wolfe and Wiessner were by that time off for Europe to buy equipment, and Cranmer, Cromwell, and Sheldon were about to board ship in New York. A frantic search was begun to obtain the services of one more participant.

With the approval of Dartmouth students Cranmer and Sheldon, attention focused on Jack Durrance, who had already been mentioned as a possibility. He was a premedical student at Dartmouth who had worked summers in the Tetons as a mountain guide and had led a number of fine ascents, notably, in an amateur capacity, the first ascent of the North

Face of the Grand Teton.[2] Jack had little money, but he was known to Bob Underhill and other influential American alpinists. Unidentified American Alpine Club angels promptly reached into their pockets to facilitate his inclusion on the team. After hurriedly arranging a leave of absence from college, Jack accepted.

Durrance was the only expedition member who had never met its leader (though Wiessner was certainly aware of his record) and also the only one not subjected to Wiessner's hand-picked scrutiny. Meanwhile in Europe, Wiessner, unclear about what was going on in America, still expected Robinson. Durrance arrived as a complete and unwelcome surprise.

John Randall Durrance was born on July 20, 1912, the eldest of several siblings. In 1927, when he was fifteen, the family moved to Bavaria, Germany, where Jack achieved fluency in the local language. He and his brother, Dick, both lovers of the outdoors (Jack was already developing a passion for flowers), also became excellent skiers. On top of this, Jack studied climbing techniques from Bavarian friends and became a proficient rock climber. When Jack reached his twenties and was settling into German life in the Weimar Republic, as Fritz had settled into American life, he found employment as a trainee to become a knowledgeable English-speaking salesman. After 1933 his employers discontinued production of civilian goods for what had suddenly become the more fashionable and profitable business of manufacturing machine guns. Jack didn't like what he saw.

Jack was alone in Germany because his family had returned to America in 1931. In 1935 he, too, packed his bags and returned to the United States. Jack and brother Dick entered Dartmouth, where they continued to ski and where Dick won most of the racing prizes. Concentrating more on alpinism, Jack became known primarily as a mountain climber. From 1936 through 1938 he worked summers as a guide in the Tetons, where his ascents, though varied and notable, included little experience on ice and snow.

Like many young men, Jack had his wild moments and liked to poke fun at those who took life too seriously. Endowed with a brilliant mind, he also had a sparkling sense of humor. This trait would lead to difficulties with Fritz, whose idea of a joke was at best ponderous and who never appreciated remarks that might subject him to the slightest ridicule. Jack, on the other hand, knew how to poke fun, even at himself.

Jack differed from Fritz also in that he had the perception of a realist, while Fritz, at least on the 1939 expedition, had the vision of a romantic. On the mountain, Jack, with his guiding experience, more than once warned of impending disaster, whose prospect kept repeating itself in his dreams, while Fritz beamed perpetual optimism no matter what the odds. Jack never expressed concern for Fritz, who could clearly take care of himself, but his growing anxiety for Dudley, Tony, and "Joe" Trench, the British transport officer, eventually translated itself into nights of sleeplessness and bad dreams. As Jack came to know the group he could not believe that a man of Fritz's experience should have hand-picked to accompany him men who ought never to have been allowed to step onto the mountain – indeed, Jack considered himself unqualified and several times protested in his diary his apprehensions after Fritz later selected him to join with the summit team.

Jack's assessment of K2 was as a formidable and dangerous challenge to be undertaken only by the most experienced mountaineers. Not only did this prove correct in 1939, but thereafter as well. Forty-seven years later, thirteen climbers, all highly trained, died on K2 in eight separate accidents. Seven of the thirteen perished as they returned from the summit.[3] If K2 could do this to modern climbers with more specialized equipment and superior techniques, of what was it capable against the ragtag band that followed haltingly in Wiessner's footsteps half a century earlier?

At the time Jack asked no questions, even if he recorded his fears in his diary. He was low man on the totem pole, a last-minute replacement. But for his part, Fritz, as leader, might have reconsidered the timeliness of the project; even before leaving the United States his party had dwindled to less than half its original strength and in no way resembled the strong team he had earlier envisaged.

4

BON VOYAGE

T HOUGH NOT EXCLUSIVE, an important source for this story is Jack Durrance's diary.[1] It consists of a four-by-six-inch, leather-bound, hardcover volume, each page of which is labeled for a specific day of the year and with one extra page, entitled "Memo," at the close of every month. The first formal entry occurs under the date of Saturday, March 18, 1939. The regular text then continues without a break until the expedition's final dissolution in Srinagar on September 20, 1939. In addition to the contemporary text, the pages prior to March 18 and following September 20 contain addenda and commentaries, some repetitive, many of them written (aside from the "Medical Notes") on Jack's way home from India and entered as afterthoughts. Among other such remarks is a particularly perceptive insight into the hardships of life at high altitude that Jack wrote on his return to Base Camp following several weeks on K2, and, toward the end, recommendations for future expeditions.

Aside from one interesting episode, nothing worthy of more than passing note occurred from the time Jack bade family and friends farewell in Hanover, New Hampshire, on March 20 with, as he wrote, "a heavy heart," until he boarded ship in Genoa. "As soon as the train pulled out," he continued,

> I realized that I was not only going to miss Maria [his current girlfriend] but was going to the country of my dreams and she was not going to be along to partake in my new experience...There she stood at the station waving good-bye knowing that there was danger in the impending adventure but still smiling with moist eyes...[2]

In New York, Jack dined with American Alpine Club Treasurer Joel Ellis Fisher and his family at their home. Among the guests was Charlie Houston, leader of the previous year's expedition. Charlie expressed to Jack and the others "his seeming regret that this year's party was not altogether balanced atop the accomplishments and findings of last year's party."[3] Whether the remark resulted, as it likely did, from observation or, instead, from envy, does not matter. It was, however, prophetic and may have influenced Jack's subsequent concerns.

MEANWHILE, IN EUROPE, MUCH REMAINED TO BE DONE. Dudley Wolfe, the expedition's chief financial supporter, followed shortly by Fritz Wiessner, was hard at work buying necessary equipment not available in those days in the United States. The two men's work was meticulous; if anything, the expedition was overequipped with the best gear available at the time.[4] It was certainly better supplied, thanks to Dudley's deep pockets, than its 1938 predecessor, but nowhere near as well as modern expeditions.

The tents were strong but heavy; thermal padding had yet to replace bulky, leak-prone air mattresses. There existed a limited choice of stoves, all of which required careful priming and were hard to light, especially at altitude. Eiderdown sleeping bags were much like today's, but down clothing was unknown. Boots had edge, or tricouni, nails. On most terrain, nails provided poor traction, at least when compared with the cleated rubber soles today known as Vibram in honor of their Milanese inventor, Vitale Bramani. Nails wore down rapidly, pulled out, and conducted cold with distressing efficiency. The best ropes were of Italian hemp, water absorbent, only half as strong as the kernmantel nylon that appeared a few years later, and totally unmanageable when wet and frozen. Freeze-dried foods had yet to make their appearance, but a limited choice of dehydrated products existed: tomatoes, potatoes, celery, and carrots. Aside from pemmican, much of the food, being canned and containing water, was heavy in relation to its nutritional benefit.

As noted by Jack Durrance in the back of his diary under the date of November 10, nutrition at Base Camp and above consisted primarily of the following:

> Diet: Tea, Ovaltine, Cocoa for beverages, on rare occasions George Washington coffee.
> Meats: Wurst–bacon, Ham (tins), salmon, Corned beef, Boned Chicken, (Pemmican), sardines, tuna fish.
> Cheese: Edamer & Swiss (Gruyère).
> Bread: Rye Krisp.

Klim [the powdered whole milk of the era], Butter, Jam, Honey, Chocolate, Nuts, Life Savers, Sugar.
Veg: Dried Potatoes, Tomatoes, Celery & Carrots.
Breakfast food: Grape Nuts, Oatmeal, Cream of Wheat, Cornmeal, Ralston.
Dried Fruits: Pears, apples, raisins, prunes, apricots.
Soups – Varied Maggi varieties . . .
Yeast cakes and vitamin pills were also carried along.

It was, in short, a balanced diet: fats, proteins, carbohydrates, vitamins, and roughage, all quality. Fritz, the main purchaser, appreciated good food wherever he went.

As with all expeditions, no matter how carefully planned, there were oversights. Not enough snow goggles were purchased for the Balti porters who were to carry loads up the Baltoro Glacier to Base Camp. Jack's high-altitude boots, ordered from Munich, did not arrive in time, and for the first month on the mountain he had to make do with an old, leaky pair with worn-down nails that severely handicapped his performance. Boots supplied the Sherpas were not much better; apparently people considered Sherpas less subject to frostbite than sahibs. The same was true of Sherpa sleeping bags, which, intended for small people, were barely half the size of those supplied the Americans.[5]

One item the expedition did not include, and whose presence might have averted tragedy, was two-way, short-range radios. These were bulkier and much heavier than modern versions, but they were available and considered by some to be practical. But when the suggestion to include them was made, Fritz flatly turned it down. He always distrusted mechanical or other artificial devices.

Other mistakes were typical of every expedition. Most presented only a nuisance factor; others could be corrected by improvisation. There was not enough winter underwear; wind suits might have been better designed; trousers should have had double or even triple seats to avoid wear and tear. No expedition is perfect; every quartermaster makes mistakes, corrects them, then runs into new problems next time.

JACK DURRANCE'S VOYAGE TO EUROPE held nothing out of the ordinary. He traveled third class on the North German Lloyd's *Europa,* pride of the German merchant fleet, which (allegedly at Hitler's order) served no butter to anyone outside luxury class, and which, as it had since its maiden voyage, lived up to its reputation for vibration. Then Jack made a whirlwind visit to Paris, enjoyed a day's skiing at Kanderstegg in Switzerland with guide Fritz Ogi[6] (during which his leaky boots underwent another nailing) and moved on to Genoa, where on the morning of March

29 he boarded the Lloyd Triestino's *Conte Biancanamo* for points east of Suez. Thanks to expedition generosity, he now had a first-class cabin of his own. Last to leave America, Jack found himself the first of the expedition aboard ship for India.

Hardly had Jack rested a bit from his overnight journey by train from Switzerland than he received information that an elderly gentleman had come aboard in search of expedition members. On deck he found "a diminutive, gray-haired, red-eyed man" waiting: it was Vittorio Sella, master photographer of the Duke of the Abruzzi's 1909 Karakoram party.

Though difficult to have anticipated, an awkward situation now arose. Jack and Sella began a lively conversation next to the ship's gangplank. Suddenly, not five minutes later, a short, bald-headed man appeared, followed by a large, heavy man marching up the gangplank. Jack recognized Fritz Wiessner as the first; of the second he wrote in his diary: "...some physical specimen, was my first impression – wonder what kind of mountaineer he is."[7] It was Dudley Wolfe.

At their meeting, Fritz was visibly taken aback. He had intended to be the first on the expedition to greet Vittorio Sella, and he had expected Bestor Robinson. Instead, he found Jack Durrance, whom he had not invited, deep in conversation with the great Italian photographer. When Jack introduced himself and announced that Bestor would not be coming after all, Fritz froze and at once turned his full attention to Sella. Jack felt the ice. "Can't quite forget Fritz's look of disappointment at finding insignificant Jack filling Bestor Robinson's boots," he wrote in his diary.[8] Though he did not show it, Jack felt slighted, and this at the very start of a difficult undertaking. Fritz's reaction, though understandable, suggested a lack of consideration. In later years Jack indicated that, had he had the funds, he would have resigned from the expedition then and there and gone home.

After a moment the matter faded. The important thing was to pick Sella's brains. Sella's main thought was to urge the party to take another look at K2's Northeast Ridge, judged impractical by the 1909 and 1938 parties, but out of the violent winds that sweep the Abruzzi Ridge. Fritz promised to do so. As the two parted, Sella, eighty years of age, had tears in his eyes: "A dear [gentleman]," Jack wrote in his diary on March 29, "[who] envied our chances to see Karakoram... [and who] also gave us valuable hints and advice."

In Naples, the *Biancanamo*'s first port of call, Chappell Cranmer, Tony Cromwell, and George Sheldon came aboard. According to every account, and in spite of the momentary incident in Genoa, the men made a compatible group. Much later, on April 24 in Srinagar, Fritz would echo this sentiment: "Our party," he wrote to Joel Ellis Fisher, "is really exceptionally congenial."[9]

- *Overleaf:* K2 from Broad Peak. (Voytek Kurtyka)
- *Above:* Fritz Wiessner, leader of the expedition, in Srinagar. (Durrance collection)
- *Right:* Passing a ship in the Suez Canal. (Durrance collection)
- *Below:* Aboard the *Biancanamo*, from *left to right*: Sheldon, Cromwell, Wolfe, unidentified woman. (Durrance collection)

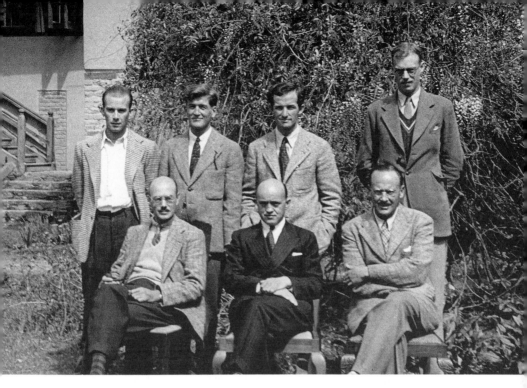

- *Above:* Official photo of the K2 1939 expedition members, from *left* to *right*, standing: George Sheldon, Chappell Cranmer, Jack Durrance, George "Joe" Trench; seated: Eaton O. (Tony) Cromwell, Fritz Wiessner, Dudley Wolfe. (Durrance collection)
- *Below:* Sherpas in Srinagar, from *left* to *right*: Sonam, Pemba Kitar, Tse Tendrup, Pasang Kitar, Pasang Kikuli, Pasang Lama, Tsering Norbu, Phinsoo, Dawa. (Durrance collection)

- *Above:* Punjab Motor Express with expedition gear. (Durrance collection)
- *Right:* Noor, the cook. (Sheldon collection)
- *Far right:* Major Kenneth Hadow. (Durrance collection)
- *Below:* Campsite in Balti village. (Durrance collection)

- *Above:* Resting in apricot grove on march to Skardu. (Durrance collection)
- *Below:* Pasang Kikuli and Sonam on march. (Durrance collection)
- *Below right:* Conference on route to Base Camp. (Durrance Collection)

■ *Above*: Trail along cliff edge above Indus. (Durrance collection)
■ *Below*: Crossing Indus on "Alexander's Barge." (Durrance collection)

- *Left*: Goatskin raft used to cross Braldu at Dassu. (Durrance collection)
- *Below:* Rope bridge crossing. (Sheldon collection)
- *Bottom:* The Baltoro at last! Porters on the march. (Durrance collection)

■ *Above:* Sheldon among ice ships of Baltoro; Masherbrum in the background. (Durrance collection)
■ *Below:* Resting on the Baltoro, from *left* to *right*: Cromwell, Wolfe, Sheldon. (Cranmer collection)

Overseas travel in the 1930s (and earlier) may have been slow, but it provided vastly more comfort and ease than the frantic, if faster, pace of modern air transport. Shipboard travel was leisurely, pleasant, and usually uncrowded. Food was generally fresh, plentiful, and often superbly prepared. Only on the last day of a trans-Atlantic voyage did cream, untreated with chemicals, turn sour. There was ample room to walk around. Various diversions, such as motion-picture shows, boxing matches, "horse" races (wherein wooden horses are moved on the throw of the dice), and card tournaments, filled leisure time; plenty of exercise could be had at deck tennis, shuffleboard, swimming in the ship's pool, or just walking the decks. Dudley Wolfe's films, taken on the *Biancanamo,* highlight the activities of a young, and obviously happy, group of men.

To the expeditionaries' delight, the ship carried more than its share of attractive and sometimes adventurous young ladies who easily succumbed to the lures of handsome, athletic men traveling on a romantic quest to the ends of the earth. The names of Catherine, Susannah, Lotte, and an American, Mrs. Dunn,[10] with long hair and flashing blue eyes, recur in Jack's diary. Most important to him appeared to be a certain Dorothy, with whom he later maintained a lengthy correspondence.

Also aboard were some dignitaries, among them the Duchess of Savoia, a member of the Italian royal family en route to Eritrea to visit Italy's expanding colonial empire. And there was Germany's financial wizard, Hjalmar Schacht, no longer head of the Reichsbank but still an influential Hitler confidant who would reappear in Srinagar on the expedition's heels. He described his trip as a "vacation" but may have had other responsibilities during his forthcoming visit to India. A pleasant, ingratiating man of great charm, Schacht provided more than one round of champagne to expedition members. Fritz, who had once met Schacht on a train in Germany, spent much time in his company.[11] The man had real attraction. Jack was impressed by his gaiety "and perhaps," he wrote in his diary on April 9, "the fact he was such a charming human." The two spent a couple of hours' conversation together under the stars one evening on the *Biancanamo*'s prow as it cut through the waters of the Gulf of Arabia.

Debarking at Bombay on April 10 and still living in luxury, the party took rooms at the Taj Mahal Hotel, then and later famous as one of the finest in the East. Aside from essential errands, the expedition members managed some sightseeing to the nearby island of Elephanta to view caves and carvings and also visited the famous Towers of Silence, where Parsee dead are to this day exposed to be scavenged by vultures.

On Tuesday evening, April 11, the six Americans boarded the Frontier Express for a torrid, dusty, premonsoon, forty-hour journey to Rawalpindi and a first real taste of Indian rail travel: restless nights because of the heat, which by day surpassed 100° Fahrenheit; the clickety-click of wheels over the tracks; the recurring din of human voices at every rail station; and a parched, grim countryside, some of it reminiscent of the South Dakota Badlands. An hour before arrival in Rawalpindi, Major Landers, the expedition agent, boarded the train to provide the party with a proper briefing of what to expect in Kashmir.

After repacking loads in Rawalpindi for motor transport to Kashmir, the six men started out in two cars, a Buick and an Oldsmobile, for the 190-mile journey over Murree Pass (7000 feet; 2130 meters) to Kashmir's capital, Srinagar. As on all winding mountain roads there were moments of apprehension. George Sheldon, in a letter to Joel Ellis Fisher dated May 6, some three weeks later, supplied a description he had not forgotten:

> The road along which we drove was bad for a nervous driver . . . sort of stuck halfway up tremendous cliffs. Occasionally a small slide would block the road and we would wait while coolies cleared it . . . two coolies per shovel – one to push, one to pull . . . [12]

Jack told somewhat the same story in his diary entry of April 15:

> Our driver was a rather stupid fellow anyway, we had a mechanic fix the carburetor near the height of the pass . . . Took several colored shots (Agfa film) of valley with innumerable terraces at odd moments while car was deciding to percolate. Fritz & Chap were my travelling compatriots and all 3 of us spent considerable time cat-napping. It is like a night-mare to wake up suddenly and see a car approaching completely over on your right – but after you have just passed safely you remember the "keep to your left" system.

Not far beyond the pass, the party descended into the cool and pleasant Vale of Kashmir, whose capital, Srinagar, was to serve as its staging area. The men had traveled 11,000 miles (18,334 kilometers), 7000 (11,667 kilometers) of them together by ship, by rail, and by car; and in the course of the journey they all had become friends.

5

LAND OF THE LOTUS EATERS

LEVEN THOUSAND MILES. And K2 now only 330 miles (550 kilometers) away–but what a 330 miles! It had taken Jack only three weeks to cover the distance from America to North-west India. The expedition must travel another month–briefly by car, then on horseback, finally, and most of the time, on foot–before it would even sight its objective. And here in Kashmir much remained to be done ere the party, yet to be fully fleshed out, could start on the final leg of its adventure.

The Vale of Kashmir had, and still enjoys, a reputation as a land of Lotus Eaters, especially for those persons fortunate enough to live on lake and river barges, whose configuration is almost unique to the area. Elizabeth Knowlton, who accompanied Fritz Wiessner to Nanga Parbat in 1932, had written of Kashmir: "Men stepped out of the world into a region of timeless ease." Westerners briefly became Oriental potentates, "rhythmically borne by native rowers up and down the Jhelum river, gliding past boats laden with half naked men and cargoes of women and children among rugs and pots," past houses and balconies "of elaborate wood carving, over which leaned women in such colors as made one catch one's breath...."[1] This was, in short, the world of Scheherazade.

The British rulers of India had not been slow to appreciate the vale's merits. By the time the 1939 expedition took place, it had long served as a cool and pleasant vacation spot for Westerners bent on escaping the heat and epidemics of the Indian lowlands. Regularly, British officials and business people traveled to Kashmir with their families at the start of the hot season; the men remained as long as their leaves allowed, while the women stayed on alone until such time as conditions down below became more pleasant.

As in all British colonial "watering places," the social activity in Kashmir, and more specifically Srinagar, could represent a full-time occupation even if otherwise unproductive. But with servants at thirty to forty cents a day, or even less in those times, there was plenty of room for leisure activity of almost every preference. For the British and their friends and guests, life was a continual round of parties, with long lunches, still longer dinners, plenty of gin and tonic, whiskey and soda, wine, beer, and what-have-you, and with constant dances, receptions, and other entertainments, a large proportion of which ended in the bedrooms of British memsahibs.

In this atmosphere the six American climbers were especially welcome. They came from a distant country on a glamorous and dangerous quest; they were handsome and entertaining; above all, they had high credentials and were socially acceptable. The grass widows of Srinagar were eager to meet them.

On top of everything else, Kashmir was a treasure house for Jack Durrance's hobby, flowers. He was dazzled by the display of Chenar trees, magnolias, palms, and tulips, which he described as "brilliant." And, as he wrote in his diary on the "Memo" page at the end of April, "The experience of shikaras [local river boats] around Dal Lake to the Mogul's Garden & to the Club is an experience in itself and must excell [sic] anything Venice has to offer."

Fritz Wiessner had arranged a pleasant interlude in Kashmir for himself and his weary, dust-covered, mud-caked companions. Seven years earlier, on his way to and from Nanga Parbat, he had made friends there with a large landowner and rug manufacturer, Major Kenneth Hadow, grandnephew of the famous Douglas Hadow, who was killed on the first ascent of the Matterhorn in 1865. Hadow had influence. In addition, he was helpful and extremely hospitable. It was he who had arranged the prompt clearance of the expedition's gear at customs and its duty-free entry into nearby Baltistan.

Hadow, described by Tony Cromwell as "the most hospitable of men," had invited the Americans to stay in his spacious home during their sojourn in Srinagar. "To do Major Hadow's hospitality and estate justice," Jack Durrance wrote in his diary on April 16, echoing Tony, "I should need several pages... The Major—a charming English gentleman in his thirties... engaged servants all around who do everything for you except eat and perform other personal activities." They even woke you in the morning with preprandial tea and toast, an enduring custom in South Asia known as *chota hazri*. They also kept stoking the fireplaces, for the weather, unlike that in the plains, was rainy and still cold.

Hadow had also arranged the election of the climbing team to honorary membership in the Ski Club of India so that it might have free use of the club's Killmarg[2] Hut, situated at 10,000 feet in the mountains above the Vale of Kashmir. There the men would enjoy an eight-day interlude in order, as Wiessner put it, to get a bit of altitude, know one another better, and enjoy some final moments of leisure. To the Americans' delight, two English women, Rose Biscoe and Leona Williams, invited themselves along for the ski tour. Good exercise and fun was had by all. During these days the men regularly climbed to the summit of Al Pathi, a 13,838-foot (4229-meter) Himalayan pygmy of the Aphanvat Range, from which they could ski down directly to the hut, a vertical distance of nearly 4000 feet (about 1300 meters). Activities took place on perfect spring snow, usually in the mornings because the afternoon sun tended to soften the slopes. The Americans had never experienced anything quite like it: "Long sweeping runs," George Sheldon wrote to Joel Ellis Fisher on May 6, "with no sign of obstruction anywhere." George had never skied outside New England and was entranced.

In the same letter, George, who easily succumbed to the temptations of luxury, and who seems to have adopted some of the colonialist spirit of the times, supplied the true meat of the idyll:

> To give you the full flavor of the atmosphere under which we skied, we had all our equipment carried three thousand feet up to the hut, we had a cook and two servants and a general caretaker. Also a sweeper – and did he earn his pay! Quite a bit different from Tuckerman's, but you really have to do it here. Prestige, and all that. But frankly it's a damn fine custom, especially when you pay a coolie the terrific sum of twenty-five cents [per day].

The days of relaxation, during which the men ascended five summits on skis, paid off. Fritz wrote Joel Ellis Fisher on April 24:

> Our party is really exceptionally congenial. We have lots of fun. I am terribly pleased with it. Today's ski ascent seemed exceptionally easy to everybody, and it makes me very happy and hopeful to see that the physical condition of the party is so good. It is a pretty good dose for our untrained group to climb 4000 feet in 3 1/2 hours over steep snow and broiling sun at an altitude of between 10,000 and 14,000 feet.

Good things come to an end. On April 27 the group returned to Srinagar, where the job of packing would combine with the inevitable round of parties. Even during the short interval at Killmarg much had changed below: rice fields were now ready for planting, and the greenery was, if anything, more pronounced than before.

WAITING IN SRINAGAR FOR THE PARTY was Lieutenant George Trench, aged twenty-two and promptly nicknamed "Joe" so as to avoid confusion with George Sheldon. Trench, like Durrance, had come aboard late; the originally designated liaison and transport officer, a certain Lieutenant McLeod, had been unable to obtain leave because of the worsening European situation. At the last moment, Hadow, with help from Lieutenant Colonel D. M. Fraser, the British resident in Kashmir, located a substitute from Peshawar. Initially "Joe" Trench seemed suitable enough: "a tall, blond, pleasant fellow," Jack wrote of him. On the same afternoon, April 27, the nine Sherpas from Darjeeling also arrived.

The Sherpas, wrote Jack on April 27, were a "very jolly looking group all with previous experience on K2, Everest, Nanga Parbat, and Kangch. [Kangchenjunga]." Their sirdar, Pasang Kikuli, was a veteran of many Himalayan expeditions and a survivor of the terrible 1934 catastrophe on Nanga Parbat, where nine lives were lost in a storm. The frostbite he suffered affected him thereafter, but he was extremely reliable and, unlike a lot of other Sherpas, had mastered many mountaineering techniques. He had been sirdar on Houston's 1938 expedition (and also Charlie's personal attendant), and the two had become close friends.[3] On that expedition he was the only Sherpa permitted by his employers to climb above Camp III (21,000 feet; 6400 meters) and had reached Camp VII, the highest, at 24,700 feet (7530 meters).

The others were Pasang Kitar, Pemba Kitar, Pasang Lama (strong, not as experienced as Kikuli, but solid and reliable, and, in Kikuli's absence, head of the Sherpas), Phinsoo (or Pintso), Tsering Norbu, Kikuli's brother Sonam, Tse Tendrup, and Dawa Thondup. Of these, five had been on K2 the previous year: Kikuli, as Houston's porter; Phinsoo, as Bates's; Pemba Kitar, as Petzoldt's; Sonam, as Burdsall's; and Tsering Norbu, as House's.

Insofar as possible, each Sherpa was again assigned a sahib. As might be expected, Fritz got Kikuli. Since there were eight other Sherpas for the other six sahibs (including Trench), straws were drawn to see which six would be assigned a sahib. After the drawing, Jack chose Dawa, a diminutive man of thirty-one who seemed always to be in good spirits.

MANY PEOPLE ERRONEOUSLY BELIEVE that all Sherpas are genuine mountain guides. Until very recent years that was simply not true. Real guides in Europe and Canada (though for arcane reasons not in the United States) are required by statute to undergo long and strenuous apprenticeships because the job is considered a serious one not to be undertaken by uncertified persons. Over several years guides learn not only the fine points of rock, snow, and ice climbing and how to look after their clients, but also first aid, ski-mountaineering, and rescue techniques.

Only after passing strict examinations, both on paper and in the field, are they permitted to exercise their trade. Sherpas in the 1930s, many of them illiterate and few with more than a grade-school education, had no such opportunities for schooling, even though some of them became excellent mountaineers in the hard school of experience. Their role in these years was to carry freight to the high camps and look after the day-to-day requirements of their employers, much in the manner of Asian servants generally.

Though not invariably observed, there existed until well after World War II an unwritten rule in the Himalaya that climbers had a responsibility to attend to the welfare and safety of their Sherpas. If at all avoidable, Sherpas were not to engage in climbing where ropes were necessary unless led by one of their sahibs. This tacit regulation had its origin in 1922 on Mount Everest when several unaccompanied Sherpas perished in an avalanche below the mountain's North Col.

Sherpas, in no way related to the military-oriented Gurkhas, belong to a minority group of Oriental origin domiciled in Nepal and northern West Bengal in the Darjeeling and Kalimpong areas. In Tibetan their name means "People of the East." Like Tibetans, they practice Buddhism, not Hinduism, and there is much mountain-related superstition in their religion. Before World War II they had little incentive to climb the great peaks around them; except as a way to make a living, they saw nothing practical in mountaineering. They gained their reputation because they were sure-footed, native to the region, reliable, hard-working, and willing to serve for modest pay. In 1939, Sherpas spoke little English. The resulting difficulties in communication sometimes had unfortunate consequences.

TWO MORE PERSONS FLESHED OUT THE 1939 EXPEDITION. At Major Hadow's recommendation, an Indian teacher and linguist from Canon Eric Tyndall Biscoe's Mission School[4] in Srinagar joined the group. Chandra Pandit, who loved the outdoors and had an interest in mountaineering, turned out to be a valuable addition as an interpreter. He knew all the languages and dialects of the regions the expedition was about to enter, and, in addition, he could also converse in the language of the Sherpas. But he was not a serious climber nor a load carrier. Some members of the expedition, especially those who spent considerable time at Base Camp, felt that in time, and with little to do except interpret, Chandra became a bit of a gossip and something of a schemer. Outwardly pleasant, he did have a predilection for hearsay and too often reported as fact matters about which he only had second-hand knowledge.

Finally there was the cook, Noor, from Kashmir. He prepared copious and excellent meals and kept a tidy kitchen. Except for one Sherpa, taken ill on the march in, he was the only one of those who left Srinagar who never ventured above Base Camp.

Thus the team was now complete: six American climbers, a British transport officer, nine Sherpas, an Indian interpreter, and a cook–eighteen in all. They were Buddhist, Christian, Hindu, and Moslem; Caucasian, Indo-Aryan, and Oriental; and belonged to at least four different nationalities–a real melting pot, with participants who did not understand each other's languages. All major Himalayan expeditions, before and since, have had somewhat the same composition. 1939 on K2 was nothing new.

6

BLISTERS AND FLEAS

A HAPPY, CONGENIAL, RATHER CAREFREE GROUP set out from Srinagar on Tuesday, May 2, 1939, for what was to prove a fateful journey. Fritz Wiessner had moved the departure date up since all packing had been done and there seemed no sense in prolonging the stay among the fleshpots of Srinagar. The last, somewhat liquid "good fortune" party took place on May 1, and, aside from headaches and hangovers, everyone was ready to go the next day. The men thanked Major Hadow for his exceptional hospitality and drove to the end of the road at the Woyjil Bridge. After that, with porters and horses carrying their loads, the party began its long march on foot and animal back to the first stop at Sonnemarg. Already suffering from blisters acquired on the ski outing, George Sheldon and Jack Durrance lagged some distance behind the others.

Three wonderful things happened one early night. Noor prepared a much better than expected dinner; Fritz, the former pharmacist, demonstrated his ability to lance his companions' blisters (Fritz was the only member of the group who never developed any, a testimony to his tough feet), and after dark the party watched a total eclipse of the moon.

Little adventures, little thrills, badly blistered feet. The party approached its first obstacle, the Zoji-La, at 11,000 feet (3352 meters) the lowest pass between Kashmir and neighboring Baltistan. It was still blocked by winter snow, but Fritz, remembering his experiences of 1932, had taken precautions: he hired local porters rather than animals and traveled by night to take advantage of frozen snow. George Sheldon wrote of this stage of the journey in a May 6 letter to Joel Ellis Fisher:

At midnight, the fifth of May, we were aroused for breakfast and by one o'clock were starting uphill over the Zoji-La under a splendid full moon. The Zoji-La is the lowest of the big passes over the main ranges of the Himalaya. It was the original silk route from China to India, so the path we were forging was by no means a pioneer route. We reached the top of the pass by three o'clock and were treated to a sight which comes only to a privileged few. Deep hard snow echoed back our crunching boots with soft moonlight. On either side of us high snow peaks stretched out endlessly. . . It was cold, but underneath our windsuits we were warm and elated, for the pass was our gateway into the real Himalaya. We reached our rest station. . .

The next day a 12-mile stage took them to Dras. They now began to experience the scenery and flavor of Baltistan: arid valleys almost denuded of vegetation through which run vast and turbulent rivers, and here and there the gorgeous green of irrigated hillside terraces beside mud villages that looked like something dating back to the era of Marco Polo.[1] In one of these, perhaps Dras, Jack made the error of entering a local house to see something of its interior. That night he began to scratch; he had picked up fleas.

An atmosphere of conviviality prevailed on the march. The men seemed happy and to be having fun. It was an aura that dominated the expedition for a month, all the way to Base Camp, even though each individual had his personal peculiarities. George supplied further details in his often-quoted May 6 letter:

You probably want to know how we individually are getting along. Fritz, despite an enormous amount of work, is doing nicely. We have named him Baby Face Sahib. Chap, wise and silent as the owl, is brown as a berry. Jack and his lusty sense of humor, which once in a while draws howls of disapproval, is the acting doctor because he is considering the medical profession. Tony, or Pop Sahib, is the Voice of Experience and doing very well at it. He came out with this amazing statement today; "Climbing is fun." Such perception! Dudley immortalizes us all in celluloid each day which I fear you will have to sit through upon our return. The two Georges are bearing up amazingly well. Seriously though, we are all well and having a good as well as happy time.

Fritz echoed George. At Kargil, on May 8, also writing to Joel Ellis Fisher, he said, with a touch of paternalism:

The boys are such a nice lot, taking everything from the easy side and hitting hard when necessary, it is fun to be a member of such a congenial group. Sometimes they may be a little too carefree but one word suffices to make them do their duty and work hard. I feel quite certain they will do well on the mountain, and that I will have no difficulties whatsoever in the running of a careful, efficient and coordinated climb.

As for the Sherpas, George told Fisher:

> *Our nine Sherpas are the staff of our existence. They get us up in the*
> *morning – a difficult feat at times – and they whack the coolies with their*
> *tongues whenever any of the sahib's equipment is endangered. We*
> *have a fine cook, Noor Muhammed, who has us putting on weight in-*
> *stead of losing it. Yes, indeed, we are doing very well.*

The three-plus tons of supplies and gear were, of course, carried either by local porters, beasts of burden, or sometimes both, depending on who or what happened to be available. At the end of every three or four stages, porters or wranglers were paid off, usually after long arguments about proper amounts and at the rate of about $.50 a day per man or $1 to $1.50 per horse. Then new men or animals were hired for the next three or four stages. A head man, or *jammadar,* managed the various teams, and the party had a local *chuprassi,* or policeman, to maintain order and prevent theft.

The usual stage was about 15 miles. The climbers traveled on foot, although for a considerable time most of them, suffering from blisters, rode horses. Occasional foot or leg injuries – shin splints in Dudley's case, a torn tendon in Trench's, a sprained ankle in Jack's – also made riding preferable. George, exuberant, often raced ahead of the others around noon to find a good lunch spot. There were also informal contests to see who could get to the proposed campground first. At day's end, dusty and tired, the sahibs sought out green terraces on which to pitch camp, often in the shade of an apricot grove, where they sipped tea while snowy spring blossoms drifted about. So entranced was Jack by these oases that many times he would stay up at night to watch the silent, snowcapped peaks in the distance and the stars and admire the beauty and atmosphere of the Indian night. Once he became so enamored with his surroundings that he took an oath to return someday at the same season and not alone if at all possible.

Jack may have had another reason, too, for staying up late in the evenings. By now the fleas had made a home of his sleeping bag.

AS NOMINAL DOCTOR, Jack, who had yet to attend a single class in medical school and who did not even know how to draw blood, ministered conscientiously to the minor ailments common to all treks. First priority, of course, was reserved for his companions and the Sherpas; then, if there was enough time, he tried to attend to the swarm of local villagers who came in search of the presumed medical help they knew existed somewhere, but which they had no way to obtain. Jack's "Medical Notes" for the period of May 2 through May 18 (recorded in his diary on the memo page preceding November 1 through November 4), when the party had its first rest day, make interesting reading, even though some of his remedies did not conform with modern medical practice or, for that matter, with those of his contemporaries who held medical degrees:

MAY 2: Gund. All have pregnant feet – blisters will be borne soon: George & I recovering from bunions.

MAY 3: Sonnamarg. Sheldon, Cranmer, Dudley & myself victims of blisters (I acquired mine in Srinagar the night before leaving). Fritz opened all & filled with his tannic acid containing 'Wonder Tan'.

MAY 4: Baltal. Snow travelling produced several cases of mild snow blindness. Use drops in them. More blisters.

MAY 5: Motayan. Filthy little village over 10,000 ft. Mud houses, goats & livestock share dwellings, & all eat together on flat roofs. Goiters! Several sore eyes – lots of blisters. I had a bad cold from Sonnamarg-Baltal march. Fleas must love me.

MAY 6: Dras. Pasang complains of the S_____. Diarrhea no doubt. Stomach cramps, slight temperature. Stayed up several hours feeding him aspirin & applying hot water bottle. Gave him dose of castor oil that afternoon. Sonam's shin splints & trick knee cartilage or tendon on the bum since Zoji-La or shortly before . . .

MAY 7: Shimse Karbu. Pasang still sad looking. Gave him Toni's opium pill to slow his bowels down, next day he walked [he had previously been riding]. Sonam somewhat better, still limps. Blisters for party – Chap has a doubleheader.

MAY 8: Kharal. God forsaken, barren spot at junction of Dras and Shigar Rivers and China-India and Tibet-India caravan routes. Old man appeared with wife & child – pills and few annas[2] . . . Dudley complains of tendon strain & swollen leg. Chap rode horse today because of blisters. Our head man has bad eye.

MAY 9: Olthingthang. Most beautiful village on earth if one does not get too near the houses and their stench. Mud, wood & reed structures, low, smoky, smelly & crowded – dusty, dank and dirty. Several goiters visible. Polyandry practiced by Mohammedans here provided for good spread of venereal diseases. People of this section have little or entirely no medical examination or care; worthy location for medical missionary if he is able to break through traditional and religious prejudices. Blisters improving. My slight case of sore eyes again well after drops of – – [diary here is a blank space] and dark glasses. It was indeed a surprise to see my grey-bearded patient of Kharal turn up in Olthingthang for further treatment, or was it for further baksheesh? Flattering nevertheless to have a patient follow you 14 miles or so. He got an aspirin and some Life Savers as a reward.

MAY 10: Bachaich. Quite positive that I picked up my circus of fleas here – either directly off contact with coolies, off the ground where others had camped or maybe from tent & sleeping bag carried by infested coolies. Father appeared with son who seemed to have stomach cramps (fits) at various intervals – asking the father what he did in such cases he answered – "nothing, we just let them die." A few harmless pills & a coin sent them off happy.

MAY 12: Parkutta. Village head man complained of constipation so he immediately got a big dose of castor oil. Contrary to all reports, namely that the natives love castor oil, he made a very wry appearance and had trouble keeping his dose. It worked!!

Sprained my ankle en route from Tolti. Right after lunch attempted to jump stream from 6 ft. pier as it were, slipped on large patch on opposite bank – got wet and felt "wringing." Continued march on ankle – also next day too but then rode from Gol to Skardu and from Skardu to Shigar. One more day's walk and nearly all well again.

MAY 15: Dudley found it advisable to ride to Shigar from Skardu on account of his shin splints. Had local Indian doctor look at his ankle & shin at Shigar – he prescribed salt water (lukewarm) baths. Also took a look at Chap's prize blisters. As George's feet were not too hot all three continued next day mounted.

MAY 17: Dud, George & Chap continued riding just as far as possible – to sheep skin rafts at Dassu. Usual number of belly aches among curious villagers during last few days.

MAY 17–18: Dassu.

1. Dud's foot soaked. Shows considerable improvement.

2. Old man led his blind wife for cure! Pitiful! Gave digestive powders and 4 annas to each of couple.

3. Pemba had cough & fever. Quinine fixed it. Notice many, many cases of goiter & trachoma.

Such, generally speaking, were the medical problems during the early stages of the march to Base Camp. Nothing that an informed layman could not handle, except for severe illnesses among the natives, many of which, doctor or no doctor, could not be treated without hospital facilities, if they could be treated at all.

STAGE FOLLOWED STAGE, with the men going ever deeper into mountain country. The only large settlement was Skardu, with its extensive bazaar and its uncommonly dense Hindu population. And there was Shigar, with its many apricot groves, then Koshumal, and finally Dassu for rest and reorganization. For the moment, the main job was to walk – or, if not possible, to ride. But every man had a special task that he did well. Fritz and "Joe" Trench busied themselves, with help from Tony, with porter and animal loads: each porter – or, when horses were used, wrangler – was issued a numbered identification card corresponding with his load, a duplicate of which was kept by the sahibs so that no mistakes could be made at payroll time. Chappell did odd jobs, while the energetic George, when not forging far ahead of the others, prepared newspaper articles and wrote letters home. Jack had his task cut out as medical officer. Taking into consideration his lack of training and experience, he acquitted himself well. And, of course, there was Dudley, always busy with his many still and motion-picture cameras recording everyone's movements for posterity.[3] These films corroborate the diary reports of a harmonious and happy approach march.

Despite its beauty, this was stark country. Tony, in a letter to Joel Ellis Fisher dated May 14, commented:

> This is indeed a bleak and barren country, and how the inhabitants manage to live fills me with a constant admiration and wonder. The hills are entirely bare of vegetation, which indeed only exists on the irrigated alluvial fans. We camp in these, and generally manage to make ourselves very comfortable. As there is much water in the canals at this time of year one can generally manage a bath, which is a great comfort after a hot and dusty march.

Two obstacles had to be overcome before Fritz permitted the caravan to take its first rest day. First, at Skardu, the party must cross the swift-flowing Indus. This was done on an ancient barge, which, according to legend as well as appearance, had been in service for the twenty-three centuries since Alexander the Great's conquering Greeks had constructed it to cross the river into India.[4] The crossing, and the work connected with it, required several hours. Saltwater navigator Dudley Wolfe, in a letter to the American Alpine Club dated May 13, but obviously written some days thereafter, described what took place:

> May 15 was to be a most interesting day, as we were to cross the Indus by ferry. This was a lengthy procedure as the current is swift and the boat small. The crew consisted of two helmsmen, who also sculled, and eight rowers. To negotiate the current it was necessary to take the boat far upstream above the point of embarkation, then by rowing as hard as they possibly could, directly for the opposite bank, the rowers, carried down by the current, got their boat to a point where we went aboard. It took about six ferry loads and a great amount of time to get our 39 horses, 9 coolies [Sherpa porters] and the seven of us to the opposite bank.
>
> The rest of the march was mostly through the flat sandy bottom of the Shigar River. Once more the heat was intense. In order to make use of a shortcut, we crossed a wide ford which in one place was at least waist deep. In crossing this some of the horse loads got wet. But no appreciable damage was done as the hot sun dried them out quickly.
>
> Some of us rode that day, including Jack Durrance, who, fortunately, had what for these parts might be called a fiery steed, the fire being either natural or the result of a stout switch. Anyway, by jumping his

mount over the stone wall of the polo field and finishing at a gallop, he was the first man in. We had come eleven miles in eight hours, including the fording of the Indus . . .

The next river crossing, that of the Braldu, two days later proved even more interesting. Dudley described what happened:

Again a ferry must be used. But here the situation was much more interesting than on the Indus. The Braldo, although narrow, is extremely swift with a series of small rapids. The boats consisted of two small skin rafts that had been carried in parts from Shigar. Each raft had 29 inflatable goat skins attached to a framework of poles. The crew used the same tactics in crossing as on the Indus. Although on the Braldo, in order to come down across the current, the crew carried the rafts far above the point where the baggage train was located. Having reached the point of embarkation, they hauled this raft out, blew the skins up again, launched it and took a sizeable load of baggage across. Although the passage was short, the crew managed a snatch of song in midstream. Flimsy as the rafts looked they managed to get the heavy loads over without getting them wet. The horses were not taken over. We must say goodbye to the little animals . . . and rely henceforth on Balti coolies.

Jack gave a somewhat shorter but equally graphic version in his diary (May 15 and 17):

Each trip across as the boat . . . started out, a cry would rise in loud prayer to Allah and Mohammed to protect and bring them safely across, rather impressive . . . Crossed river in first boatload just opposite [Dassu] campsite. Quite a thrill to float over wildly racing Himalayan torrent on 26^5 inflated sheepskins with loud prayers of the oarsmen for "safe voyage."

They were now in Dassu, another filthy, God-forsaken village with the usual share of goiter, cretinism, trachoma, and parasitical diseases. There all loads had to be reorganized for transport by porters, each cargo consisting of from sixty to sixty-five pounds. While this work proceeded, letters were written, newspaper stories prepared, and food sorted for the rest of the march in. Jack had the job of weighing and making up some 123 loads, each of which had to bear an identifying number and a listing of its contents. He enjoyed the task, but it took all day, so he wrote neither letters nor diary entries at the time. George, on the other hand, spent the entire time composing a story for the press. One Sherpa, Pemba Kitar, was found to be running a fever; Jack gave him quinine bisulphate and two painkillers, and by the next morning he felt better.

From Dassu to Gomboro to Chokpo, ever more dismal villages with equally dismal and wretched inhabitants, most of them diseased and barely able to scratch a living from the stubborn native soil. The sahibs kept reminding themselves that all water must be boiled, as well as most food.

More torrents–tributaries of the Braldu, to whose source they were heading–had to be crossed. But this no longer could be done by boat. Instead, the locals had devised an even more ingenious form of river torture. In a letter to the American Alpine Club dated June 4 and mailed from Base Camp, George described the event:

> *All three marches were notable for one reason or another. The first might be characterized by a twelve hundred foot climb over an ugly hill with greatly increased loads. The second march we crossed rope bridges. These bridges are truly remarkable and not all as pleasant and solid to cross as, say, the George Washington Bridge. They consist of three ropes thrown across the river and fastened to pilings. One rope is for the feet, the other two for the arms. As the ropes are merely woven from twigs and the river swirls gaily along many feet below, we naturally used the best mountaineering clutch on the side ropes. The bridges have two very unpleasant characteristics: they continually sway and threaten to turn over on you, leaving you and your rucksack suspended upside down; secondly it is reported that these bridges are never replaced until they break with somebody on them . . .*

The third march to which George referred took the caravan to Askole, the last settlement before entering the great Karakoram. By Balti standards, Askole was rich. In those days it produced more grain than its inhabitants needed. But the natives, profiting from a growing experience with expeditions, had learned how to get the most out of foreign visitors and by 1939 bore a reputation as "bad boys."

The stage to Askole had been short, just 6 miles. This gave the party many valuable hours in which to hire a new complement of porters for the march to Base Camp. It also provided Jack a chance to practice his growing medical skills, as his "Medical Notes" attest:[6]

> *MAY 20: Chongo. One porter scratched knee–iodine. Small child with boil in middle of back–cleaned. Had father squeeze out pus and then applied Mercury ointment bandage–gave father to know the pus was the devil himself and unless killed by boiling water when he came out he would cause more boils. Hope he doesn't boil his child! Left extra dressing with anxious father who was quite grateful.*
>
> *Massage for Dudley's shin splints and Trench's tendon with Histamine.*
>
> *MAY 21: Askole.*
>
> *1. So called leper (?) who at any rate was paralyzed and had to be carried on the back of another man. Gave him digestive powders, 1 aspirin*

and prescribed daily bath in 4–5 mile distant warm sulfur spring. He was already quite old.

2. An aspirin for a strong but curious young man with pain in the chest. He was bluffing, I believe.

3. Eye drops for Shuprasi from Skardu with warning to keep his dirty fingers out of them and to wear dark glasses.

4. George Sheldon ate too much fudge on 21st and a whopping big dinner on top of it – consequences: indigestion with vomiting and diarrhea. Felt too bad on 22 to get up and start but left at 10:00 AM. Though weak he is O.K. again. Had no fever but chills in the night.

Sanitary conditions in Askole very poor with houses crowded together – narrow paths between hovels. No one seems to be personally clean and syphilis is supposed to flourish here where polyandry is practiced. Eye trouble (Trachoma) and goiter are predominant maladies. People here suspicious & typical wild bad boys of the original Aryan stock.

On Monday, May 22, having rearranged loads and hired 123 porters, the party left Askole – the last, frail human settlement – and took off into the wilderness. Together with enough food to last the porters about twelve days, the total baggage added up to an estimated four and a quarter tons. The men of the expedition were as happy and congenial as on the day of their departure from Srinagar three weeks earlier. The venture so far had proceeded well, with a diverting multitude of minor adventures and no major problems. The tests, however, were yet to come.

7

THE ROAD TO XANADU

SLOWLY THE CARAVAN CONTINUED on its way. On May 22, after crossing its first glacier, merely the rock-strewn tongue of the Biafo, the party camped near an enormous boulder at a place called Korofon. George, less exuberant than usual because of his recent overindulgence, reached camp last; Chappell continued his quiet, gentle reflections; Fritz, the leader, with Tony, his deputy, and Trench, the transport officer, scurried around everywhere. Dudley, of course, kept taking pictures. As for Jack, he still endured his plague. "Went over all my clothing for fleas," he wrote in his diary, "as I continue to be bitten beyond all decency every night and can't sleep. Found only four–one escaped..."

Jack also had his medical work. In addition to the consequences of George's gluttony, there was the Sherpa Pemba Kitar, whose cough and fever had now recurred. Jack almost had a misunderstanding with Fritz over the case, but after a bit of discussion it was decided to send Pemba back to Skardu to obtain a doctor's certificate that he should be allowed to proceed. The ever eager Pemba protested, but in the end he agreed to turn back. Of this Jack wrote in his "Medical Notes" on the diary page for November 6, 1939:

> Pemba very weak on march, complains of cough with pain near diaphragm – carried his pack for him over Biafo tongue and still he staggered into camp. Fritz diagnosed possible pneumonia symptoms and ordered his return to Skardu for Dr's O.K. A very wise decision in view of the complications which usually arise with such bronchial ailments in high altitude.

No longer did the expedition have to contend with the filth of wretched villages, but camped on clean ground, albeit in ever starker and more forbidding country. Korofon, Bardumal, Paiju–the path, built by shepherds, now petered out almost entirely. The men alternated between walking on the edge of the Braldu and along steep, rocky hillsides. No more rope bridges, no more rafts; they had to ford every stream–and there were plenty. The men removed shoes and stockings, rolled up pants, and waded until they emerged on the far side with icy feet–except for Fritz, who opted to have a porter carry him across. On one such venture the porter slipped and plunged his fully clothed cargo into the water. Everybody except Fritz laughed.

On the fourth day out of Askole, just beyond Paiju at 11,500 feet (about 3500 meters), on a cold, rainy morning, the expedition members first stepped onto the Baltoro Glacier, source of the Braldu River.

The Baltoro runs west for 40 miles from the highest peaks of the Karakoram Range. With its neighbors–the Biafo, the Hispar, and the Siachen–it is one of the largest icefields outside polar regions and surely one of the most spectacular. On its north rise a myriad of sharp granite spires that vary in altitude from 18,000 to almost 24,000 feet (5500 to 7300 meters), culminating in the spectacularly steep Mustagh Tower. Fritz Wiessner, primarily a rock climber, was deeply impressed as, one by one, the summits peeked out through the dissolving clouds. So was everyone else.

The spires were a mere prelude. On the Baltoro's south rise two of the world's great summits: Masherbrum and, farther along, but still hidden, Chogolisa,[1] each short of the magic 8000-meter mark dear to mountaineers, yet both princes of the realm. At the glacier's head, still out of sight, waited those enormous wonders of nature: the six Gasherbrums, Broad Peak, and, finally, soaring above all, K2.

Ever since leaving Askole the weather had been cloudy and raw–good for hiking but poor for sightseeing. On May 26, the second night beyond Paiju, the party camped in a green oasis, called Urdukas, on the south edge of the Baltoro. That night it snowed. That night, too, as he lay awake in his tent while his companions slept, Fritz, to his wonder and delight, heard the distant cry of a snow leopard.[2]

Rare are the expeditions that escape a porter strike in Urdukas. The 1939 expedition experienced its own version–demands for more gear, shorter hours, and, above all, better pay. Fritz began to worry that if idleness were prolonged, there would be insufficient food for all the porters to reach Base Camp with their loads. Indeed, some did have to be left behind in the care of Sherpa Tsering and a couple of Baltis until arrangements could be made to move them forward.

The porters, as Jack noted, had a point. It was snowing and cold, and they were at 13,900 feet (4235 meters). "Poor coolies," he wrote on May 27, "were done in and found only wet snow & wet tarpaulins to soothe their misery."

Two grim days of enforced idleness passed in Urdukas. Finally, May 29 brought good weather. There was a brief but conclusive palaver, the strike terminated, and the caravan moved on.

Anyone who has traveled up the Baltoro becomes increasingly overwhelmed with the setting, one of the most spectacular in the world. Black rock and grey moraine contrast with the clean, white, distant walls of eternal snow, all under the deep blue of the high-altitude sky, while men only a hundred yards away seem like tiny specks on the horizon. And halfway up the glacier, the visitor runs into a unique local formation called the Ice Ships, towering pinnacles of pure white ice that soar almost 300 feet into the air.

Only in recent years have the causes for these spectacular ice mounds been determined by geologists. Jack, reflecting about them some days later in Base Camp, came up with a theory closely approximating the official modern version and used the extra monthly space entitled "Memo" at the close of May to elaborate his ideas:

> *My theory or shall I merely murmur my hypothesis concerning the ice ships expressed in a layman's tongue is this: There were no perceptible ice ships beyond the influence of the Younghusband Glacier. None are found beyond the entry of the Mustagh Glacier into the Baltoro, both entering from the N. They seem then to originate under side pressure influence of the side glacier (Younghusband) – quite some size and comparatively steep descent. Hence after being forced up at some point of the junction of the two separate ice streams (travelling at different speeds) they retained their height (which never exceeded the highest glacier hillocks of the Baltoro) by pressure from below which seemed to be in balance with their mass (height) so that while floating down in perfect alignment from the Y. Gl. to the Mustagh Gl. pressure kept them up as quickly as the sun melted them into such shiplike (sails) forms.*

Jack's language, for perhaps the only time in his journal, seems a bit confused, but the general idea is there.

The expedition spent the night of May 29 camped for the first time on bare ice. The Americans and their Sherpas had the protection of warm sleeping bags and air mattresses. Not so, however, the porters. Of these Jack wrote in his diary that night:

> *The coolies slept huddled together on rock-slab nests they either built or had found from previous expeditions – one of our tarpaulins held in the warmth and Balti stench, & their discomfort.*

The hardships had begun to tell. One man stubbed two toes badly, tearing off the nails. Another slipped, fell, banged his knee, and fainted; but Jack got him back on his feet in fifteen minutes with a caffeine pill. Still others began to complain of snow blindness. Though equipped with footwear, the porters preferred to march barefoot, even on ice and through snow. The heavy callouses developed therefrom probably protected them from frostbite, but at the same time their centimeter-thick epidermis often cracked and bled. Jack treated the condition with the then-popular suntan ointment Skol.

Despite growing hardships, both among porters and, to a far lesser degree, sahibs, things were still going well, with all obstacles handily overcome and morale high. On May 30, however, an event occurred that in all likelihood contributed strongly to the expedition's first major setback.

At the time, what happened did not seem important—just one of those things that rasps a bit and is soon corrected. Somehow a porter dropped a tarpaulin, which fell into a crevasse. Pasang Kikuli tried to retrieve it and failed. Fritz then asked the ever-willing Chappell Cranmer whether he would like to give the matter a second try. Chappell had a stubborn streak. Rather than admit defeat, he spent a long time deep in the cold, damp hole, and at an elevation of 15,000 feet (4500 meters), to which he was not yet accustomed, looking for the missing item. Finally recovering it, he was hauled soaking wet, chilled, and exhausted back into the sunlight.[3] The incident could not have helped improve Chappell's state of health, good as it seemed. Rather the contrary, for the exertion had been severe and the conditions bad at a time when acclimatization was still incomplete. (See Appendix B for the dangers and diseases of high altitude.) But for the moment no one took notice of the incident; in later years Fritz forgot it entirely, denying that anything of the sort had ever happened.

A second incident occurred on May 31, this one laden with immediate consequences. Camped in snow about a mile below the confluence of the Baltoro, Vigne, Godwin-Austen, and West Gasherbrum glaciers, some twenty-five to thirty porters suddenly refused to carry farther. The reason: no snow goggles. Somehow, when purchasing equipment in Germany, Fritz and Dudley had failed to include a sufficient number of goggles to equip all load carriers, who would now have to either stay behind or risk the extremely painful ordeal of snow blindness. Fritz was already on his way to Base Camp, but his deputy, Tony, suggested that everyone pitch in at once and manufacture twenty or thirty pairs. Chappell and Jack promptly produced the necessary equipment, which they made of cardboard with slits in the manner traditionally used by Eskimos.

Not long after leaving the campsite with the improvised-goggle-equipped porters, Jack and Chap caught up with George Sheldon and "Joe" Trench, now in Fritz's tracks, with three weeping porters at their feet, all suffering from snow blindness, one of them severely so. As he wrote that evening, Jack "puzzled over some sort of relief for the poor devils. We cut up my polaroid goggles and pasted them over the slits of their cardboard masks and sent them perforce back to Askole," accompanied by two men who could still see. As the casualties departed, Wolfe's camera recorded the dramatic incident.

Not only did the shortage of goggles cause suffering among the porters, but it had an indirect effect on the team as well. The resulting manpower shortage obliged those who had stayed behind to assist the porters— specifically, Chappell, Jack, "Joe," and George—not only to attend to the casualties, but to add the extra, now abandoned porter loads to their own, distributing the weight among the persons available. This made for what was in effect a double-carry for Jack, Chappell, "Joe," and George at altitudes where they had never been before. Chappell, recently out of the crevasse, must have found the ordeal very trying.

In all other respects, however, May 31 stood out as a banner day for the expedition. At noon, three marches above Urdukas and in splendid weather, the advance guard of the caravan reached Concordia[4] at 15,092 feet (4600 meters). Now higher than any point in America's forty-eight contiguous states, the men stood at the junction of the region's mightiest local glaciers: the Godwin-Austen, Upper Baltoro, Vigne, and West Gasherbrum. As they turned the corner, there, suddenly, it emerged, regal and resplendent in a fresh raiment of snow. K2!

They stared. Sella's splendid photographs paled before the reality that soared above them. What a challenge! And what, too, the toil and danger. For Fritz Wiessner, who had made the commitment months before, the words he would later put into his typewritten diary ran through his head: "Everything that I have learned...is dedicated to this—cool and deliberate, but with a warm heart." K2 for him could never be an enemy; rather it was one of nature's great bastions. His companions, as they stood awe-struck before the mountain, were not so sure.

As Jack, George, Chappell, "Joe" and the last of the porters slowly straggled into Base Camp, heavily laden, the early arrivals were already hard at work pitching tents and sorting supplies. The location was a few miles above Concordia on the Godwin-Austen Glacier at 16,500 feet (5010 meters), not far from its predecessor's site of the year before. Fritz felt pleased; aside from a few rare differences of opinion and minor confrontations such as occur to all people trying to do a job together, everyone had worked hard and performed harmoniously, a sign that the men were rapidly evolving into a real team. As he had indicated earlier in his letter to Joel Ellis Fisher, they should do well on the mountain.

16,600 ft.

Base Camp   **MAY 31**   *Wednesday*   100

[handwritten diary entry, largely illegible]

Last night's camp 3rd on Baltoro — sheltered vale in ice hillocks. Two porters quit on us at start next morning because of snow blindness. Sheldon scolded them a bit harshly not realizing quite the discomfort of the affliction. Gunner and I last to leave camp. Gunner very slow — we took shots of Mitre, Bride and Gasherbrum IV + Broad. Soon caught up with two Georges who had three weeping coolies at their feet — all more or less snow blind — one pretty bad off. (Forgot to mention the critical moments at beginning of the day when all coolies without dark glasses refused to go on. At Tom's suggestion we quickly pitched in + manufactured 20–30 pair cardboard slit glasses.) Chaps + Joe left George + I to puzzle over some relief for the poor devils. We cut up my polaroid goggles and pasted them over the slits of their cardboard masks and put them on. Force back to Askole. & he. Then greatest thrill of trip — K2 hove up way above the Baldwin-Austin Gl. In spite of wonders the 6–7 mile push up the very exhausting — arrived B.C. all in. Helped put ... tents, burnt stove ...

Durrance's diary entry for May 31

Not to cut off all communications, arrangements were made for a mail runner to come up from Askole on specified dates. Then all but a few of the best porters, selected to stay on for a few more days, were paid off and sent home. Absent new instructions, they were to return on July 23 for the homeward journey. This gave the team fifty-three days in which to ascend the mountain, ample time Fritz believed; by then someone would have reached the top or the attempt would have been abandoned. Even if a few people were still not off the peak, they could remain a few days more inasmuch as the camps would be amply stocked.

In due course, the seven loads left behind in Urdukas arrived with Sherpa Tsering. The expedition was now alone: six Americans, and thirteen British subjects of various backgrounds and races–nineteen persons altogether–at the end of a frail and uncertain line of communication with the outside world.

On June 1, Fritz Wiessner, Tony Cromwell, and Pasang Kikuli left for a three-day reconnaissance up the glacier. Fritz, following Vittorio Sella's suggestion, wanted to see the Northeast Ridge for himself–not that he intended to follow it, but just to make sure. He also wanted to have a good look at the Abruzzi Ridge.

A month had passed and many events had taken place since the expedition had left Srinagar so happy, carefree, and congenial. Throughout their journey to the mountain the men had retained that mood. But the preliminaries were about to end and the real job to begin.

A MAJOR PERIL FOR ALL UNDERTAKINGS with limited personnel is attrition. It can easily rout small parties. But even in large expeditions, by the time the team gets the chance to grab the prize, several of its members are usually out of action. A man falls and sprains or fractures an ankle; another contracts malaria or dengue fever on the march; a third comes down with high-altitude pulmonary edema (HAPE); a fourth eats tainted beef a thousand feet below a mountain objective and must descend; a fifth succumbs to exhaustion; a sixth and seventh, day after grueling day, simply lose heart. The 1939 American Karakoram Expedition to K2 was in no way immune. Attrition hit the very first day in Base Camp.

June 1, the morning that Fritz and Tony departed on reconnaissance, Chappell stepped out of his tent and announced he didn't feel well. At one time or another everyone had felt a bit down, notably "Joe" Trench and George, so no one worried when he crawled back into his sleeping bag. At noon, Jack, delayed until then by camp chores and by a renewed search for the still active and elusive fleas, went to see him. A bit later he emerged from the tent, with a serious look on his face. "I'm afraid we have a sick man on our hands," he announced.

Chappell was more than ordinarily sick: in a few more hours he would be close to death. "He coughed profusely," Jack wrote in his diary that day, "and expectorated quantities of flegm & slime." There was a deep rattle in his cough. He had no appetite, his temperature rose to 102° Fahrenheit (38.9° Celsius), and his pulse began to race. Jack, with no medical experience and in an age when high-altitude pulmonary edema was generally unknown, diagnosed pneumonia or cardiac decompensation – not too far off. Rightly or wrongly, he administered two tablets of ammonium chloride and one of phenobarbitol, and then spent the entire afternoon with Chappell. The patient did not improve. (For the seriousness of Chappell's ailment, see Appendix B.)

Jack's diagnosis may have been primitive, but his treatment of Chappell was heroic. "He called for me," Jack wrote in his diary on June 1, "while I tried to get some supper. Hurried to his tent around six and administered artificial respiration for at least 2 hours." The crisis was reached at 8 P.M.

Jack's memories of the event lasted all his life. During interviews with one of the authors in December 1986 and again in February 1987, he described the scene as follows:

Chappell was coughing up a huge quantity of clear, frothy fluid, or mush, from his lungs. I must have collected at least three coffee cups full. Horrible, bubbly stuff. Poor fellow, he was completely out of it, delirious, unconscious, babbling nonsense from time to time about a baseball game he dreamed he was playing back at Dartmouth. I fought a losing battle to keep him and the immediate vicinity clean. But even the tent was becoming a mess and everything inside smelled to high heaven. Then the worst happened: Chappell developed diarrhea and simultaneously lost control of his body functions.

Well, I reached outside the tent, grabbed a piece of plywood, cardboard, or whatever, and shoved it under Chappell's butt. But the damage was done. I could only keep the filth from growing worse. It was hours before I managed to clean things up – even then everything stank of vomit, mucus, urine, and, above all, just plain shit. I never knew anyone could be so sick and stay alive – especially here at 16,500 feet. But I stayed with him; I held his head; I reassured him; I tried to keep him warm, dry, and as clean as I could. In those days I wasn't very good at that sort of thing, but I did what I could, everything I thought could be of help.

You know, I'm an old man now, and I've practiced pulmonary medicine for over thirty-five years. I've seen patients get well, and I've seen many die. But from the day I entered medical school until now, at seventy-five, I've never had a worse patient than my first one, Chappell Cranmer.

Jack would never admit it, but he surely saved his "first" patient's life – and then slowly nursed him back to health. This kind of loyality on Jack's part repeatedly expressed itself before the season was out. It showed in his acts and it permeated his diary.

Even after the crisis Chappell's condition was still touch and go. In his diary entries for June 1 and 2, Jack commented as follows:

> *All Sahibs very worried. Started to give codein hypodermic at 9:00, but his condition seemed better and my lack of skill made me decide against such an action–also he obviously seemed to improve. No sleep that night! He expectorated all night–two tins full. Also had 3 bowel movements–as he was very weak it proved to be a workout to help him. He was too weak to hardly lift his arm. Thank God for the dawn and for sparing Chap!*

Chappell Cranmer would live, but for all practical purposes he could not participate in the ascent. It would take weeks for him to recuperate. At one blow, the expedition had lost one-sixth of its American manpower, one of the more determined and experienced. But if Fritz, on his return from his reconnaissance, had any misgivings about the undertaking as a result of Chappell's illness, he did not display it. Rather, he observed, "My best man seems to be out of it for some time."[5] The show, he announced, must go on.

If Fritz, albeit concerned about Chappell, brushed off his illness as a minor incident on the road to his objective, George's June 4 letter from Base Camp to the American Alpine Club contains not a word about Cranmer, as if the most dramatic and important event since the team's departure from Srinagar merited no comment. Most likely his silence resulted from fear that the news might alarm people back home – especially Chappell's parents, who might hear of their son's illness in a roundabout and garbled way through the climbing community.

8

THE ABRUZZI RIDGE

U NTIL RECENT TIMES, when small parties climbing alpine-style have whittled away the job's importance, virtually all large expeditions had an official leader whose task consisted of coordinating and supervising major activities from before departure until return. On any such expedition, in modern times or earlier, the leader has by far the most important duties. But these are usually thankless ones involving drudgery, hard work, dedication, and constant attention to detail. On a successful venture, the summit party–often a couple of tough, determined climbers who understand mountaineering, but perhaps little else–gets the laurels. The leader, who rarely has the time or opportunity to go high, is often conveniently forgotten. But if something goes wrong, you can bet the leader will be the one to catch the flak.

To provide relief and give the leader at least some opportunity to go high, most expeditions appoint a deputy to take over in the leader's absence or incapacitation. In addition, someone, usually the fittest and most experienced member of the climbing team, is selected point man (the military term), or lead dog (the Eskimo term). This is the person who takes care of the actual climbing problems on the mountain. The expedition leader and deputy cannot be expected to take over the role of point without seriously endangering the flow of supplies and support that is their basic responsibility.

On the 1939 expedition to K2, Fritz had appointed Tony Cromwell to be his deputy as well as to serve as expedition treasurer. Tony freely accepted these jobs, as he wrote Joel Ellis Fisher on May 14. But Fritz failed to select anyone to serve as point, and at Base Camp it became increasingly clear that he was reserving that position for himself, either because he didn't trust his companions' abilities, or because he had always been in the habit of going first. There was no doubting his ability as a mountaineer.

Good mountaineers are abundant, even though the very finest are rare. Good expedition leaders, however, are hard to find. Fritz had little experience or training as an expedition leader. On Nanga Parbat, where he served as deputy, matters were run, more or less well, by Willi Merkl, and Fritz's experience in World War I had been that of a common soldier. On short trips and day climbs he was superb as a rope leader for a small party of two or three, and almost invariably he excelled as point man. But to him, in all climbing ventures large or small, the leader's job was, quite simply, to lead: in short, it was Fritz who had to go first. And with his heavy personality it was natural that he would want to be in the position of making all decisions. Fritz was also brought up in a culture in which no one ever questioned the orders of a higher authority – a far different environment from that of a New England town meeting.

Fritz had a good sense of organization, and, if anything, on balance he

CAMPS ON K2

Camp	Altitude		Location
	Feet	(Meters)	
Base	16,500	(5030)	On Godwin-Austen Glacier
I	18,600	(5670)	On Abruzzi Ridge at 1909 campsite
II*	19,300	(5882)	In a sheltered hollow on ridge
IIa	20,000	(6096)	Merely a dump after tents hit by stones
III	20,700	(6310)	Only a cache; no tents
IV*	21,500	(6553)	Below House Chimney at Red Rocks
V	22,000	(6705)	Just above House Chimney
VI*	23,400	(7130)	At base of ridge's Black Tower
VII*	24,700	(7529)	Crest of ridge at summit plateau
VIII +	25,300	(7711)	In embayment on summit plateau
IX +	26,050	(7940)	On terrace south of summit cliffs

* important, well-stocked camp
+ reasonably stocked assault camp

overequipped his party. Certainly, there was the oversight of the porter goggles, and the Sherpa sleeping bags were diminutive; but these things in no way derailed the expedition. On the march in, Fritz had been indefatigable; he would remain so on the mountain.

As far as Base Camp, Fritz, in the manner of good leaders, had stayed with his troops except for one or two forays to seek future transportation. And with everyone together, harmony prevailed. To be sure, minor friction had arisen from time to time: once when Jack, in an effort to be helpful, interfered with Tony's job of distributing porter loads; again, a near misunderstanding between Jack and Fritz at Korofon about what to do with the sick Pemba Kitar; and a difference of opinion between the same two over location and map interpretation on the Baltoro. Nothing important, however.

From Base Camp on up the mountain the group would gradually become separated, and this separation, far from making the heart grow fonder, tended in time to polarize the party into two groups. The rift did not visibly open up until the expedition's return to Srinagar, but when it did, it provoked a major explosion.

Of course, some separation was necessary beyond Base Camp in order to get the job done. Fritz's first action had been to set off on reconnaissance. As noted, he took with him his deputy, Tony, and the Sherpa sirdar, Pasang Kikuli. He had all the chiefs. The braves stayed behind to cope as best they could—and the town meetings began.

As noted earlier, a chain of circumstances, with links sometimes apparently unrelated, rather than a single event, led to the expedition's ultimate undoing: first the dropping out, even before the start, of the strongest expedition candidates, Bestor Robinson, Al Lindley, Sterling Hendricks, and Roger Whitney; the loss of Pemba Kitar near Askole; and now Chappell Cranmer's illness and resulting incapacitation. Another chain of events, which started with Fritz's surprise and consequent icy reception of Jack Durrance in Genoa, was to exacerbate the terrible controversy that took place after the party's return.

LEADER OR NO, a major mountaineering expedition requires a general plan of action that all members understand and accept. Fritz contrived a simple and practical strategy. It was nothing new, having evolved from experiences on many prior, major-summit expeditions. It followed the same camp plan as the 1938 K2 expedition, whose reports had been studied by all team members and in which four of the eight Sherpas now at Base Camp had participated. George Sheldon described it tersely in his later article in the *Saturday Evening Post:*

Our plan was to establish a series of camps to within striking distance of the summit. Each of these camps would be stocked with tents, sleeping bags, petrol and a two week supply of food in case a storm should maroon a party. The camps were to be near enough together to maintain constant contact... [1]

In practice, certain camps had to be pitched far apart for terrain reasons, notably Camps II and IV (Camp III was merely a cache), while Camps I and V soon outlived their usefulness and were largely eliminated.

Presumably understood by all was the rule that no camp should be dismantled until everyone above it had descended safely, or until there was convincing evidence those above had perished. The troops, however, were expected to obey the instructions of leader Wiessner, or, in his absence, those of deputy Cromwell.

Fritz's packing plan for the loads provided for almost every contingency, down to spare bootlaces and matches. But plans on paper and in execution do not always coincide because they depend on a complex web of human factors. There had been the shortage of Balti porter sunglasses. And now in Base Camp there arose a problem for one of the best climbers, Jack Durrance. His high-altitude boots, ordered at the last moment from Sporthaus Schuster,[2] had still not caught up. Jack's only footwear consisted of an old, leaky, badly worn pair of boots totally unsuited for the cold conditions above 20,000 feet (6100 meters) in the Karakoram – or, for that matter, even lower. Bad footwear handicapped Jack's performance severely.

LEADER FRITZ, DEPUTY TONY, AND SIRDAR KIKULI returned from their reconnaissance at four o'clock in the afternoon on June 3. They had climbed to 19,000 feet (5791 meters) on Sella Peak, east of and across the Godwin-Austen Glacier from K2. Following Sella's recommendation they had examined the Northeast Ridge. It looked no better than it had to Houston's party the previous year. At their high point, Fritz and Tony conferred at length while studying other aspects of K2. Houston had been right; the Abruzzi Ridge was it – but were they sufficiently strong? Tony trained his binoculars on its upper levels and grinned optimistically. If last year's team could do as well as it had, he told Fritz, this 1939 party should do better. Why, he might even change his mind and accompany the summit team. Tony had a habit of blowing hot or cold; before long it was usually the latter.

The Abruzzi Ridge, at least in its lower half, is a misnomer. It consists of a series of rock outcrops, snow faces, and ice couloirs that gradually converge as one proceeds upward. Only in its upper part, above 22,000 to

23,000 feet (6700 to 7000 meters) does it merit the name of ridge. The lower portions, subject to stonefall, are steep, messy, and by all accounts dangerous because of loose stones.

The principal difficulties on the Abruzzi Ridge are: (l) the long section between Camps II and IV, exposed to loose stones and culminating just below Camp IV in a difficult overhang; (2) a demanding 80-foot recess, known as the House Chimney, just above Camp IV; (3) some delicate rock passages, ice-covered in bad weather, above Camp VI; and (4) a dangerous ice traverse below Camp VII. With fixed ropes and under good conditions the ridge could, however, be ascended or descended by trained and experienced persons in a single day. In fact, in 1939, Sherpas several times moved on various sections of the ridge without sahibs: two climbed from Base Camp to Camp VI in a few hours, and one descended from Camp VI to Base Camp between sun-up and afternoon of the same day.[3] But then everything depends on the weather and one's climbing skill and physical condition. The Abruzzi Ridge is no place for the clumsy or the inexpert and, in bad weather, is no place for anyone, however skilled.

What makes the Abruzzi Ridge formidable are its altitude, its length, its steep ascent to ever higher levels, and its unrelenting nature. Moreover, the climber, while working against gravity, must carry heavy supplies to stock camps up in what physiologist Edward Wyss-Dunant defined, a bit arbitrarily, as the "Death Zone" (see Appendix B). Once committed there is no alternative line of escape, and nowhere, for more than 7000 feet (more than 2100 meters), is there a place where a climber can let his or her guard down–this in circumstances where with every upward step there is an unseen potential for "dulling of thought."

A major debilitating factor on the ridge is the cold, penetrating, persistent west wind that howls down from Turkestan, sweeps around the mountain, and whips up great clouds of flying snow that penetrates through tents, sleeping bags, and clothing to chill the marrow of one's bones. A perpetual and unwelcome companion, this wind is considered by the Sherpas to be their worst foe. Even from below, one sees an almost constant reminder: the great plume of spindrift that streams, like a flag, in the lee of the mountain's summit. Everyone, not just Sherpas, who has been on K2 complains of the wind. Other nearby giants–Broad Peak, Masherbrum, Chogolisa, even Hidden Peak and the Gasherbrums–receive kinder treatment and appear better protected. But K2, because of its size and location on the northern, more exposed rim of the Baltoro massif, acts as a windbreak for its lesser neighbors.

FRITZ, AS HE HAD WRITTEN IN HIS DIARY, was distressed to learn of Chappell's illness, but it didn't shake his resolve. Indeed, each day that passed strengthened his determination. Surely a party that so far had gotten along well without the likes of Robinson and Lindley could persevere without Cranmer; there was plenty of manpower around, including eight of the best Sherpas available. The mountain remained Fritz's chief concern.

Not so Jack, who had become more and more involved in the human factor. For the moment Chap was his main concern. On June 4 he wrote in his diary about Chap:

> *He shows more improvement—was set out in sun for sun bath by Fritz... washed Chap's hands & face—brushed his teeth & combed his hair. Cooked him bouillon with butter & a shot of lime juice with slice of boiled ham & Rye Krisp which he ate without too much help—hurray! Got him back in tent as wind blew up (cold). Then tried to continue house cleaning I had begun earlier in the day (got Chap's junk out but my personal affairs still in upheaval).*

And on June 5, returning from his first carry to Camp I, he added: "Chap is recovering quite rapidly—He can even help now when the necessity for personal relief arises."

Just why Chappell fell ill when no one else did is unclear. The long stay in the crevasse on May 30 and the double-carry to Base Camp the next day both played a part in creating a favorable climate for the onset of something that, in retrospect, was probably high-altitude pulmonary edema (HAPE). In interviews years later, Fritz showed skepticism and attributed the illness to a "minor lung problem" mentioned at one time by Chappell's mother.

ON THE MOUNTAIN ACTION BEGAN as planned on June 5. Fritz, Jack, George, Dudley, the eight Sherpas, and two temporarily retained Baltis shouldered thirty-five-pound loads for the sahibs and fifty pounds each for the porters. Fritz, going ahead, as expected, on the first rope, set what Jack described as a "stiff pace" for the first 2 miles while the party wormed its way around big crevasses. But he also allowed two prolonged rests, one just before a large, avalanche-swept section and the other below the Godwin-Austen Glacier's icefall. Jack, with little glacier experience, marveled at Fritz's pathfinding skill and ingenuity: "a masterpiece of route finding," he wrote in his diary that day. Then followed a 700-foot (213-meter) climb from the glacier to Camp I, at 18,600 feet (5670 meters) on the 1909 Italian campsite.

The duke's old tent platforms were still serviceable, and debris left by past occupants lay strewn about. Here the party deposited some 700 pounds (about 300 kilograms) of gear. Eventually that, and later equipment, would move upstairs so that in the end Camp I would become no more than a staging area. For the time being, however, it represented an important step in the expedition's upward march.

It was on the way back to Base Camp that, for the first time since Genoa, an uncomfortable situation briefly developed. Apparently George, always chomping at the bit, sprinted off well ahead of the others. Fritz became irritated by the display of flamboyance. He caught up with George and chewed him out. "George caught hell [from Fritz] for spurting ahead," Jack wrote in his diary on June 5.

Questioned about this incident several decades later, Fritz pointed to a different culprit: it was Jack, not George, who had behaved impishly.[4] But by then memories had faded, and Fritz had built up a lasting, if irrational, prejudice against Jack. Jack's diary, written at the time, seems a better source than Fritz's reconstructed memory. Besides, Jack's boots were far too worn to permit a gallop over the icy glacier.

Everybody carried loads, even "Joe" Trench, who was growling more and more that menial work, such as pack bearing, ought to be reserved for Asians. Sherpas and Baltis, then and now, carry more than their Western employers. Teamwork, the essential ingredient for success, kept improving, at least at this time. The work was hard, especially for Jack, whose tendency was to do more than the others and whose footwear gave him much grief. But despite wind, altitude, and long, heavy carries, no one complained openly. Privately it could be another story: "There is no expression," Jack wrote on June 7, "to describe how awful I felt physically today–back ached–short winded and despondent spirits." The wind, too, hurt: "I thought my tent would turn into a magic carpet," he added. And the fleas in his sleeping bag seemed immune to altitude sickness. Jack was doing his best, but perhaps already his heart, unlike Fritz's, was not on K2.

Fritz Wiessner, Jack Durrance, and Pasang Kikuli occupied Camp I overnight for the first time on June 8.

On June 9, Dudley Wolfe, having made three relays to Camp I, and loaded with cameras, left Base Camp with a fourth and final cargo. He would never return.

That same day, Fritz, Jack, and Kikuli pushed the route to Camp II, where they found the same wind-protected nook that had served their 1938 predecessors. This camp became the most important on the lower part of the ridge; in time it replaced Camp I and represented one of the key, fully stocked shelters defined in the original climbing plan.

As he had from Base Camp to Camp I, and true to his belief that the leader must lead, Fritz forged the route. "...[He] did the lion's share of step kicking," Jack wrote in his diary on June 9. "I, the whale's share of freezing." Jack, behind and dodging stones, could help only modestly. "My shoes were most inadequate to cope with yesterday's workout," he wrote on June 10. "Three hours standing still in the snow [while Fritz, ahead, carved a route up the steep spots]. Toe exercises warded off any form of frostbite, Gott sei Dank!"

On the descent, disregarding his earlier admonitions to George, Fritz, with new tricouni nails on his boots, left Jack behind and galloped down the ice patches to Camp I. Kikuli, always solicitous, stayed behind to assist Jack on the slippery places where his decrepit footwear was holding him back more every day. "I just wanted to see whether you could take care of yourself" were the words Jack heard from Fritz to explain his Sheldon-like conduct. The incident, not grave in itself, made Jack uneasy. It suggested insensitivity and a double standard on the part of the expedition leader. Still, Jack had enjoyed one of his best days so far: "Tired but had glorious day & magnificent Himalayan [scenery], late arrival back in camp with most famous of Himalayan porters, Pasang Kikuli."

Jack had by now developed great admiration for the Sherpas. He was clearly awed in the presence of their most distinguished veteran. And though he was an accomplished rock climber and, in fact, a better mountaineer than he thought himself, Jack still retained deep respect, almost a reverence, for Fritz, especially as a climber.

At Camp I they found Dudley, Tony, and "Joe" plus five Sherpas, ready to start moving the ton and a half of accumulated supplies upward to Camp II. Fritz, however, decided to declare June 10 a rest day. Tony, "Joe," and Dud took the decision literally and barely moved out of their tent. Fritz and a still tired but plucky Jack rested not at all, but set to cooking, checking gear, and doing other chores. At day's end Jack, weary even when writing, observed: "That's the effect of the altitude – every step & word is an effort."

Fritz and Jack were, for the present, seeing eye to eye and getting on well. The rest of the party, however, was in the doghouse. Nobody wanted to do any work, and "Joe" Trench, with slovenly habits, transformed one tent into a pigsty. There was a brief blow-up between Dudley and Tony, and then things calmed down; but in his diary entry of June 12, Jack let it all hang out:

> I hope from now on the others will help a little more with less criticism (phenomenon of this altitude). Spent my rest day working like hell – cleaning dishes and pigpen, drying raisins, putting things on to soak, testing High Primus, etc. Joe more hindrance than help & exasperates me with his Indian Sahib attitude – he can't help it, but it is annoying, by God. I'm no Indian servant.

Camp I Rest Day. **JUNE 10** *Saturday*

My shoes were most inadequate to cope with yesterdays work out. 3 hrs. standing still in the snow. Toe exercises warded off any form of frost bite — Gott sei Danks! Pasang & I roped down Talus slope while Fritz had run on ahead. Tired but had glorious day & magnificent Himalayan late arrival back in camp with the most famous of Himalayan porters Pasang Kiguli going ahead on my Klay. Toni arrived at Camp I from B. C & 8 day with Dud & Joe. He had tea & soup for us which along with a warm bed was a great comfort. Today is rest day for 5 Whites & 5 Sherpas at Camp I. Toni & Dud & Joe hardly got out of their tents all day. Fritz and I untangled second spool of Peep tchnur and but seven or more ropes which were stretched over the snow to make them pliable & straight. Also we did the cooking which kept us two busy all rest day. Managed to write two pages of diary otherwise "fussy." But that is the effect of the altitude — Every step & word is an effort. Making up loads some proposition too.

Durrance's diary entry for June 10

Then, on his ferries to Camp II, in addition to his thirty-five-pound load, Jack was given "Joe" Trench to conduct. Clumsy and constantly tired, "Joe" proved a real hindrance, especially since Jack had developed a lame leg as well as a toothache that was to bother him until his return to Srinagar two and a half months later. The only consolation was that after they finally settled into Camp II on June 14, the fleas from Dras seemed to go into an altitude-induced hibernation.

"Joe" was not the only butterfingers in the group. The more experienced climbers, Fritz excepted, were beginning to view Dudley with more than a little apprehension. All the more so because in every way Dud was so lovable and such fun as a companion. During a descent to Camp I to carry up loads on June 16, Dudley seemed particularly awkward, whereupon his companions (chiefly Tony) openly expressed their reservations about his presence on K2. Dudley, a sensitive person, felt hurt. Thereafter he gravitated steadily toward Fritz (temporarily absent in Base Camp), who had begun to treat him as a favorite. It almost looked as though the team members were beginning to take sides, thereby threatening the cohesion and unity that had hitherto prevailed.

EVER SINCE BASE CAMP'S ESTABLISHMENT, Fritz had managed successfully to wear two hats, that of commander and that of point, or, as Jack preferred to describe it, "lead dog." On June 14, faced with unfinished administrative duties, Fritz descended to Base Camp, taking with him George and three Sherpas. He left Tony in charge, with instructions to proceed with the advance and, if possible, to push as high as Houston's Camp IV, just below the "Red Rocks" at 21,500 feet (6553 meters). In retrospect he may have expected too much.

At Base Camp Fritz learned good news and bad. Chappell continued to improve. The first mail runner had just arrived, bringing more than sixty letters from the outside world. There were the usual greetings from family and friends, but he also found references to warlike rumblings in central Europe. Hitler, whom Fritz had hoped to leave behind when he became an American citizen, seemed to have an insatiable appetite. Of greater immediacy was the fact that Jack's boots were not in the mailbag. Without them the party's second most skilled member, and a harder worker than most of the others, would be unable to climb high.

Aside from the persistent wind, the expedition had enjoyed good weather until June 15, when the first brief storm arrived. It cleared in a day, but it shook the men in Camp II and only somewhat less so those at Base Camp. It warned of things to come.

Fritz and George departed Base Camp on June 16, escorting four others as far as Camp II for a long stay on the Abruzzi Ridge. Most supplies had now reached Camp I or II. Chappell was moving around now and would be able to attend to whatever needed to be done below, while deputy leader Tony surely could supervise activities on the lower sections of the ridge. Fritz itched to resume his job as point.

As he bade Chappell good-bye, Fritz took a last look around. Certainly the mountain was dangerous and his commitment total. He expected to return alive, and in triumph, but he might be wrong. He stared at K2's imposing structure, and his inherent optimism returned: "Cool and deliberate..." he said to himself, as he had written in his diary some days earlier.[5]

Fritz's six-man caravan – the Indian interpreter, Chandra, came along for his second visit to the mountain – reached Camp II on the afternoon of June 17. Fritz expected to learn of real progress. Instead he found a disconsolate Dudley brewing tea for Jack and Tony, with Jack, who had until then been a heavy cigarette smoker, inveighing against tobacco, which, he had decided, was positively harmful at altitude. What had they done all this time, aside from engaging in bull sessions? Not much. They had not even reached the site of the old Camp III. The brief storm and bad conditions, Tony said, had made progress difficult, even dangerous. Finally, in anticipation of Fritz's imminent return, Tony had made an about-face. Jack noted on June 17:

> *[Tony] has decided to push up in spite of recent snowfall, also wisely decided to leave George Trench & Dudley behind until route has been reconnoitered. Sherpas late in getting ready, start around 7:00 AM. Sun strikes tents at 6:15 AM. Froze feet [Jack's bad boots again] on way up to dump. Dawa rubbed them and applied Histamine ointment... Pasang K led way straight up past many rope slings & fixed ropes of last year – going very slow – placed our fixed ropes and pitons. Had to make dump of loads 200 feet under old Camp III – winter climbing – ice & snow & cold feet.*

Omitted at the time from his diary, but mentioned later, is the fact that the vertical rise from Camp II to IV (2200 feet; 671 meters) made for an extremely long carry at altitudes mostly above 20,000 feet (6096 meters). In addition, the risk of stonefall was constant and severe – so severe that Fritz vetoed the idea of an intermediate Camp III, preferring to use the old site merely as a cache.

Unlike its smoothly oiled 1938 predecessor, all of whose participants had expedition experience in wet and frigid Alaska or similar spots, most of the 1939 team belonged to what must be termed the "fair-weather climbing set." Even in the Tetons, where Jack had guided, summer storms, occasionally severe, usually did not last long. On top of this, expedition deputy Tony Cromwell was extremely cautious and almost fearful, accustomed as he was to accepting his climbing orders from paid guides.

With nothing to do, or rather, consequent on reluctance to do anything, morale, so high a week or two earlier, had begun to sag. The strong winds and the brief, violent storm further disheartened the climbers, and besides, Tony's and Jack's extensive experience was telling them that they simply did not have the right make-up to be on K2 at all, nor, in their opinion, did their three less experienced comrades: "Joe," George, and especially Dud.

Yes, especially Dud. He was strong and enthusiastic, yet clumsy. After Dud had departed Base Camp, George had exclaimed in his letter to the American Alpine Club of June 14: "Dudley is on the mountain and you can't get him to come down." Whether going up or down he required assistance, and while a delightful tent-mate, he hardly knew how to light a Primus stove or prepare any food except tea. "This trip & mountaineering," Jack wrote in his diary on June 16, "is simply a bit more than he expected and he is sensitive about 'roping up,' 'belaying,' etc." Still, he was game. Dudley's tenacity and his great strength were beginning to work on Fritz's mind; perhaps Dudley did, after all, have it in him to go for the top.

Fritz had little comment about the lack of progress, but surely he must have been disappointed. If the mountain was to be climbed at all, somebody had to do it, and those fellows at Camp II seemed completely lacking in initiative. So it was up to Fritz because there simply wasn't anyone else. The alternative was for them all to go home. But that was unthinkable. Henceforth it was he, Fritz, who would serve as point, all the way up, and, if necessary, all the way down. Administrative and support duties would simply have to be delegated.

Thus on K2, except for a few hundred feet of step-cutting above Camp II, Fritz Wiessner, whether by design or necessity, became the point man every inch of the way. Other expeditions have rotated the job, while solo climbers have used the tracks and equipment of their predecessors. But nobody in the history of Himalayan mountaineering has outperformed Fritz Wiessner, alone responsible for his expedition's progress and saddled with companions who were more of a hindrance to him than a help.

The major problem with Fritz's support was Tony Cromwell's attitude. The man had accepted the job of deputy leader and knew that his task was to keep things moving up the mountain. Yet he repeatedly called off proposed carries, citing a variety of flimsy excuses–the threat of bad weather, poor climbing conditions, Sherpa reluctance–anything that would delay exertion. Nor did he at Camp II, in Fritz's absence, try to instill in his companions, Sherpa or American, a sense of initiative and will to perform. That was Tony's job; even if he himself could not or would not climb higher, his duty was to encourage the others to keep going. Jack's diary for the mid-June period contains repeated references to Tony's irresolution.

Unfortunately no one, especially faced with so formidable an antagonist as K2, can do two full-time jobs simultaneously. By taking over that of point man, Fritz in effect disassociated himself from his appointed responsibility as overall leader. The change from administrative leader to climbing leader had a major impact on events to follow.

Even with Fritz in the lead it took two more days before the site for Camp IV could be reached. As Tony and Jack already knew, the going was hard and dangerous over long, steep, often stone-swept slopes. Finally, on June 21, a large, heavily laden caravan on three ropes – Fritz, Dudley, Sonam, and George on the first; Jack, Dawa, Tsering, and Norbu on the second; and Kikuli, Tse Tendrup, and Pasang Kitar on the third – established Camp IV after a gain of 2200 feet (671 meters). Jack, in his old boots, felt the cold. He provided a general description of the event in his diary entry the next day (June 22):

> [The final overhang, just below the top, is a] fancy piece of rock work...Hand over hand pullup with ample loose stones about to make it interesting for those below.In fact whole route from Col [site of Camp IIa] to Camp IV requires continual caution for loose stones & some places require good klettern [rock climbing] if it is to be done safely.

At 4:00 P.M. that day, Jack, unable to stay because of bad footwear, began the task of escorting Dawa, Pasang Kitar, Sonam, and Tsering back to Camp II, looking forward with little enthusiasm to further carries over the dangerous slopes. Meanwhile, the other six – Fritz, George, and Dudley with Kikuli, Norbu, and Tse Tendrup – set about pitching three tents (one for sahibs, one for Sherpas, and one for supplies) on the platforms constructed the previous year.

It was cold and windy. But somewhere far below and distantly, summer had arrived.

9

PRELUDE TO DISASTER

ODERN PHYSIOLOGISTS, as indicated earlier and as discussed in Appendix B, know that above about 22,000 feet (6700 meters), with personal variations, there is, over a period of time, perceptible deterioration of human functions. Some recent studies even indicate that, in severe cases, there may be lasting damage to the brain. Even the sturdiest individuals, some of whom, like Fritz Wiessner, can tolerate a higher elevation and for a longer time than others, are in the long run not spared. Just as somewhere around 17,000 feet (5181 meters) ends the zone of permanent biota habitation, so, somewhere around 22,000, give or take a thousand feet, begins the zone of sustained deterioration. Nor do those exposed to it notice their gradual decline, but rather the erosion masquerades as apparently continued strength, only to strike suddenly at the moment least expected.

In 1939 little was known except in rare medical circles about high-altitude deterioration and the need to descend for recuperation. Rather, it was traditional policy to climb a little higher, day by day, and remain at the new altitude in the expectation that sustained exposure would assist the acclimatization process.

Except for one very short break, Fritz would remain at 21,500 feet (6553 meters), and much of the time, far above, for the next twenty-four days after establishing himself at Camp IV. Dudley Wolfe, now seeming to show ever-increasing physical strength and, as George Sheldon had observed, insistent on remaining at ever loftier aeries without once descending, was to spend more than a month in what Wyss-Dunant later called the "Death Zone."

THANKS TO THE EXPEDITION LEADER'S LAST RESORT DECISION to become point man, things were moving again. Camp IV was secure and reasonably stocked. The next day, June 22, Fritz planned to lead the House Chimney, the Abruzzi Ridge's severest obstacle, now only a couple of hundred feet above him, and set up Camp V. He had looked forward to this job ever since learning of its first ascent by his old Waddington and Devil's Tower buddy, Bill House.

But fate often spoils the best plans. That night a violent storm shrieked out of Turkestan. The eternally cold, piercing wind rose to hurricane force (at Camp II, Jack recorded gusts of eighty miles per hour) and swept down on the little camp. Tents reeled, guy ropes tautened to the breaking point, and canvas clapped like thunder. Bang! Bang! Bang! . . . A pause as the tempest gathered new strength, then again . . . Bang! Bang! Bang! So strong were the gusts that at times George believed the wind "would launch them into a maiden flight into Tibet. Even Fritz," he wrote in his July 8 letter to the American Alpine club, "a man who had endured several storms on Nanga Parbat, uneasily called it the worst storm he had ever been in." The men, imprisoned in their tents, huddled in their sleeping bags. Melting water from ice over flickering Primus stoves took hours; cooking food took even longer. The stove fumes poisoned what little oxyen remained in the air and caused mild disorientation. Sleep became impossible. It turned cold, with temperatures dropping to $-2°$ Fahrenheit ($-19°$ Celsius). Even in sleeping bags, hands and feet suffered.

During one lull George stepped outside to film the gyrating tents. In the process his fingers turned numb and the wind almost blew him away. He dove back into the relative safety and comfort of his sleeping bag. During another lull, this on June 25, Jack, hit almost as hard in Camp II, began to be "a bit anxious for their [those above] welfare or at least comfort," as he noted in his diary. He prodded two Sherpas, Phinsoo and Sonam, to carry supplies, together with a note for Fritz, to Camp IV. The pair got through, and remained.

Camp II received its share of the storm, although because it was lower and better protected, things were somewhat more tolerable – this despite the fact that, in due course, snow would fall there on the next twelve out of fourteen days. Nonetheless, conditions and forced confinement had a bad effect. "It is," Jack wrote on June 27, "far too windy & dangerous to relieve oneself at our eagles' nest privy." Even the hardy and usually reliable Sherpas became apathetic. "Negligent Sherpas left one end of their [empty] tent half open, which finishing the equation gives a half tent full of snow," Jack told his diary. To which he added: "Blast their indifference to details anyway!"[1]

Toward the end of the storm, Jack had the most pleasant surprise of his sojourn. On June 28, Tsering, who had gone to Base Camp because of temporary illness, arrived with the mail. It was, said the weather-worn Jack, "more than any Xmas to me – my expedition boots arrived. Now, weather permitting," he gleefully added, "and all other things being equal, I may be able to go higher."

Altogether the great storm lasted eight days.

Suddenly, on June 29, all was quiet, and a lingering fog settled over the mountain. At Camp IV, George, toes nipped by cold and shaken by a fall, descended with several Sherpas. Fritz climbed out onto a little promontory to see them off. He shouted encouragement and advice as they vanished down into the mist. Long after they disappeared Fritz kept his post, his loud, encouraging voice calling out comfort and good cheer through the fog to those who had kept him company during the past nine trying days.[2]

Fritz would not see George again.

MORE THAN CHAPPELL CRANMER'S ILLNESS, more than the heavy relays between camps, and more than the raw throats, sleeplessness, and constant fatigue, the terrible weather of late June shattered the morale of almost all the climbers. There were only two exceptions: the ever-optimistic Fritz and Dudley, whose trust in Fritz had become almost absolute.

If Fritz and Dudley bubbled with confidence up in Camp IV, those in Camp II labored under a cloud of pessimism. The early optimism and carefree spirit were gone. Eyes turned away from the hardships of K2 and toward the comforts of home. The "most discussed topic," Jack told his diary on June 26, "is what we shall do when once again in civilization – a week's stay in Srinagar – sightseeing in India (Taj Mahal, etc.) and in my case several short "Bergfahrten" in the Dolomites as I land in Venice to be followed by a short visit to Munich . . . and Garmisch-Partenkirchen."[3] However much battered, Jack retained his love for the mountains.

Psychologically, the expedition had begun to pull apart: Fritz and Dudley focused on the summit; the others wanted only home. It was no longer the cohesive group that Fritz had held together earlier by his constant and dominant presence. Now that he had been forced to appropriate for himself the assignment of point, and now that all participants had experienced a taste of what K2 and its meteorological allies could do, things changed. The psychological gap was about to be widened by the physical gap created by Fritz's sustained absence far above everyone else. And without the presence of a strong and enthusiastic deputy to cover the rear, the essential elements to unity needed for success were lost.

Fritz had already once witnessed what was likely to happen in his absence; without his presence, the others were likely to do nothing. But, optimistically, he ignored this warning.

THERE NEXT TOOK PLACE AN INCIDENT that in more than one way illustrates the prevailing state of expedition communications. On July 1, the day after George Sheldon's arrival at Camp II and following a trip to Camp I to carry up the last remaining loads, Jack Durrance sent another note to Fritz Wiessner by way of the Sherpas:

Camp II, July 1
Dear Fritz: Thank heavens for Camp IV that the weather has taken a turn for the better. George S. arrived in II around 4:30 P.M. with four Sherpas rather tired and cold – but safe. Everything here hung on during the storm with the exception of Joe who blew in on us, one day late, the 28th of June. The last mail brought my boots at last which with all the new snow was very much like Christmas. Your mail is being sent up with Dudley's by the Sherpas: Sonam, Pasang Kitar and Tse Tendrup. Incidentally the 60 lbs. of sugar did not arrive with the mail so that our sweet tooth will have to take it easy until our order does come. Also Dud's 1000 ft. [of] Kodachrome was missing. A new camera of some sort with much film did come for him, but, and with many apologies, Joe found it too heavy and rather a luxury to haul up as Dud now has three cameras above Base Camp. Also Pemba Kitar, the sick Sherpa, arrived with the mail runners and Chap and Joe immediately sent him back. He had still a bad cough and no Drs certificate – professing the later [sic] was in the next mail. However, after 3 hrs. argument with Chandra he returned to Askole or parts thereafter.

Toni[4] has been here since June 24 and we are go [sic] down to I to conclusively move everything up to II. All that is left in Camp I after today will be two Yak tents, sleeping bags, stove for passersby or anyone trapped there for an indefinite period. There is also a tin of gas there partly full. It may be had upon request or emergency or if not used taken back to Base Camp for return journey.

Toni and I will remain in II until further orders from you and in the meanwhile try to push all loads to Camp IV providing an understanding is reached that parties will not be working from IV to III while we pack up. In our opinion we would be nearly useless above as you and Dud and Pasang are as large "Spitzen" party as is necessary. There is not much use in eating expensive Camp IV food and sitting . . . [last line of letter illegible][5]

The note merits comment because of Fritz's (and probably also Dudley's) reaction. First, it is informative; it describes movements down below, George's safe arrival, and the very recent receipt of Jack's boots, without which he could not be expected to climb high, as well as noting Tony's presence at Camp II since June 24. Second, it explains that, in large part because of other cameras already on the mountain, "Joe" Trench did not carry Dudley's most recently arrived toy up the mountain. Third, it informs Fritz that the men at Camp II are ready to push loads to Camp IV, but that before so doing there must be assurances that the upper part of the route will be free of travelers because of the risk (implied but not explicitly stated in the letter) of dislodging stones on those coming up from below. Nowhere in the note is there a disrespectful word nor indication of rebellion; Jack and Tony would like to receive some orders and are waiting to be told what to do next.

Up in Camp V, which they had just occupied and where they received Jack's letter, Fritz and, probably, Dudley seem to have completely misinterpreted what Jack was trying to say and became irritated. Perhaps it was because Dudley's new camera had been left behind, or because during the storm no sahibs had pushed through more gear to Camp IV, or simply because of the effects of altitude. On July 2, via two Sherpas, Fritz sent down an acerbic reply in which he specifically named Tony and Jack: "I am very disappointed in you . . ." it began. Jack, who was by now growing disenchanted with Fritz, expressed in his diary on July 2, for almost the first time his own irritation:

> As Dear Jack & Toni preceded these encouraging words I frankly felt a bit irked for my part. Toni was furious for we see no reason for such a statement – however – we move only as puppets, it is definitely a one man's trip – all one can do is one's best and use the good reason invested in his make-up not to let Sunday [which it was] be spoiled by such a trifle.

At a time when the great storm had noticeably demoralized many in the party, Fritz, rather than encouraging his hesitant companions, was turning them off. What Tony and Jack – and, for that matter, "Joe," – needed was support, not criticism; they also wanted instructions. Fritz's charge of malingering, certainly in Jack's case, was unfair. Fritz's own movement charts (see Appendix C) show that between June 21 and July 2 he had left the vicinity of his tent at Camp IV three times, and that during the same interval, and despite bad weather, Jack had made four carries from Camp I to II.

Even in later years Fritz stubbornly continued to assert that during this period on K2, Jack was not doing his job. In the 1940 article "The Second American Expedition to K2," written with Chappell Cranmer for the

Durrance's diary entry for July 2

American Alpine Journal, Fritz suggests that Jack was in possession of his new boots on June 21, whereas in fact they did not reach him until June 28, after another full week of bad weather. And in a scribbled note to one of the authors of this book mailed in 1984 and accompanying a photocopy of Jack's note of July 1, Fritz commented: "...This is interesting, shows Durrance's state and inactivity during a time when I and 2 Sherpas were pushing up above–see chart."

Not at all. Except for the short, albeit difficult, push up the chimney to Camp V, Fritz hadn't done a thing. Jack had been out, mostly in bad boots, five times and had made four carries.

There is, however, no need to quibble. What the correspondence of July 1 and 2 between Jack and Fritz underscores is the growing breakdown, both physically and psychologically, between the leader, on the one hand, and the bulk of his men, on the other. The coolness between Fritz and Jack that had started in Genoa had turned to ice under the stress of altitude and constant peril and had now grown to include Tony and "Joe" Trench. More and more, these three sought to avoid Fritz's authoritarian personality and quite understandably turned their attention homeward, while Fritz and Dudley still longed for the summit.

Would radios have helped? They were not so reliable as a generation later and were vastly heavier. In his 1955 book Fritz states he had refused to include them "for ideological reasons." But should ideology have been allowed to play a dominant role in a life-and-death situation, such as an assault on the world's unclimbed, second-highest, and most formidable mountain?[6]

The exchange of letters between Fritz in Camp V and Jack in Camp II was just one more link in the chain of circumstances that led to the great controversy in the American climbing community after the expedition. The gap was widening. As Jack recorded in his diary, the support party in Camp II continued to do what the leader wanted. But Jack and, no doubt, Tony felt frustrated by Fritz's apparent habit of leaving his companions alone "with no or practically little knowledge of what plans are being held or made for advance" as Jack wrote in his diary (in "Medical Notes" under the date of November 21). Jack compared the sensation as being akin to "sitting on needles."

Anyway, after a morale-shaking additional three-day storm, Jack, Tony, a frostbitten George, and six Sherpas carried loads through knee-deep snow to the Camp III dump. Fresh snow had covered most of the track, so foot- and handholds had to be laboriously uncovered. On the descent an accident occurred that, had it not been for Jack's promptness, might have been fatal; Tony, descending last, slipped in an ice couloir and, calling loudly for a belay, went down some dozens of feet before being stopped by the rope Jack had anchored to a large block. For a long time thereafter, Tony complained of pain in his side.[7]

The Camp III carry exposed yet another casualty: George's toes, nipped by frost during the storm, got worse. As the weather warmed, his feet became swollen. At best, he hobbled with difficulty. Deputy leader Tony ordered him back to Base Camp for attention. Down he limped and there, crippled, he remained.

K2 had struck again. One-third of the American climbing party was now out of action – if you added Tony, who fortunately remained ambulatory, it was one-half. And the critical days still lay ahead.

In addition, there was growing anxiety among the more experienced of the party about the wisdom of allowing Dudley to keep climbing up the mountain. Gentle, trusting, lovable Dudley just didn't seem to belong on K2, especially when more experienced people like Jack and Tony had come to believe that they had no business there either. Dudley's strength and determination were his only assets; aside from those, he was helpless, as both Jack and Tony had noted. He could not move in any steep place without expert assistance. Yet there he was at 21,500 feet (6553 meters) on K2, being hauled ever higher by the expedition point man. Tony and Jack worried about Dudley, Jack all the more so because his guiding experience had exposed him to the perils that plague incompetents. From the beginning of the trip Jack had suffered from insomnia (often a symptom of altitude sickness), but now, when he thought about Dudley, he could hardly sleep at all.

10

INTO THE DEATH ZONE

U P ABOVE, AT CAMP IV, Fritz judged the time ripe to move on. The great storm had left the mountain in bad shape, but somehow on June 30, after much struggle, Fritz emerged from the top of the House Chimney, pulled Pasang Kikuli up behind him, and equipped the difficult passage with fixed ropes. The next day, with Sherpa assistance, he hauled up the awkward Dudley. Four men – two Sherpas and two sahibs – settled into Camp V.

A three-day storm confined everyone again. Fortunately Camp V was better protected than Camp IV and the storm less severe than its predecessor. The residents suffered little.

Under clear skies on July 5, Fritz, with Pasang Kikuli and Tse Tendrup, departed with forty-pound loads up the ridge to set up Camp VI and, if luck held, to carry freight to Camp VII. Dudley stayed at Camp V to receive supplies whose arrival from below Fritz deemed to be imminent.

Though disappointed with his American associates below, Fritz beamed with pleasure over the behavior of his two Sherpa companions. Kikuli reminded him of the toughest and strongest climbers in the Alps. Tendrup, too, was strong, but he had a rough personality and sometimes talked back – also had no understanding of English whatsoever. A bit of a braggart and not altogether truthful, he had a reputation for laziness and seemed to dislike his job. Kikuli, last on the rope, sometimes had to prod him with his ice axe to keep him moving.

The three, Fritz wrote, "wallowed [their] way over heavily snow-plastered rock slopes...and erected the tents for Camp VI"[1] at 23,400 feet (7140 meters). It was a grim, airy spot where the 1938 party had been obliged to carve out platforms from the steep slope. So precarious was the stance that on one occasion in 1938, a teacup, left at the tent door, tumbled, unprovoked, never to be seen again.[2] The next morning, with less weight, they climbed what is known as the Black Tower – a long, narrow, exposed segment of ridge with one rotten overhang, and pushed to about 24,500 feet (7467 meters) at the start of a very steep and delicate snow and ice traverse. This, in turn, was situated just below a flat area at the crest of the ridge that had been used for Camp VII in 1938. That spot marked the top of the Abruzzi Ridge. Except for a few hundred feet far below, Fritz had been first on the rope and broken the trail all the way!

The upper part of the Abruzzi had more than once reminded Fritz of Mont Blanc's famous Peuterey Ridge, with its steep flanks of broken granite, which he had scaled more than a decade earlier. Though considerably harder, it also resembled that same mountain's normal route up the Aiguille du Gouter above Tête Rousse: long, outward-sloping ledges with ice patches, where one rarely needs to use hands, but where a single slip could mean a long, probably fatal fall.

Fritz fully expected to find a shipment of supplies at Camp V or at least at Camp IV on his return from above. But there was no sign of anyone except, of course, Dudley, whom he had left there alone three days earlier. Dudley seemed puzzled; every day, he told Fritz, he had crawled down to the top of the House Chimney and called to Camp IV, but there came no reply. What, Dudley and Fritz asked themselves, was going on?

Because of the lack of an energetic and dedicated administrator below, the lines of communication between those above and those below broke down again, the only connection having been the unsatisfactory exchange of notes some days earlier. Fritz did not stop to wait at Camp V. He left Dudley in care of Kikuli and Tendrup and, exchanging his point-man hat for his administrative fedora, raced down alone to Camp II.

"LO AND BEHOLD," Jack wrote in his journal on July 10, "Fritz came forth from the hanging fogs of K2 alone yesterday aft. It was about 3:30 P.M. when he appeared, looking somewhat worn since I saw him last 18 days ago. He had accomplished the impossible by fully establishing Camp VI and pushing one set of loads within 300 yds. of Camp VII." Tony, "Joe" (who had just arrived from Base Camp with laden Sherpas), and Jack could hardly believe their eyes. Unable to reach Camp IV in a single trip because of snow and storm, low on morale, and with dwindling hopes of success, they had been much concerned about their comrades above. Either through choice (Fritz's claim) or necessity (Tony's) they had talked much and accomplished little aside from two trips to the Camp III dump.

Fritz's unexpected apparition like a latter-day Odin out of Valhalla's mists, and the news that the Abruzzi Ridge was all but conquered and fully equipped, acted on the disconsolate crew like a shot of adrenaline. Morale soared.

With the ambulatory contingent of the party united again, Fritz could at least temporarily resume his dual role as point and administrative leader. Everyone, he directed, would pack up with the Sherpas and rejoin Dudley at the head of the line for the push to the final camps and the assault on the summit.

Four Sherpas, unescorted, moved up on the day following Fritz's arrival at Camp II. They were Dawa, Pasang Kitar, Sonam, and Tsering (Norbu). They were told to pick up the gear left earlier at the Camp III dump; but being unsupervised, they took practically nothing, leaving almost everything for the main party the next day. It began to look as if many Sherpas simply could not be counted on to do their duty when out of sight of the sahibs. Or equally likely, they could not understand orders given them in English or by sign language.

Shortly after reaching Camp IV, one Sherpa, trying unassisted to reach Camp V, had an accident. "It seems," Jack wrote under the date July 12, but referring to events of July 11, "Sonam fell half way down the House Ch., then several hundred feet[3] down snow slopes at its base, headed, no doubt, for Camp I, had his brother not seen the incident from below & run out quickly enough to catch him at level of IV as he rolled into a scree patch. Result: disabled Sherpa with numerous bruises but nothing serious. One notch for Pasang Kikuli." K2 had struck still another blow!

On July 11 Tony, Jack, "Joe," and Fritz, along with remaining Sherpas Phinsoo and Pasang Lama, slowly wended their way to Camp IV. Fritz led on the first of two ropes. Jack commanded the second. It was not Jack's favorite climbing day; he told his diary that evening:

> Route freshly buried so that going was slow and III reached around 2:00 P.M. Found to our dismay that yesterday's Sherpa caravan had taken practically nothing from the old dumps other than 1 tin of gas... Three ropes from III to IV. I had Joe and Pasang on last rope. Some ordeal! Belayed Joe on practically every pitch. Sometimes in the midst of difficult pitch would suddenly feel rope go taut, Joe despondently gazing into scenery... Very hard getting up over overhang with heavy pack. Strong N.E. wind at IV. Joe all in.

This trip to Camp IV undid what Fritz's appearance at Camp II had done for morale two days earlier. The route was long, steep, and dangerous. The lead person (Fritz) kept dislodging stones onto the men below. Everyone was heavily laden, on top of which they had to pick up and carry what the Sherpas had left behind at the Camp III dump the day before. No wonder that by the time they reached Camp IV, the men–except for Fritz–were demoralized.

Except for the lame, the halt, and the sick, everyone was together under Fritz's command at Camp IV. Most people had somber faces. In his July 10 entry Jack had already examined the situation as realistically as he could:

> *Pop Sahib [Cromwell] declares he is now used up and no good above IV. George Sheldon is an invalid with frostbitten toes in Base Camp, Chap Cranmer still too weak to visit I and II so that Fritz, Dud & I are the only ones left.*

"Joe" Trench was unqualified as a climber, and Dudley, in Jack's opinion, no better. Of Dudley, Jack wrote a few days later (under "Medical Notes," probably written on July 20):

> *It is unfair to take a man along and use valuable time hauling him about just because he was able to finance the undertaking–and also dangerous if conditions hit him just right when he is dependent on his own resources.*

Jack, examining Dud at Camp V on July 12 was also concerned about Wolfe's feet, which showed signs of frostbite. Whether Jack communicated his observations to Fritz is not known, but if he did, then Fritz should have ordered Dudley off the mountain. As for Jack himself, he indicated in his diary ("Medical Notes," under November 19) a sense of "emotional upset that I had been selected to make summit dash with Fritz." He really wanted no part of it–just to do his duty and let it go at that. Dwindling manpower and human reserves led Jack to believe that Fritz, at this point, should perhaps think of abandoning the project altogether.

But Fritz entertained no idea of surrender. Always an optimist, he decided to push on, preferably accompanied by at least one American. Of the sahibs, he would take the strong, still determined, but slightly frostbitten and bumbling Dudley, as well as the thoroughly unenthusiastic and exhausted Jack, whose heart was not in it but whose sense of duty kept him moving, and whose state of depression was not clearly understood by Fritz. There were seven healthy Sherpas to carry the loads. Tony, "Joe," and Sonam could stay at Camp IV or return to Camp II, as they chose, as a "reserve force"–whatever that, under the circumstances, might mean.

The forces parted on July 12, but not until, at "Joe's" request, Jack had spent a couple of hours hauling Trench up the House Chimney so that he could claim some sort of altitude record. At nearby Camp V, Dudley crawled out of his hermitage and joined the fun. He had spent the previous five nights there, apparently unwilling to descend for fear lower altitudes might adversely affect his acclimatization.

After Jack had, with difficulty, hauled "Joe" up the House Chimney, he then had to lower him. Meanwhile five Sherpas and Fritz took off for higher ground. When Jack finished his thankless task with Trench, he found himself alone with two Sherpas and Dudley, plus ten pounds of sugar and maybe twenty-five pounds of iron pitons and steel carabiners left behind by the others, all of which added to already heavy loads. With two Sherpas going first on the rope, and Dudley next, Jack came last to observe the others and serve as anchor man. The route was easy, but steep and treacherous. One slip and it was "down to the glacier." There were few belay points. Again and again, Jack watched in horror as Dudley stumbled and almost fell in areas where there was no way to stop him or prevent him from dragging the entire rope team to a fatal fall. Dudley's clumsiness reinforced Jack's belief that Dud had no business climbing high on K2.

Fortunately nothing dire happened as far as Camp VI. Though a poor climber, Dudley seemed strong. Jack, having climbed with heavy loads from 19,300 feet to 24,400 feet (more than 4000 feet, or 1220 meters) in two days and supervised the movements first of the inept "Joe" and then those of the stumbling Dudley, became extremely weary. He had a terrible time keeping up with the others. Meanwhile the Sherpas flitted back and forth almost as though they were at sea level. Not surprisingly, they were the first to reach Camp VI.

Jack felt exhausted; in the past two days he had worked himself to the bone. The long climb with a heavy pack, and then hauling "Joe" around and later Dudley, had consumed all his reserves and more.

At Camp VI for the first time in weeks, Jack shared a tent with Dudley while Fritz roomed elsewhere with some of the Sherpas. Extremely apprehensive about Dudley, Jack decided to speak frankly. In a diary entry not under that day's heading (but instead under October 18) and written several days later, Jack described what happened:

> *Quite surprised at Camp VI when I heard Dudley intended to go on to VII. Somehow I was definitely under the impression that he remain at VI and took it upon myself that night to speak to Dudley about it (we slept in same tent). I strongly advised him not to go higher, if so at his own responsibility, for he could not return on his own – therefore dependent. Next morning as usual he took the matter up with Fritz – the leader, who said he could not refuse anyone who could carry a load & keep up with the party – logical but misplaced judgment.*

As might be expected, Fritz was neither pleased nor amused that Jack should have attempted to counsel Dudley. Years later he supplied his own interpretation of the incident by suggesting that, in fact, Jack had become jealous of Dudley and was trying to eliminate him from the com-

OCTOBER 18

considerably aware of this — really
on of the above & the expedition and
its future success.

16. It should be very clear and
distinctly understood that success
depends largely on luck with the
weather. Maybe the ~~Himalayas~~ aren't
technically as stiff or anywhere near
as difficult as mountain achievements
to date in the Alps & elsewhere but combined
with high altitude effects upon man
& high altitude weather changes they
become very difficult indeed — also
quite dangerous if one becomes over-
confident and over Alps-minded.

_____

July 13th. Quite surprised at Camp VI when
I heard Studley intended to go on to VII
somehow I was definitely under the impression
that he remain at VI and took it upon myself
that might to speak to Studley about it (we
slept in same tent) I strongly advised him
not to go higher if so at his own responsibility
for he could not return on his own — therefore dependent

Durrance's diary entry for October 18 but dated July 13

petition. Had Fritz understood Jack's state of morale and total lack of interest at this juncture whether he, Fritz, or anyone else for that matter reached the top of K2, he might have told a different story. Fritz's subsequent diary version of the incident ran as follows:

> *Dudley tells me that Jack tried to talk him out the previous night to go higher. He considered it quite annoying as Jack in Dud's opinion had no business after Jack had done so poorly during the past weeks that he better would remain at 6. Dud considered it even sillier after Jack had to return and he made it so easily. If he should get slow or find it too difficult higher he should stay in reserve. Dudley seems determined to go high and intimates jealousy Jack's and Tony's part.*[4]

The above passage underscores the great chasm that had opened among expedition personnel, something Fritz should have noticed and corrected. It seems ludicrous that Dudley, who never left his sleeping bag except to climb higher, could say that Jack had done poorly. In the forty-two days from the establishment of Base Camp to their arrival at Camp VI, Jack had climbed a total of 28,200 feet (8595 meters) and made twenty-one heavy load carries, fourteen of them in old, leaky, untrustworthy boots, often as leader and therefore with the added duty to safeguard Sherpas and incompetent companions. Dudley had climbed 22,300 feet (6797 meters), of which 800 feet (243 meters) were without loads, and he had not been responsible for leading anything or caring for anyone.

The next morning, in roped teams, the column resumed its advance. As was customary on this expedition, the climbers made a late start: 10:30 A.M. In the thin air everyone moved slowly; it took one and a half hours to gain barely 400 feet (121 meters). Jack could not catch his breath and decided to sit down. His head ached and he felt faint.

A brief conference ensued. Fritz proposed that Jack return to Camp VI and wait to see if he felt better the next day, something Fritz indicated would surely happen. Fritz, Dudley, and three Sherpas would occupy Camp VII; the other four—Kikuli (who had developed frostbite), Norbu, Dawa, and Phinsoo—would return to Camp VI overnight. Jack could accompany the Sherpas back up with more loads the next day. If still unwell himself, Jack was to send them up anyway. Meanwhile Dudley and Fritz, with Pasang Lama, Tse Tendrup, and Pasang Kitar, would establish Camp VIII and maybe a Camp IX.

Fritz seems to have had no idea that Jack's illness might be long-lasting or serious. But even if Jack did not climb the mountain, his presence at Camp VI would secure movement of supplies upward. Just to be sure, though, Fritz, with Sherpa help, carried enough materiel for a protracted stay up high, an action that might permit him not only to cut his supply line, but his communications as well.

Fritz, Dudley, and the Sherpas crossed the Abruzzi's final, steep ice traverse and set up Camp VII on the same spot that had been sirdar Pasang Kikuli's high point the year before. The next day, June 14, with Dudley, Pasang Lama, Tse Tendrup, and Pasang Kitar close on his heels, Fritz moved up through knee-deep, crusted snow to a small, sheltered embayment where the men pitched Camp VIII. There Fritz retained Pasang Lama and sent Tendrup and Kitar down with express orders that their next move was to carry up additional supplies. Lama, as Kikuli's deputy, placed Tendrup in charge of the Sherpas who were now to reside at Camps VI and VII and maintain supply lines.

Whether Tendrup and Kitar understood their assignment is unclear. Fritz, as his writings suggest, thought they did. But according to Jack, Tendrup and Kitar, of all the Sherpas, had the poorest comprehension of English, and Tendrup did not like his job nor his position high on the mountain. Also, there seems to have been confusion on Lama's part in turning over the high-camp Sherpa leadership to Tendrup, for he believed Kikuli to be at Camp VI and, according to Fritz, it was generally believed Kikuli, despite his frostbitten toes, would remain on the mountain.

It had taken Fritz's party thirty-six days, or twenty-five allowing for eleven days of storm, to ascend from Camp I to Camp VIII. The more close-knit 1938 party had gained the same altitude plus 700 feet (213 meters) in twenty-one days, or eighteen, allowing for three days of storm. If speed can be considered a measure of competence, the 1938 expedition outperformed its successor of 1939 by seven days, or about 25 percent.

THE ESTABLISHMENT OF THE ASSAULT PARTY under the summit had three immediate consequences: (l) the unsupervised Sherpas at Camp VII had to make their own decisions, and their inability to speak or understand English sometimes caused them to get their instructions mixed up; (2) with no sahib at Camp VII, Fritz and Dudley, holding a different idea from those below as to the proper course of action, were in effect cut off; (3) given the summit team's inability to communicate with those below, and with the entire support team either sick or demoralized, there was no one who could be counted upon to perform vital supply tasks, except perhaps one or two Sherpas.

Both physically and psychologically the expedition was split. Above at Camp VIII was Fritz Wiessner, strong and confident, with his equally dedicated and constant companion, Dudley Wolfe, their eyes hypnotized by the summit. Below was an exhausted band of men – Cranmer, Durrance, Sheldon, and Trench – under the command of a vacillating and irresolute leader, Cromwell; all had done their best within their limitations, but their interest in climbing K2 had now dwindled to nothing.

Three men were now alone, less than 3000 feet (914 meters) below the crest of K2–still a long way at this altitude, but within striking distance. Although they did not know it, they would not see another human being here nor on the Abruzzi Ridge for more than two weeks, and then only in the direst circumstance.

All Fritz had left of his American companions was Dudley. Fritz would never quit. The summit was at hand. With Dudley and Pasang Lama he would go for broke.

JACK DURRANCE, ALONE AND SICK from altitude 400 feet (122 meters) above Camp VI, thought it would be easy to descend to the tents. Instead, every step was torture. He could move no more than ten or fifteen steps at a time before being forced to sit down, exhausted, and catch his breath. It was hours before he crawled into his sleeping bag. He barely managed to prepare tea for the porters (Kikuli, Dawa, Tsering, and Phinsoo) returning from Camp VII.

The July 14 entry in Jack's diary reads as follows:

> *Felt so rotten last night that I had Dawa to sleep at my side while I groaned and moaned all night with difficulties of getting enough air and a revolting heart action. Decided during long, uncomfortable & impossible hours of the night that the best plan for me was to get down to II or lower immediately while I still had strength. Got Sherpas up at 5:00 AM and started down with all four at 8:30 AM. Howling cold wind from the S.W. (bad sign). All in IV at 11:00 AM.*[5]

At Camp IV Jack left Phinsoo and Tsering with instructions to carry supplies to Camp VI and on to Camp VII. Tsering refused to climb above Camp VI–he feared the ice traverse below Camp VII. But at least Jack had assurances the supplies would get as far as Camp VI. Presumably Tendrup and Kitar would descend to Camp VI and, with Phinsoo, restock Camp VII and possibly carry to Camp VIII. Jack, however, was at this time too ill to think clearly on those alternatives.

By his own account, Jack was in pitiful condition during the descent from Camp IV to Camp II. He carried no load, yet had to sit and pant at the end of each pitch. He could hardly talk; he had developed a severe, irrepressible, dry cough, a terrible headache, continued shortage of breath, tachycardia, and a touch of cyanosis on the lips and fingernails–sure indications of hypoxia. Dawa and Kikuli, the latter with what appeared to be serious frostbite on his toes, because of which he could not stay high, had almost carried him down the 2200 feet (670 meters) from Camp IV.

The sight that greeted Jack at Camp II was also disheartening: he found an exhausted Tony and "Joe" and the still battered Sonam, three beaten men surrounded by unwashed pots and pans filled with the remnants of a "horrible stew concoction" Trench had prepared. Rather than touch it, Jack threw it all out.

Tony, ever cautious, considered Jack's condition sufficiently serious to require several days' rest before resuming activity of any kind. So while Tony, "Joe," Sonam, and Dawa returned to Base Camp, Jack remained with Kikuli at Camp II, where they became good friends keeping each other company. Despite a continuation of his ever-present insomnia, Jack slowly improved.

The precise nature of Jack's illness has never been determined, for there was no one present capable of supplying a medical diagnosis. It was probably a case of early high-altitude pulmonary edema (HAPE), though it may well have been high-altitude cerebral edema (HACE), or a touch of both. Had Jack remained in Camp VI, 4000 feet (1219 meters) higher up, in obedience to his sense of duty and not yielded to instinct, he might well have died.

Jack's descent completed the isolation of the summit team. The only link with the outside, a link already weak and unreliable, was the presence of two Sherpas at Camp VII and two more presumably at Camp VI. Aside from these four, there was no one else on the Abruzzi Ridge above Camp II, and neither of its denizens felt in any condition to travel. Though it was a problem to which he certainly contributed, Fritz could maintain with some justice that he was being abandoned.

But there are two sides to every coin. In another, different sense Fritz can be said to have abandoned the expedition in order to pursue his obsession, K2. In his presence things usually went well; in his absence they tended to fall apart. He had had plenty of warning: the onset of Chappell's severe illness while he and Tony were off on Sella Peak; the failure of others to push to Camp IV while he descended to Base Camp, something that may have forced him into a permanent point situation; the breakdown of the supply system between Camps II and IV, occasioned in part by the storm but later by morale problems; and, finally, Tony's refusal to go above Camp IV and Jack's illness at Camp VI, where, to be sure, Fritz had been present. Rather than stay behind, keep an eye on his men, and urge them forward – if this was still possible – Fritz persevered at the head of the column with a sort of "devil take the hindmost" attitude. He was ideally suited for the point job, but he desperately needed a more forceful deputy than Tony.

Abandonment, however, is not quite the right term in either case. Rather, the two segments of the expedition, mentally and physically, were headed in opposite directions, an almost certain prelude to disaster.

11

THE NEW EVIDENCE

T HE CRITICAL DAYS HAD ARRIVED–July 15 to 19, 1939. High on K2, completely cut off, unaware of what was happening below, Fritz, Dudley, and Lama pushed for the summit. At the wretched Camp VI, with no room to move around, and for a time at Camp VII, sat four uneasy and uncomfortable Sherpas. Jack, still ill but in command of his senses, and the frostbitten Pasang Kikuli occupied Camp II. Deputy leader Tony, "Joe," Sonam, and Dawa were at Base Camp, along with interpreter Chandra, cook Noor, George, and Chappell, the last two preparing to start for home after a brief geological sojourn part way down the Baltoro. The Askole porters had been notified to show up on July 23 to pick up gear for the return journey.

For the moment the decisive action would take place around Camp II. Fritz, who was not present, averred to his dying day that Jack, on his own responsibility, initiated measures that were directly responsible for catastrophe. Over the years Fritz's self-serving, if honestly believed, version unfortunately became widely accepted.

On July 18, at Camp II, Jack made a routine entry in his diary to record developments and vent his growing frustrations. For fifty years thereafter, he never disclosed to anyone just what took place,[1] nor did he allow others to have access to his diary:

> Camp II, July 18: Dawa danced up here yesterday aft. with notes from Toni and Chap: "Salvage all the tents & sleeping bags you can, we have ample food." Easier said than done! I have only two Sherpas and am in no tip-top shape myself for walking, much less packing... In order to fetch 4 Sherpa sleeping bags from IV, two Yak tents from III [the dump],

two Sahib sleeping bags from III & a tin of beef and one of ham from III Dawa & Pasang must go aloft and return rather heavily loaded – meanwhile to avoid a double passage from II to I tomorrow, I must pack down 55 lbs. of equipment to I and return to-night. The boys are more than willing – so that is precisely what we did. I had some time with my bulky load alone over several icy places and dodging stones in the large couloir. Took 4 hrs. to return and empty at that. Picked some flowers to press on way back up. Dawa brought down 65 lbs. and Pasang 75 lbs. from above!! We arrived simultaneously. Big feed!

Then, on July 19, immediately on the heels of the above passage, Jack made another entry, which, in a slightly different context, proved of equal if not greater importance:

Pasang [Kikuli] caught Sherpas from VI trying to sneak down to more comfortable quarters at IV yesterday. He sent them up [one word here illegible] with matches, fuel & food to their "support" station at VI where they are to await developments above. Found out Camp VIII established July 14. Hurrah!

Jack acted precisely as he should have, despite the fact that, for logistical reasons rather than in consideration of the overall plan, he had protested the action to his diary. What he did was to carry out the orders of Tony Cromwell, who, in Fritz's absence, was in charge. Presumably Tony knew what he was doing. It was up to Jack, if at all possible, to obey, and obey he did.

The orders did not seem unreasonable; every camp above Camp IV was well stocked, and Sherpas were in attendance at two of them who had instructions from their sirdar Kikuli "to await developments above," which meant exactly that, absent an inability to understand orders or an unwillingness to obey them. Equally important, everyone knew the Askole porters were expected in a few days to evacuate most of the baggage, and the more they carried, the less would be the burden on the last persons to leave the mountain. July 23, in short, was a real deadline.

At Camp II, therefore, Jack had simply done his tasks as the agent for his superior. So one might rightly inquire as to whether Jack merited blame for stripping the midmountain camps. Indeed, Jack had expressed doubts whether, with only two men, he might be physically able to carry out his orders at all.

In addition, the last sentence of the second entry says much about Dudley's charge of jealousy. The words "Found out Camp VIII established July 14. Hurrah!" are not the privately expressed observations of a presumably jealous man.

On July 19, Jack, Kikuli, and Dawa, having secured the Camp II tents, trudged with heavy loads into Base Camp. Only Tony, who in later years

Durrance's diary entry for July 18

would comment about it to Kenneth Mason (author of *Abode of Snow*), had any appreciation for Jack's wasted state: not heavy to begin with, he had lost close to thirty pounds.

For the trials of existence at high altitude on prolonged climbing expeditions and, more personally, Jack Durrance's reaction thereto, an essay he wrote in the back of his diary while at Base Camp a day or two following his return from the Abruzzi Ridge is worth citing in toto:[2]

Beginning July 8 through 13 no sleep at all on my part. Even catnaps were only embryonic. Finally broke down under it all at Camp VI the 13th. Sleepless nights combined with emotional upset that I had been selected to make summit dash with Fritz, long stay at Camp II (weeks) and two day haul from II to VI with heavy pack (and not to forget "little" job of hauling Joe Trench around) consumed all my reserves and more. Decided 1/3 way up to VII that there was no use going further for never in my life before have I tried to conceal my condition more before myself and the others and what !! laborious effort to make the few hundred feet that I did on the 13th July. (Where is my southern [illegible]?) Being human I seek an alibi—naturally.

(1) The poor weather conditions that completely wore George Sheldon and Toni Cr. out (admittedly). The physical strain of 5 or more weeks in high altitude must be considerable (I've lost 20–30 lbs) and then not to be forgotten is the ever present mental drain on one's energies. All one talks about is the weather, climbing conditions, risks, chances, good and bad judgment + leadership, effects of altitude, etc., etc.

(2) Then there is leadership: Left alone with no or practically little knowledge of what plans are being held or made for advance (there are as many things to be done behind as there are ahead) has a tendency to place one in the position of "sitting on needles." Then one should not be yanked according to my way of reasoning out of one level immediately to 4000 or 5000 ft. higher without proper time & consideration for acclimatization. All men are not equal and some can take, others cannot! Maybe the only way to climb these hills is to force force everything, but my theory is if the weather is definitely agin you—to buck it you are overstepping reasonable caution (Nanga Parbat '34–'37 !!!). Certainly it isn't the actual technical climbing that taxes one—that is comparatively easy. It's the weather & altitude. When at night you almost suffocate from the exertion of turning over in your cursed sleeping bag it doesn't take much imagination to realize how the body is taxed carrying 30–40 lbs uphill (really climbing too) above 20,000 ft. A point likely to be forgotten also is that once worn out up here the body has a devil of a hard job repairing damages (if this can be done at all?). Of course everybody tires, puffs and pants with hardly any exception, but upon a few moments or minutes rest he is ready for more. But as soon as that certain point of fatigue is overreached the anabolic action cannot balance the

catabolic action. Result: you are very tired and your reserve credit is low-ered. The effects of the altitude are varied: One member of the party simply went around in a daze – a dreamer going through all actions mechanically above Camp I. His every reaction slowed down to half normal at least, with carelessness a threatening vice. Another carrying on smoothly by sheer will until his heart began to flutter. Another pant-ing vigorously at every slight exertion but with an ox-like constitution recovering each time with a considerable rest. In view of those observed facts (granting the observations themselves might be affected by alti-tude) I feel the high Himalayas should be approached somewhat differ-ently than perhaps climbs of nearly the same altitude difference in the Alps, Rockies, etc. There every ounce of willpower & energy may be placed on the table & used for soon they are replaced, the main point being that they are at all available. In the Himalayas these tactics seem as much misplaced as the wooing of a princess with a Bronx technique. Perhaps I should "forget it," not complain nor criticize, but I can't help having the feeling that I'm a near – guinea pig and have to jot down my observations, criticisms & ideas while still in the laboratory.

Being a member of a drastically unequal party [as] regards age, posi-tion and ability combined with experience (& I shall not try to judge my own position) I might say the experiment has been a failure in all except congeniality and that has been impaired by the other factors to some degree. If at all possible and in face of all difficulties mt. experience & ability should be on par for all members. (Otherwise why not some in-dividual hire expert guides to rope him up?) This relieves the task of the leader and more important his anxiety in bad weather or emergencies. Energies may be distributed then so all are practically fresh for the "dash" or high work. Every party should see to it that tempers are enough under control & personalities near enough alike to avoid open quarrels, these are frequently found among Himalayan Exped. This last consideration is a serious one & extremely hard to avoid – leader can do a lot. It is unfair to take a man along and use valuable time hauling him about just because he was able to finance the undertaking – and also dangerous if conditions hit him just right when he is dependent on his own resources. Once a Canadian won the Kandahar [ski] downhill race by simply risking everything and going straight (he could hardly execute a decent turn. Well he was lucky that he did not break his neck which he certainly risked and the other participants were lucky they did not con-tact him). In the mtns. you are bound by a rope. I hope I've made my point clear.[3]

July 20 was Jack's twenty-seventh birthday. He celebrated by taking his first bath in seven weeks, over and, to the extent possible, inside a hollow vessel filled with warm water. Greatly refreshed and feeling clean at last, he crawled into his sleeping bag. At once he began to itch. The fleas had come back to life.

A LIGHT STORM DESCENDED ON THE MOUNTAIN. It lasted from July 15 through 16. Fritz, Dudley, and Lama huddled in the small tent at Camp VIII. Tendrup, the strong, lazy Sherpa who had been placed in charge when it seemed to Lama that Kikuli might be forced to descend, and Kitar waited it out at Camp VII, and Tsering (Norbu) and Phinsoo sojourned at the uncomfortable Camp VI, having climbed back up after their descent to Camp IV with Jack on July 14. The Sherpas' instructions, first from Fritz and then from Jack, were to continue to ferry supplies whenever possible, first to Camp VII and then onward to Camp VIII. They did nothing of the kind; perhaps they had not understood.

When the weather cleared on July 17, Tendrup and Kitar, rather than carry to Camp VIII, descended to Camp VI and urged Tsering and Phinsoo to join in further descent. These last two, loyal and obedient, and disregarding their cramped quarters, refused. Thereupon the first two continued down without them. At Camp IV on July 18 they were surprised by Kikuli's and Dawa's arrival in search of sleeping bags and other equipment. The sirdar administered a sharp verbal rebuke and ordered Tendrup and Kitar back upstairs with loads to Camps VI, VII, and preferably VIII, telling them to stay at the high camps until they received news from above. The two got as far as Camp VI on July 19.

According to subsequent reports by the Sherpas involved, on July 20, Tendrup, Tsering, and Kitar left Phinsoo at Camp VI and went the distance to Camp VII. Only Tendrup, the head man, proceeded farther— alone. Cautiously he climbed a short distance and stopped.[4] He did not wish to venture onto what he considered to be avalanche-prone slopes below Camp VIII, now barely 500 feet (153 meters) above him. Having climbed as high as he dared, Tendrup began to shout in the direction of the higher camp. There was no reply.

He shouted again. No answer.

He shouted a third time.

Silence.

12

A MOUNTAIN WAS LOST

SINCE TENDRUP HAD HEARD no sounds of life, he looked around. In the direction of Camp VIII he spotted traces of large avalanches. The party, he reasoned, might have been carried away. Worse, they might have been eaten by mountain demons. These considerations convinced him there had been an accident. Moreover, Tendrup had had his fill of hauling loads in poor boots and lodging in inadequate sleeping bags. He was by now almost as demoralized as his American employers below. Back at Camp VII he expressed his fears to Tsering and to the relatively inexperienced Kitar. The two accepted Tendrup's story as fact. Therefore, since everyone above was obviously dead, and everyone below scheduled to go home in another three days, what was the point in staying at inhospitable Camps VI and VII any longer?

Kikuli and Dawa, as Tendrup had seen, had stripped Camp IV of sleeping bags. Why not do the same at Camp VII? The sleeping bags, in Sherpa eyes, were the most valuable possessions of expeditionaries. Traditionally they were given away to worthy Sherpas at the end of each trip. Would not Tendrup make himself worthy by hauling as many bags as possible off the mountain? So down from Camp VII came the bedding.

At Camp VI Phinsoo caught the infection. The four Sherpas loaded themselves with all they could carry, which meant, among other things, every last bag, and hurried down the mountain past the already abandoned Camps V, IV, and later II. They left behind only a few unsecured tents, scattered food, and, except at Camps VII and II, not even a stove. By

July 23 the four were at Camp I, where they had just spent the night. In effect, they were off the Abruzzi Ridge.[1]

BY JULY 22 ONLY THREE SAHIBS WERE PRESENT at Base Camp: deputy leader Tony Cromwell, transport officer "Joe" Trench, and a still weak Jack Durrance. George Sheldon and Chappell Cranmer had left on July 18 for a geology trip near Urdukas, far down the Baltoro, and from thence planned to journey home. Neither was in any condition to assist the expedition further, and they wanted to be back, if possible, at Dartmouth for the beginning of the fall term.

The others at Base Camp were Pasang Kikuli, still somewhat frostbitten but, as he had shown from his trip to Camp IV, rapidly recovering, strong, and high in morale; his ailing brother, Sonam; and Jack's loyal porter, Dawa. Also present were the Indian interpreter, Chandra, a pleasant meddler in every affair and now known as the camp gossip, plus the obliging cook, Noor. By late afternoon of July 22 all eight had begun to feel uneasy about what might be happening above. They had spotted the Camp VI tents on the morning of July 21 and noted by afternoon that these had been struck. Under the prevailing good weather and with the route equipped, people should be able to descend from Camp VI to Base Camp in a day and a half at the most. Besides, even the summit party knew that the expedition's stay on the Godwin-Austen Glacier must terminate on July 24 or 25 at the latest, and should be trying to meet its schedule; it had had plenty of time and the proper weather to get to the top. Yet no one had shown up.

On July 23 a worried Jack wrote in his journal:

> Last night [I] called Pasang Kikuli in for a conference. I asked if he cared and was able to go to II today to see if others have started to vacate mtn. yet or not. Coolies arrive today (or are supposed to) and under the circumstances (which are quite different than those agreed upon when the coolies were ordered) Toni and I cannot leave until we have word from above that all is O.K. Pasang & Dawa left this morning at 5:30 to fetch news and some extra, needed food from II . . . According to my observation of Camp VI Fritz should turn up this afternoon . . . therefore we shall begin to worry should Dawa & P. fail to get contact. In which case Toni, Pasang, Dawa & I shall go up the ridge tomorrow ourselves to establish contact, sending Trench with main baggage and coolies to Askole . . .

The entry not only summarizes Base Camp thinking, but as in so many earlier portions of Jack's journal, it underscores his concern. Even though forced down for physical reasons, he remained ready to sacrifice his last strength in an emergency.

His diary for July 23 ends with the dramatic statement: "Pasang Kitar, Tsering Norbu, Tse Tendrup & Phinsoo came down today with alarming news!" To which he added the following day:

> *[They were] a weather-worn lot, worried with a guilty conscience for having quit the mtn. without orders or contact with Bara Sahib since July 14th! They have fears that something has happened to the advanced party consisting of Wolfe, Wiessner and Pasang Lama whom they left at Camp VIII on July 14 camped beneath a threatening ice cornice.*
>
> *Their story & presence caused considerable alarm at Base Camp for aside from the bad weather of July 15–16 the weather since then has been exceptionally good and three days are really all necessary to make the top & back again from site of Camp VIII (on the nose of the ridge). Toni, Pasang Kikuli & Dawa have gone to search campsite with field glasses from upper God. Austen Gl. & find out what else they can.*

Even at Camp VIII, at more than 25,000 feet (7620 meters), the three-day storm had been mild–so mild, in fact, that later during his first hours of descending to Base Camp, Fritz could not recall it and thereby managed for a short while to compress the passage of time into less than it really had been, a phenomenon Jack observed in a diary notation ("Medical Notes," under the date of December 20) entered some time later:

> *Fritz had peculiar effect from high altitude–after-effects, I should say. When listing the activities of his stay above Camp III [i.e., Camp IV] he completely forgot a two-day hideout in Camp 8 from stormy weather nor could he recall the same for a very long time. He accused me of shoving the calendar up two days! Matter of fact only the more important events seem to stick to his memory–e.g. he couldn't recall where stoves had been on descent etc. without extra concentration.*

Whether Fritz's thinking capacities were impaired by altitude cannot be known. For the rest of his life he vehemently denied this. But Jack's observation is supported by the contention of modern-day high-altitude physiologists that exposure to altitude can at least temporarily result in dulling of the mind. And a 1989 article published in the *New England Journal of Medicine*[2] indicates that too much time at altitude results in at least some permanent brain impairment. The matter is not worth quibbling about, and one can choose to accept or reject Fritz's opinion. What is certain is that, if Fritz's thinking became slowed and his memory a bit shaken, this would explain and perhaps in part excuse the unorthodox decision that he was to make on his way down at Camp VII, a decision that had catastrophic consequences.

DECEMBER 20

July 31. Fritz had peculiar effect from high altitude - after effects I should say. When listing the activities of his stay above Camp III he completely forgot a two day hide out in Camp 8 from stormy weather nor could he recall the same for a very long time. He accused me of shoving the calendar up two days! Matter of fact only the more important events seem to stick to his memory - e.g. he couldn't recall where stores had been on descent etc. without extra concentration.

Aug 2. From second hand information from Pasang Kikuli through Tsering it seems Dudley Wolfe did not recover or improve from his 6 day stay at Camp VII but was terribly weak when the 3 sherpas arrived unable to descend. One doesn't recuperate therefore all too well above 20,000 ft or more.

Durrance's diary entry for December 20 but dated July 31

BY JULY 17 THE SKIES HAD CLEARED. Fritz had now spent twenty-four days total in Wyss-Dunant's "Death Zone"; Dudley, twenty-six. Both were going strong, a tribute to their physical and mental make-up. Lama, too, moved efficiently. Camp VIII was adequately stocked; more supplies were due that day; and with Tony and "Joe" perhaps still at Camp IV and Jack at Camp VI supervising the upward movement of supplies, things looked good. Fritz resumed the lead. The other two followed.

One more camp and the summit was in reach. The moment they had so labored for was at hand. Yet now, just above Camp VIII, unexpected difficulties slowed them. Fritz wrote about them in his typed diary entry for July 17:

> Below the bergschrund the snow is bottomless. It takes me a long time to plow through this and cross over to the other lip. I could only see this one place to cross the 'schrund. It was just to the right of an ice cliff, which continues to the rock ridge. One could in case the 'schrund offers no other crossing, go over to that ridge and climb up from there.
>
> Dudley just cannot follow, even in my and Pasang's tracks. He will go back to the tent and either follow up later with another party or stay there and maintain contacts between us and the rest of the party. We soon reach the ridge, having better snow above the bergschrund. After the exhausting and long work below the 'schrund we are not able to go much farther. After our tracks are frozen it will be much easier for Dud and the rest of the Sherpas to bring up loads.
>
> We pitch our tent across the shoulder on the line between the snow and the rocks. It was a very hard day, and we just cannot make the apparently short distance to an excellent camp site somewhat higher on the flat top of a great rock pillar. From there a rock ridge leads up towards the summit rocks. The ridge is west of the shoulder ridge, and ice, which may fall from the ice-cliff above the shoulder, will not reach the ridge.[3]

It took the pair several hours more, on July 18, to climb to the rock platform, 350 feet (107 meters) higher and so tantalizingly near. Here at 26,050 feet (7940 meters) they set up Camp IX, barely 2200 feet (723 meters) below K2's summit. The weather was perfect, with hardly a breath of wind; the surroundings, Fritz wrote later, were "indescribably magnificent."

For some distance above Camp IX the route was obvious, over easy rock and a bit of snow. Next came two possibilities: a traverse right led to a steep snow and ice couloir offering easy access to the summit cone. It had one drawback: as far as Fritz could see, it appeared threatened by ice falling from the summit cornice and ice cliff. To the left, safe from avalanches, Fritz spotted a route up the steep rocks. These were no doubt iced over, certainly difficult to climb under the best conditions, but they were sheltered from objective dangers. Safety prevailed; he chose the rocks.

It was July 19. He and Pasang had slept well – too well, for they only got under way at 9:00 A.M. – a surprisingly late hour for the final assault of a great mountain.[4] The rocks, glazed with ice, proved more difficult than anticipated. In view of the altitude and conditions, Fritz later judged many passages on the rock to be in the sixth (at that time the most severe) grade of difficulty. Lama would sit and belay while Fritz led the next pitch. Lama, belayed by Fritz, would then climb up to join him. As he had since the day he left Base Camp, Fritz remained in the lead.

Rock climbing of the caliber Fritz encountered that day had seldom before been done anywhere in the Himalaya, certainly not above 20,000 feet (6096 meters), let alone more than a mile higher. Nor has such climbing been done at equivalent altitudes since. Those summit rocks of K2, the mountain's final defenses, taxed the utmost skill, courage, and strength of one of the world's finest high-angle climbers. "It is very steep where Fritz climbed," Lou Reichardt, who in 1978 was the first American to scale K2, related years later. So steep, in fact, that rather than follow in Fritz's footsteps, all subsequent parties have carefully avoided the cliffs and followed the far easier snow ramp.

For nine hours they moved upward, testing one line after another in an effort to select the most promising passage. By late afternoon Fritz found himself separated from the easy summit snows by only a 25-foot traverse of moderate difficulty.[5] He estimated his altitude at 27,450 feet (8367 meters). The remaining 800 feet (244 meters) on good ground could be covered in three or four hours at most.

Fritz wrote on July 19:

> *It was 6:00 PM by then. I had made up my mind to go to the summit despite the late hour and climb through the night. We had found a safe route and overcome the difficulties, and with the exception of the traverse, had easy going from now on.*
>
> *The weather was safe and we were not exhausted. Night climbing had to be done anyway, as it would take us a long time to descend the difficult route up which we had struggled.[6] Much better to go up to the summit slowly and with many stops and return over the difficult part of the route the next morning. Pasang, however, did not have the heart for it: he wanted to go back to camp once he realized night was not far. He refused to go on, even did not pass my rope while I started the traverse. His reasoning and my lack of energy made me give in.[7]*

In some ways Fritz was a peculiar person. He could show the highest degree of kindness and consideration for those in his immediate vicinity, but once out of sight he seemed to care little what became of them.

Pasang Lama had been a friend, a loyal companion, a gallant follower – and he was on Fritz's *rope*; he was right *there*. So Fritz decided to go down and try again rather than leave his companion and continue alone. Whether out of magnanimity or influenced by weariness, the decision cost Fritz the greatest dream of his life. Yet never thereafter did he have a harsh word to say about Pasang Lama or his performance.

It was well after 6:00 P.M. when they turned back. Fritz informed Lama that the next day they might move camp upward, and then, on July 21, make another attempt, this time by the couloir, or ramp. On the way to the high point he had been able to look into it from above and had seen that, contrary to his earlier apprehensions, it was completely safe.

Fritz's narrative continued:

> *We returned over the difficult rocks and soon it was dark, which slowed us further. We could not consider a bivouac, it was much too cold, only moving kept us reasonably warm.*
>
> *When we had to rappel over a difficult, partly overhanging zone, Pasang got tangled up when he came down on the rope and seemed in great distress. I could not give him the quick help he needed as I had gone down first to make sure that the rappel was laid out well and ended at the right place. I was just trying to climb up again when Pasang cleared his rope tangle, but [in the process] lost our 2 [pairs of] crampons which he carried.[8]*
>
> *We continued down and reached our camp at 2:30 AM.*
>
> *I regretted many times on the way down that I had given in. It would have been so much easier for us to go on to the summit and return over the difficult part on the route the next morning.*
>
> *We were quite tired when we arrived in camp.*

They did not move their tent upward the next day, as Fritz had planned. Instead they rested, for the previous diary entry had been a masterful understatement. Fritz wrote:

> *July 20th. The first rays of a beautiful morning touched our tent when we had finished preparing the warm drinks and food after our nightly adventure and were relaxing in our sleeping bags. A lovely warm day was spent in the wide-open tent; I lay for hours naked on my sleeping bag and energy and new strength came back by afternoon; also Pasang, who seemed very tired at 2:30 AM told me he had recovered.*
>
> *I discarded the idea of moving the tent as nobody had come up from Camp VIII with additional supplies which we would have needed if we were to stay more than two days.*

Now that the high point of July 19 had been reached, and what turned out to be a vital two pairs of crampons lost, there began a long chain of disappointments that led up to the expedition's tragic outcome.

Fritz and Lama slept very late that morning, even sun-bathing naked on their sleeping bags enjoying the unusual warmth throughout most of the day in the dry, thin air. July 20 may well have been a well-deserved rest day, but it was very expensive for the two men at Camp IX. The leader's diary continued:

> *July 21: I prepare breakfast at dawn and we leave camp at 6:00 AM.*[9]
> *Good going to the foot of the pillar, then disagreeable traverse several hundred feet to the upper part of the rock and ice couloir, which leads up to the foot of the ice cliff and east of our ridge.*
>
> *Much snow is on the rocks of the traverse and makes it difficult and treacherous. It takes me a long time to lead across. After climbing out of the couloir, I reach a short, steep slope just beneath the ice-cliff. The slope is in bad condition, a hard crust demands step-cutting; if only we had not lost our crampons the previous night! [sic]. With them we could have walked right up this slope and following Schneemuelde [snow trough] to the highest point. But it is impossible to cut all the necessary steps, it would be a full day's work at this altitude, so again we return – it is too late to continue towards the summit on the other route . . .*

On July 22, after a restful night, Fritz and Pasang Lama descended to Camp VIII to pick up new supplies. Fritz had promised the weary Sherpa that he would be replaced by a fresher man for the next assault. Thinking he would be gone only a few hours, Fritz left his bedding behind, but Lama toted his small Sherpa sleeping bag and mattress in his pack. En route, near the bergschrund, Lama fell, but Fritz, ever alert, quickly stopped the tumble. As they approached the Camp VIII tent there was at first no sign of life. Suddenly they saw Dudley crawl out of his shelter; he had been alone for five days and had run out of matches, which made it impossible for him to cook or to obtain water except by melting snow on a tarpaulin exposed to sunlight.

"I cannot understand," Fritz wrote, "why our Sherpas [who] had definitely promised to stock up Camp VIII, had not come. I also wondered where was Jack."

Interestingly, Fritz never expressed any wonder as to where all the other sahibs were or what they had been doing in his absence. Nor did he seem aware that a nine-day separation from the others without giving news of what was going on up above might lead to the conclusion below that something had gone seriously wrong.

It was then necessary to descend to Camp VII, which they had left in good condition and well stocked nine days earlier. Dudley took his sleeping bag with him after deciding not to remain at Camp VIII, but, for one of the few times during his stay on K2, to descend the short distance to the next lower camp.

Fritz described in his diary the dramatic and startling events that next occurred:

> We had a little difficulty to find the route to VII as the afternoon was foggy. Pasang, whom I let go first, had a tendency to go too far E. I finally took the lead and soon was sure to go the right direction.

On the descent, the leader usually comes last to watch the movement of his companions. In this instance, Lama had been going first, with Dudley in the middle, and Fritz behind–the accepted order. Because of the need to find the route, Fritz reversed the order, a very sensible decision under the circumstances. The snow on the slope became very hard on the steeper part above the bergschrund and the few seracs about 500 feet above Camp VII:

> Here Dudley was slow: he did not like the technique which had to be applied and the slow moving was annoying and made us cold.[10] We soon got in soft snow and then had to cross a hard stretch. As Dudley found it difficult to go down face to the slope and kicking steps in the snow, I started to scratch while facing forward [outward]. After having prepared the third step a sharp jerk from the rear pulled me away and I started to slip down the hard slope and calling the attention of the other two. As I was still holding my axe at the other end ready for cutting the next step I had difficulties to regain a hold on the [axe] head quickly. I succeeded in getting this grip and slow down sliding, before the rope between me and Dudley tightened and Dudley and Pasang started to slide. However I had not regained complete control at that point and, as Dud and Pasang slid down with ever increasing speed, the played out rope between us gave me a bad jerk away from the slope, just when I was about to anchor myself and catch the other two. I somersaulted and began to slide very fast, the two others sliding ahead of me. I had now a good grip on the axe and worked hard with the pick to stop. A little better snow on the ever steeper slope made me succeed and even the next jerk could not throw me off any more. I had Dudley and Pasang on my rope.
>
> It was a narrow escape: the two had been stopped about 60 feet above the edge of the big rim behind which steep rock and ice slopes fell directly on the Godwin-Austen glacier [7000 feet (about 2000 meters) below]. Dud did not recall at VII why the rope gave me the jerk; but Pasang, who was behind Dudley, told us that Dudley had got tangled up with the rope; he always used to belay carefully and correctly.

Fritz's description of this incident seems a bit confused, but his confusion stemmed from the fact that, being in the lead, he could not know precisely what was happening behind. Apparently Dudley stepped on the rope between him and Fritz, and the sudden pull caused Fritz to lose his balance. Then, when the rope tightened as Fritz fell, Dudley got torn off.

Not known are Lama's efforts, if any, to stop the tumble. His resulting kidney injuries may have been caused by an effort to supply a body belay with the rope. Any account of this incident, even Fritz's, contains speculative elements.

Proceeding with extreme care, they reached Camp VII around dusk on July 22. A great shock awaited them. The tents had been completely cleared. One had collapsed under the weight of snow, poles broken and holes everywhere, useless; the second, covered with snow, had to be repitched, a forty-five-minute job. All bedding–sleeping bags and air mattresses–were gone, but there were two stoves, fuel, and scattered food. The place looked like a rat's nest.

First a terrible fall that nearly cost them their lives–a fall in which Pasang Lama sustained kidney injuries and chest bruises and Dudley a bad shaking, as well as the loss of his sleeping bag. And now this!

WE HAVE ONLY FRITZ'S WORDS for the events that took place up high in the preceding eight days or those of the next two. Except for the compression of dates at Camp VII, in effect a minor lapse that might occur to anyone, there is little reason to doubt Fritz's story. He certainly climbed very high with Lama on July 19, perhaps a bit lower than he believed, perhaps even higher than he indicated. Dudley Wolfe, extremely tired from wading through deep snow above Camp VIII, appears to have been still in reasonably good health when Fritz picked him up on the way down to Camp VII, this despite later allegations by some that he had fallen ill.[11] Except for a bad shake-up, Fritz believed him fit at Camp VII.

They passed a miserable night at Camp VII trying to share Pasang's diminutive sleeping bag and mattress.[12] Fritz's distress turned to anger.

> We could not understand... One thing was clear to me: Jack must not have been able to recover and was still at VI and possibly the Sherpas had played foul; but then they had been so cheerful when we left them. The day when we had left Camp VII it was full of food and two or three reserve sleeping bags; it was agreed that much of it would be moved on to higher camps and another group was to bring up more from below. Everything was clearly understood at that time and cheerfully acknowledged by Kikuli in charge of the group returning to Camp VI... Now this condition.

But was it so clearly understood, not so much by Kikuli, but by the other Sherpas? And what was their state of morale as the days passed and they heard nothing from up above? Along with other failures of communication, the Sherpas' inability to understand English did not help matters. Fritz continued:

It was obvious that nobody had been at VII for many days or cared about the three men above – to the [sic] Hell with them! Here we were left without sufficient protective equipment and food, even the bags and some provisions which we ourselves brought to VII taken away.

Fritz may have exaggerated a bit in the last sentence: there was plenty of food (although somewhat scattered), fuel, and two functioning stoves, which could be used for warmth. Nevertheless, the three men must have been extremely uncomfortable. As the night turned to dawn, the great question arose: what to do next?

The decision now made was to be the major cause of the ensuing tragedy. Fritz split his small party.

A cardinal rule of mountaineering, observed, certainly until recent years, is that under no circumstances does one split a small party if one has any reason to suspect trouble ahead. Only when one member of the team becomes incapacitated is an exception allowed so as to permit others to seek help. In the case of Fritz's team at Camp VII, that exception cannot be cited for what he decided. The group was undeniably small, and as Fritz always insisted in later years, all three, though a bit battered, were mobile. And because there was no one else present who could later contradict Fritz as to Dudley's health, he must be taken at his word. Even Lama later indicated that Dudley seemed fit.

Furthermore, in view of the circumstances, any rational and prudent person, unaffected by the stress of altitude, descending to Camp VII could only have concluded that something was very, very wrong down below. There had been many warnings of possible trouble, and now there was clear evidence. While on K2, every time Fritz had left the main group there had been disappointments: Chap's illness during the reconnaissance absence; Tony's failure to push to Camp IV while Fritz returned to Base Camp; the slow movement of supplies from Camp II to Camp IV; Tony's refusal to go above Camp IV; Jack's illness; the inexplicable failure of the Sherpas to push supplies up to Camp VIII and their nonappearance for eight long days; and, finally, the mess at Camp VII. If these conditions did not suggest serious problems, what could?

Surely this was a time when three ambulatory men should have stuck together rather than separate. Indeed, if by some miracle, all was well below, say at Camp VI, three backs were surely better than two or one to help haul up fresh supplies.

In spite of the evidence, Fritz Wiessner, for reasons forever unclear, allowed Dudley Wolfe to remain alone and unattended at Camp VII in the obvious knowledge that if anything further went wrong, Dudley lacked the competence to descend alone.[13] This at almost 25,000 feet (7620 meters) on the remotest high mountain on earth. Was this the decision of a leader fully in command of his faculties?

Moreover, the decision seems particularly hard to explain in view of Jack's prophetic warning to Dudley at Camp VI. It is one thing to stay high with climbers above you and all seemingly well below. It is quite another to be alone on top with things obviously amiss below.

Fritz never accepted "dullness of thought" as an excuse for his puzzling decision. To the end of his eventful and honored life he insisted that at no time on K2 did his mind in any way fail him.

So Dudley, Fritz's jolly, trusting, and loyal companion on K2, remained alone and confident at Camp VII while Fritz and Lama took off in search of elusive sleeping bags and other missing objects.[14]

Later Fritz argued that he had left Dudley behind because Dudley had wanted to remain and because he had been left alone before with no dire consequences, besides which conditions and the weather were good.

Fritz and Lama left Dudley at Camp VII around 10:00 A.M. on July 23. They had an unpleasant descent to Camp VI in cold, foggy weather. In addition, they felt in poor shape because of the bad night and the events of the previous day—not to mention the exertions even higher. They reached Camp VI and found not a soul there, just two tents laid down and a duffel bag with food, but no sleeping bags and no mattresses. Staggering on to Camps V and IV they met with the same disappointments. Almost out of strength, they reached Camp II at dusk. There they found two tents up, but not a living creature. There was food and a stove in one tent, but no bedding. The other tent was empty. They took it down, used it as a cover, and passed a second miserable night. Fritz commented:

> To describe in words the horrible feelings and thoughts I had during the day would be futile indeed. Is there any possibility for an excuse for such a condition? Does one sacrifice a great goal and human beings in such a way?

At Camp II there was no rest; they shivered through the darkness. On the morning of July 24, twenty-four hours out of Camp VII, they reached the glacier. There, more dead than alive, they stumbled, half-dazed, in the direction of Base Camp. They could hardly walk; every hundred yards or so they had to sit and rest. Fritz had lost his voice and could speak only in a whisper; his chest ached, his knees buckled, and his toes burned from frostbite. He was totally emaciated. Years later, Fritz assured his friends that those two nights had so debilitated him that he could close his middle finger and thumb around his ankle. Lama's condition, with cracked ribs, blood in his urine, and damaged kidneys from the fall above Camp VII, was even worse.

As Lama and Fritz neared Base Camp they were overtaken by Tony and three Sherpas returning from their search up the Godwin-Austen Glacier. At first Tony believed he'd seen ghosts. "Thank God you're alive!" he exclaimed.

A look of savage rage was Fritz's initial response. Then at Base Camp, in front of everyone, Fritz exploded at his deputy. Tony was guilty of attempted murder; there would be lawsuits galore; Tony would pay for his negligence – all this in a rasping whisper, but the gestures made the meaning clear. Tony, accustomed to polite and deferential society, was appalled. Even if Fritz had justification, this was going too far. He and the others had done the best of which they were capable; they were not the world's greatest mountaineers. And sometimes Fritz had kept his plans to himself. Even Fritz, after cooling off, thought he'd been a bit rough, but he did not retract or apologize. The damage was done, and in the weeks that followed, Tony, once a friend, became a foe.

Jack Durrance had watched the confrontation in silence. Anxious not to fan the flames, he said nothing about Tony's note ordering the evacuation of the sleeping bags. As the quarrel between Tony and Fritz grew in intensity, first at Srinagar and later in America, Jack decided to keep his mouth shut unless officially asked to give his version of events. But official queries, aside from an informal discussion with Charlie Houston, were not forthcoming. The matter slowly died down, and interest shifted to more immediate events, such as World War II. It would be many years before the story reappeared on front pages.

13

THE SEARCH

ONE OF FRITZ'S MAJOR COMPLAINTS upon arrival at Base Camp was that when the four high-camp Sherpas arrived with all the remaining bedding, they should have been turned around and ordered back up with the sleeping bags. That way Fritz and Lama would have had a good night's sleep at either Camp II or IV.

A good and valid idea, had not Fritz and Lama been descending right on the Sherpas' heels. Tendrup and his companions had arrived at Base Camp the evening of July 23, in need of rest. Less than twenty-four hours later, Fritz and Lama made their appearance. So, in fact, there would have been no time to send equipment back up. Better would have been for Jack, Dawa, and Kikuli to have hauled a few of their bags back to Camp II, preferably to Camp IV, on July 20 or 21. But at that time no one knew what mischief the high-camp Sherpas were entertaining, and, besides, the deputy leader seemed pleased with the partial evacuation of the mountain.

Fritz and Lama were in pitiful physical condition, but this surprised no one. In the past month Fritz had spent twenty-nine days at 21,500 feet (6553 meters) or above, of which ten had been continuously above 25,000 (7620 meters) under conditions of extreme physical activity. And at the end of this sojourn, in desperation, he had managed to arrest a fall that ought to have killed him and his companions. No question about it, Fritz was one of the most physically fit men of his time and a superb acclimatizer.

No one, of course, can say whether it was his prolonged stay at altitude or the two consecutive nights at Camps VII and II without proper insulation that caused the deterioration. Fritz always said he was still fit when he started the descent from Camp IX, and he always blamed his impairment on the two wretched nights on the way down. No doubt they contributed, but every high-altitude physiologist consulted by the authors of this book believes that by the time Fritz and Lama descended to Camp VII, their deterioration was already far advanced.

Fritz's shift of emphasis away from the debilitating effects of altitude to the absence of bedding fitted in well with his personality and theories. He admitted to error only with extreme difficulty. Besides, in 1939, little if anything was known about long-term high-altitude deterioration, and even in later times Fritz was skeptical of medical findings on the subject. For years he argued, rightly as it turned out, that Everest could be climbed without oxygen. What he never accepted was that people who remain at too high an elevation for too long will deteriorate and in time probably die. Since he would not blame his lengthy residence above 25,000 feet (7620 meters) for his and Lama's condition, he cast the onus on those he believed had stripped the camps, notably Jack, whose sustained silence lent credibility to the charge.

Whatever the reasons for Fritz's weakness, he arrived at Base Camp a very sick man. Yet his writings reflect his tremendous physical and moral resilience. No matter how desperate the situation or his condition, he never gave up. Battered, beaten, totally spent after weeks as point man on the mountain with less than help from most of his comrades, and after forty-eight of the most exhausting hours of his life, he continued to focus his attention on K2. All around him people packed for the march home while the Askole porters, who had arrived the previous day, waited for their loads. Fritz acted like a boxer who has been repeatedly floored, only to get up and receive more punches: commendable but not recommended as a way of life. Even though his diary notes for July 24 are in a plaintive tone, he redresses himself immediately:

> The mountain is far away... The weather is the best we have had so far. Will it be possible for me to go up after a short rest with some Sherpas and Jack, if he is in shape, to pick up Dudley and then call on the summit?[1]

Totally exhausted and with the expedition's situation rapidly growing critical, Fritz continued unrealistically to exude optimism. Even Dudley's predicament alone at Camp VII did not seem serious to him at this time: had he not left Dud up there in good health? Fritz's tenacity, however misplaced, merits respect and was cited subsequently by his admirers.

Now began the struggle to rejoin Dudley. Tony and "Joe" were out of it. The latter had to escort most of the porters to Askole. The former, who offered to stay, appeared so dejected to Fritz that he was granted leave to depart. That left five healthy Sherpas–Sonam and Lama were still ill, and Tendrup, utterly disgraced, was asked to go–plus Fritz and Jack.

Though united in their resolve that a party must go up the mountain at once, the two sahibs held widely differing opinions as to what should be that party's objective. Fritz, still looking at K2 through rose-colored glasses, viewed the effort as a renewed attempt on the summit. Under the date of July 25 he wrote in his diary:

> *Jack, Phinsoo, Pasang Kitar, Dawa leave for Camp VII to meet Dudley. Jack, who feels well, may go on another summit attempt with me. I plan to follow tomorrow or in two days with Pasang Lama if he has recovered and if the beautiful weather holds...*

Fritz later wrote:

> *We decided that Cromwell and Trench should leave with the porters who had come up from Askole to carry loads...Durrance, Chandra and I, together with all the Sherpas except Tendrup, who had cooked up the avalanche story and who was regarded as a devil by the other Sherpas, should remain for a further attempt. Durrance, who felt in good condition, wanted to go with the three Sherpas as fast as possible to Camp VII the next day. Only sleeping bags and air mattresses would have to be carried from below: provisions could be picked up in Camps IV and VI. From Camp VII Durrance, Wolfe and the Sherpas could provision Camp VIII. I would attempt on the third day to follow with the remaining Sherpas and join up with Wolfe-Durrance's group.*[2]

There is no indication in either citation that Fritz had the slightest worries about Dudley at this time. Jack was to "meet" him at Camp VII, not rescue him. Fritz viewed the operation as the onset of a renewed assault on the summit, to take place as soon as he caught up and resumed his job as point man.

Jack, on the other hand, had more than merely lost interest in K2. All he wanted to do was to pluck Dudley from his lofty perch. In his diary at the time Jack clearly uses the word "rescue." Nowhere does he refer to another stab at the summit. On August 3, in a letter to Tony summarizing events, Jack wrote: "July 25th–I left with Dawa, Phinsoo and Pasang Kitar to *rescue* [emphasis supplied] Dudley."

Nothing in the letter indicates the slightest interest in the summit. For Jack it was Camp VII or bust: bring down Dudley and go *home.* Apparently Fritz was utterly unaware of the attitude of his one remaining American climber.

At first Jack made good progress on his rescue mission. The party of four reached Camp II in six hours out of Base Camp. But along the way to Camp I Dawa lost his voice. The next day at Camp IV, Dawa said he could climb no higher. On the long ascent from Camp II he had complained of chest pains and an extremely sore throat.[3] The wind was blowing fiercely. At Camp IV that night, Jack began to develop symptoms suggesting a relapse of his own recent illness. Then, on the morning of July 27, Kitar, least experienced of the Sherpas, refused to accompany Phinsoo to Camp VI and points beyond to rescue Wolfe. Jack faced a hard decision, as he noted in his July 27 diary entry:

> *Knowing from previous experience that I should probably be no good at VI and not able to continue to VII (orders from Fritz were to go only to II and send Sherpas on up alone) and having Dawa sick and Pasang Kitar flatly refusing to attempt to bring Wolfe down with only two Sherpas not to mention his reluctance to move in snow & wind – I decided to return to base camp at once with Dawa & get Fritz & Pasang Kikuli to go to the rescue.*

Unbeknownst to Jack, Fritz's condition had not improved much, if at all. His frostbitten toes ached, and his throat felt so bad he could not sleep. However willing, there was no way he could give much help. Fritz observed years later to one of the authors of this book: "I still could not realize that I was out for several weeks to come."

At Base Camp, Fritz, Jack, and the others held a conference about what to do next. The options seemed pretty well exhausted. Help, however, came from the Sherpas. Fritz noted in his diary on July 27, a few hours after Jack's return:

> *Pasang Kikuli seem [sic] to feel in good shape and his toes seem improved. He tells me very resolutely that there would be no need for me in my bad condition to go up, he would be perfectly able to handle the situation. He and Tsering would go up tomorrow morning going as high as Camp 6 the next day with Pasang Kitar and Pinsoo from Camp 6 to 7 and back to Camp 6 with Wolfe Sahib . . .*

Although in his diary Fritz suggests that Kikuli volunteered to lead the new rescue team, some of Fritz's critics later charged the leader actually ordered the Sherpas up. The facts cannot be ascertained. Jack's diary comments that day about the fateful conference are inconclusive: ". . . A conference held upon my return decided to entrust rescue to Pasang Kikuli who left early this morning (6:00 A.M.) with Tsering Norbu for Camp IV . . ." But the weight of the evidence supports the contention that Kikuli acted on his own initiative, for in his entry of July 27 Fritz observes of Kikuli: "Good luck for me to have a man like Pasang left, he is dependable and always does what he plans, I could not do it better." For Fritz, the final clause of the entry represents a great acknowledgment of an-

- *Overleaf:* Near Concordia, May 31, 1939. Note heavy loads of "double carry."
  Left to *right*: Durrance, Cranmer, Sheldon. (Durrance collection)
- *Above:* Party approaching Godwin-Austen icefall below Camp I. (Durrance collection)
- *Below:* Base Camp on Godwin-Austen Glacier, Chogolisa in the background. (Durrance collection)
- *Below right:* Camp I, about 1,000 feet above glacier. (Durrance collection)

- *Above right:* Unidentified Sherpa in Godwin-Austen icefall. (Durrance collection)
- *Below:* Climbers near Camp II. (Durrance collection)

- *Left:* Camp II. (Durrance collection)
- *Above:* View toward Concordia near Camp VI. (Durrance collection)
- *Below:* Setting up Camp IV. (Durrance collection)
- *Facing page*: Above Camp II. Note fixed rope as handrail, no jumars. (Durrance collection)

■ *Facing page:* View up the Abruzzi Ridge between Camps II and III at about the 20,000-foot level. Note nailed boots. (Durrance collection)
■ *Left:* Camp IV. (Durrance collection)
■ *Below:* Upper portion of the Abruzzi Ridge. (Photo © Greg Child)

Wiessner's and Dawa Lama's high point 27,500

Camp IX

Camp VIII

Where Wolfe stayed

Camp VII

■ *Right:* On the
way home,
Paiju Peak to
the left in the
background.
(Durrance
collection)

■ *Below:* A weary
Fritz Wiessner
on the return
march.
(Durrance
collection)

other man's abilities and devotion. But then the Sherpas have always been known for their loyalty in times of trouble.

Kikuli and Tsering left, as noted by Jack, at 6:00 A.M. on July 28 and moved faster than expected. At noon, while climbing just under 1000 feet (300 meters) an hour, an astonishing pace for the altitude, they reached Camp IV. They then continued to Camp VI, where they rejoined Kitar and Phinsoo, who, after Jack had left them, had at last mustered the courage to climb to (but not beyond) Camp VI.[4] Kikuli and Tsering had ascended 7000 feet (2134 meters) in a day, every step carrying them higher into the thin air of the upper atmosphere, and anticipating the modern Himalayan, alpine-style climbing by well-acclimatized and rested persons that would some day become fashionable.

They had not finished. The next morning, as Fritz wrote on July 29, their efforts continued:

> *Around 11:00 AM [Jack's diary says 10:00 A.M.] we see through Dudley's glasses 3 men go up the snow couloir between Camps 6 and 7. Pasang had actually made the terrific distance Base Camp–Camp 6 in a single day. We watch for their return, two hours later, but nobody returned. Finally, around 5 PM three men only are descending the couloir. What is wrong?*

What indeed? And what could have been Dudley's condition when they found him – if, for that matter, they had found him at all?

Much of what follows is fact, insofar as it could be pieced together. But much, too, is conjectural, for no one can read another's mind.

Dudley Wolfe was a gentle and gracious person – and a most fortunate one, if to be born rich is fortunate. But all his life he was a restless spirit, as though some inner force commanded him to strike out into the world, brave fortune's arrows, and prove himself worthy of his inheritance.

Raised in a setting that should have made him a playboy, Dudley sought better. Yet he never found a niche where he could leave a mark. As noted earlier, he was older than his classmates in preparatory school and had run off from Phillips Andover Academy to serve in World War I.

When war ended he sought a career. A respected profession required a college degree, so Dudley entered Harvard, graduating at age thirty-three. He wanted to do much; yet all he had was sports – racing yachts, skiing, a bit of mountaineering – and, alas, he lacked an athletic physique.

Even Dudley's married life ended in disappointment. Alice Blaine Damrosch, daughter of conductor Walter Damrosch and enate granddaughter of Maine's Republican political leader James G. Blaine, was a delightful woman. She was tall, athletic, and far more than Dudley's equal on ski slopes. Even after the break-up, she retained affection for Dudley, but their relationship had simply not worked out.

Through Alice's skiing connections with Fritz Wiessner, Dudley learned about K2. The more he heard about it, the more he wanted to climb it. He asked Fritz if he could go; he would, he added, help with the expenses. Alice urged his acceptance. Fritz considered Dudley a good candidate; he had done some climbing, and his presence meant money for the expedition. Fritz said yes.

As with Fritz, K2 became Dudley's obsession, the be-all and end-all of his dreams. It represented a new lease on life. At last he had a chance to prove himself to the world, a chance to show he could become *somebody* on his own merits.

Dudley adored Fritz, and Fritz responded in kind. So Dudley could be found, invariably, at Fritz's side, always ready to assist with every detail of the expedition. Over time there seemed to develop between the two what other members of the party facetiously described as a guide-client relationship: Fritz, the guide, would safely conduct Dudley, the client, to the top of K2 and back. The cold, the storms, the altitude, the cramped confinement in tiny tents, all these and more Dudley endured with his never-ending good humor. Only once or twice, such as when someone failed to carry up his new camera or questioned his climbing ability, did he display irritation. The summit was all that counted. Fritz, also mesmerized by K2, loved him for it.

Then, high on K2, after proving himself the only member of the expedition with the strength and determination to follow the leader to the assault camps, and in full sight of the objective, fate dealt Dudley one more cruel blow. Unable to follow Fritz and Pasang through waist-deep snow at 25,300 feet (7772 meters), Dudley found himself obliged to return alone to Camp VIII.

Except in the preparatory stage, Dudley, however strong, was by no means the expedition's workhorse. He was unqualified as a rope leader; he had a poor sense of balance, bad eyesight, and, despite his ascents, only limited experience. As a camper he was not much better; he could go through a whole box of matches and still fail to light a stove.

Moving ever upward from camp to camp under his good shepherd's tutelage, rarely descending to help carry up loads, Dudley had spent much of the expedition alone or almost alone in a tent, especially when up high: seven nights at Camp V waiting for supplies that never came; five at Camp VIII, again with frustrated expectations; and now six nights at Camp VII. He had had plenty of time to reflect on a life he must have considered so wretchedly wasted. And now K2, his final obsession, had been denied him. Once more he faced the thought of failure. Perhaps, if death should beckon, as it had six days earlier on the slopes above, he would not resist.

By the time the Sherpas reached him at noon on July 29, Dudley had spent thirty-eight consecutive days above 22,000 feet (6705 meters), most of them in a tent. Of these, sixteen had been at heights averaging 25,000 feet (7620 meters). In the history of mountaineering to that time, no man – not Noel Odell of Everest, not Fritz himself – had been known to remain at such heights so long – even with oxygen support. And few have done it since.

No one knows for sure just what Dudley's state of health may have been when he parted company with Fritz on July 23. Fritz reported that Dudley looked fine, talked about another try for the summit, and by inference seemed strong enough to have descended with the other two had he so wished. There are those who doubt Fritz's testimony. So Dudley's condition on that date is an unanswered question. But six days later the Sherpas found him in a deplorable state. He seemed to have not once left his tent since Fritz's departure; he had once again exhausted his match supply and therefore had had no warm food and, worse, no fluids; his sleeping bag and the entire tent floor were contaminated with body wastes. Fritz, writing as of some days later (August 2) and citing the testimony of the one surviving Sherpa who had gone on the rescue mission, gives this description:

> *When arriving at Camp 7 at noon they found Dudley lying in his sleeping-bag very apathetic. He did not read his mail or even look at the note which I had written to him. It seemed he had not eaten for several days, nor had he been outside his tent. He had even relieved himself in the tent. He complained he had no matches. His hands and feet with the exception of some sore spots on his left hand were in good shape. F [sic] Pasang told Tse that everything was in horrible condition in spite of the good weather. The Sherpas made him tea and wanted to take him with them. He refused however and told them to come back next day when he would be ready. Pasang told Tsering that they had led Dudley outside the tent and that he staggered around.*

As Tony and Jack had warned Fritz was likely to happen, Dudley, without Fritz's support, had gone to pieces.

Unable to fulfill their mission that day, the three Sherpas returned to Camp VI, where Tsering awaited them. Stormy weather the next day kept them tentbound. On July 31 the same Sherpa trio – Kikuli, Kitar, and Phinsoo – leaving Tsering behind, departed once more for Camp VII. They planned either to extract from Dudley a chit exonerating them in case he still refused to descend, or to carry him bodily down the mountain.

The Sherpas never returned. Four men vanished in the mists. K2 had struck its last and deadliest blow.

TSERING WAITED TWO DAYS at Camp VI with fading hopes. On August 2, around 7:30 A.M., Jack watched a solitary figure start down from Camp VI. Early that afternoon, having literally run down the mountain, Tsering arrived in Base Camp, the bearer of bad news.

On the first attempt to save Dudley, Tsering had stayed behind, something he again did two days later; he still feared the traverse below Camp VII. He therefore never saw Dudley, but relayed what Kikuli and the others had told him about Dudley's condition on their first visit. Tsering's report was second-hand, but it had the ring of truth. What he had to say alarmed the remaining Sherpas – Dawa, Lama, and Sonam. "The Sherpas are certain," Jack wrote on August 3, "something awful has happened." Two of them, Tsering and the now partially recovered Dawa, went up the glacier to look around.

Fritz, still optimistic, remained unconvinced, but had begun to waver. He wrote in his diary under the date August 2:

> Tsering said it was impossible that the Sherpas should have stayed with the Sahib under the conditions his tent was in and the second tent too badly torn. Also they have no sleeping bags and there was no food for them at VII. A serious situation but we cannot believe that something should have happened to two such experienced men as Pasang Kikuli and Phinsoo, also Pasang Kitar a newer man was perfectly able to handle a difficult situation safely and had shown good rope technique. If Dudley really had not recovered and the Sherpas had transported him down the mountain they certainly would have been well roped and would have taken all precautions with belaying each other to judge from the good belaying they had done throughout the trip. No, it seems impossible that anything should have happened to such an able group.

Something had to be done. Hardly anyone was left capable of action. Jack again offered his services, but doubted his "lousy condition would ever carry me . . . far." Fritz agreed. Jack would stay in Base Camp to observe. Of the Sherpas only two, Dawa and Tsering, had retained any strength; they were once more sent up the glacier to sleep at Camp I and await orders.

Sick, emotionally drained, still hardly able to walk, much less to climb, Fritz set out one last time in an effort to reach Camp VII – now with four men to rescue. Jack accompanied him to the icefall, whence Fritz, with Tsering and Dawa, went on to Camp I. Fritz barely covered the remaining distance before dark. Of his physical condition at this time he wrote in his diary:

I can breathe only with great effort, somehow the respiration stops at my throat...August 4: We will try to reach Camp 4 today. The wind has changed again to the SW and fresh clouds appear over Broad Peak and K2. Going to II is very slow. In spite of my respiration troubles I am able to keep up with Dawa and Tsering but I realize I cannot make 4 today. We will have to stay at 2. Tsering says also that it would be impossible for him to go the distance to 4 today...I am very much afraid now that an accident has occurred.

The same day it began to snow. The storm lasted until August 7, by which time 1.5 feet (0.5 meter) of snow had accumulated outside the tents at Camp II. Elsewhere on the mountain there were no signs of life. Tsering then disclosed something only hinted at before. Contrary to what Fritz believed, there was no edible food at Camp VII; Wolfe had been lying on most of the supplies, and they were saturated with his body wastes. This news destroyed Fritz's last hopes of ever seeing the four men again. To march farther was hopeless. Fritz had reached the bitter end of his once vast human resources.

Fritz and the Sherpas trudged slowly back to Base Camp, their spirits desperately low. There Fritz finally threw in the towel and ordered operations suspended—after all, what else could be done? Jack was still unwell, Fritz a mere skeleton, and, as Jack indicated in his diary earlier (August 3), "Tsering is baulky, Pasang Lama footsore & Dawa a whispering dwarf." It was all over.

Somewhere on K2 the gentle flakes were burying ever deeper the remains of a gallant American sportsman, two brave Sherpas, and their even braver sirdar, Pasang Kikuli, whom Jack and Fritz had long since described as the best of the best.

"And so ends our sad story!" Jack wrote later in his diary (under the date October 24) in a final note covering the rescue operations from July 25 through August 8. "May God do his best by our comrades!"

14

THE ROAD BACK

T HERE ARE FOUR KINDS of expeditions: (1) those that are happy and successful; (2) those that are happy and unsuccessful; (3) those that are unhappy and successful; and (4) those that are unhappy and unsuccessful. The 1939 American Karakoram Expedition to K2 belonged to the last category.

It was a long journey home.

At last the full meaning of the catastrophe began to penetrate Fritz's consciousness. Hitherto he had been too involved with emergencies and illusions of hope to understand what had happened. With these gone he faced the truth. A quarter of those who had started up the Abruzzi Ridge were dead; eight more could be considered casualties–twelve out of fifteen.

The expedition that had arrived in Base Camp at the end of May, so full of strength and confidence, withdrew piecemeal in ragtag fashion. First to leave were the walking wounded, George Sheldon and Chappell Cranmer, on July 18, even before Jack Durrance's descent and Fritz's attempts at the summit. Then, on July 25, at the height of the crisis, the psychological victims–the despondent and woefully out-of-his-depth deputy leader, Tony Cromwell; the demoralized and inept transport officer, "Joe" Trench; and the disgraced Sherpa, Tendrup–left with the main porter caravan. Finally, August 9 brought the departure of the rest of the party–Chandra, the interpreter; Noor, the cook; Sherpas Pasang Lama, Dawa, Tsering, and Sonam; Jack Durrance; and, last of all, Fritz Wiessner, cruelly disappointed and for the moment broken in body and spirit.

There may exist records of the Sheldon-Cranmer and Trench-Cromwell return odysseys to Askole, where the two groups rejoined and thence to Srinagar, but no effort has been made to find them, for they are not relevant to the essence of the tragedy. George and Chappell were the first to get home. They had little to report because they left Base Camp more than a week before the drama's climax. Tony, who sojourned in Srinagar until well after Fritz's arrival there (after notifying his friends at home), was the next to return to America. There he was met at dockside by the American Alpine Club's secretary, Henry Snow Hall, Jr., to whom he hastened to tell his version of events. But the most significant exit consisted of the rear guard, Fritz and Jack.

Though the two men held opposing views on almost every subject, and though Fritz, from a conversation with Kikuli on July 26, knew of Jack's role in the removal of the sleeping bags (albeit not the full or exact story), the two got along well. No doubt this was difficult, especially for Jack. Fritz had a limited sense of humor, was extremely set in his ways, and could not believe the things at which he excelled could be done in any way other than his own; he had a closed mind, impervious to counsel. In contrast, Jack was a prankster, a banterer with a sharp sense of humor and sarcastic wit; he had a facile, fun-loving mind, which Fritz did not understand or appreciate. Jack liked competition; Fritz claimed he didn't. But Jack could get along with Fritz as long as his admiration and awe of the man persisted, making every effort to carry out his instructions, even though they were often hard to understand. The only issues he ever raised involved his appraisal of the competence and determination of the team's other members.

There is no record that either in Base Camp after the tragedy nor on the way out Fritz ever confronted Jack about the sleeping-bag removal. Jack's diary, so refreshingly candid on everything else, contains no hint of this topic. Nor is there any record that the two engaged in any quarrels aside from a few petty spats of the sort that happen to tired people just about anywhere.

Jack kept a rambling account of his thoughts and experiences during the march out. Above Urdukas, a still weak Fritz suffered a fainting spell of brief duration. On August 14 a Balti porter, Hasem, caught "two very small trout in a small streamlet" with his hands. "Sorry to say," Jack observed, "he ate them himself." At the inevitable rope bridges, Fritz, never afraid of heights, but shy in the presence of raging water, hesitated to cross. Jack's toothache had returned, and the fleas were really after him: "I'm an old rooster now for I've learned the art of scratching." Visiting a native house at Askole, he picked up another five or six fleas, which promptly multiplied. Two days later he "found besides two fat fleas eight of another sort of unmentionable vermin on my shirt." He had interesting encounters with beasts of burden, or, rather, nags. At the Tragbal Pass, just short of Srinagar, he wrote on August 26: "If my horse balks & causes me as much trouble as yesterday, I'm certain to lose my temper." Then, later the same day, he added: "Well, I might add that it did and that my temper was duly lost."

As might be expected from famished men, Jack's diary beyond Askole is full of references to food. Fritz and Jack seem to have feasted almost endlessly, sometimes with accompanying indigestion. They ate roast lamb, chicken, innumerable omelets, and fruit, fruit, fruit, mostly local melons and ripe apricots.

AT ASKOLE, wishing to avoid the roundabout route via the Braldu River, Fritz, Jack, and the others crossed the river by a rope bridge and cut across the mountains to Shigar by way of the Skoro Pass, which briefly took them back to about 17,000 feet (5181 meters).

In Shigar on August 18, working together, Fritz and Jack started drafting the expedition's important final report. In general the two seemed agreed on the text; but it was a long job, and the final version took form only some weeks later in Srinagar. Just who said what during the discussions about the wording has never been clarified. Fritz asserted later that Jack, with a guilty conscience, kept coming to him and crying out, "What shall we tell them? What shall we tell them?" to which, by his account, Fritz replied, "The truth, of course." Jack insisted it was the other way around, that Fritz kept crying, "What shall we tell them?" while Jack insisted on the truth.

Shigar to Skardu went quickly and effortlessly by goat-skin raft down the Shigar River and thence across the Indus: "Four Baltis manned our ship," Jack wrote, "with six-foot poles as paddles. There was quite some rough water, sometimes high waves, at other times we scraped the shallow bottom." The river journey terminated at the local rajah's estate.

On August 25 the party reached Gurais, which had a telegraph office. Fritz sent out eight or nine important wires, including a report to the *Times of India*. The night of August 26 they slept in a Dak bungalow that Jack noted was "in meadow surrounded by tall Himalayan spruce & fir & hemlock." Their host, an interesting and hospitable gentleman named Percival, warned them nonetheless about risks from local thieves – and leopards! He provided a chicken dinner, relaxing whiskey and sodas, an open fire, and, joy of joys, hot baths! Kashmir was near at hand with real civilization.

Early the next morning Fritz, Jack, Chandra, the Sherpas, and miscellaneous retinue raced down the heights by shortcut to reach the Iron Bridge at Bandipur. There Tony Cromwell met them, and there the final act took place in the chain of events that led to hostilities. The real trouble was about to start.

Tony took one look at the draft text of the expedition's final report, so painstakingly prepared by Fritz and Jack, and exploded.[1] This time it was not Fritz who made accusations, but Tony. Fritz, he said flatly, had murdered Dudley Wolfe and the three Sherpas.

Jack, as his diary (the source of almost everything in this chapter) suggests, hoped the differences between Tony and Fritz could be contained and kept private. It was, he felt, something that properly belonged within the expedition, not all over the countryside. But Tony, arriving first in Kashmir with Trench, had already spilled his sentiments onto the British colony in Srinagar, whence they were certain to spread to America. A cablegram he sent to the AAC's secretary Hall had also ensured that his viewpoint would command the first official attention. Try as he might, Jack proved unable to repress Tony and Trench, who clearly wanted a public scandal. The blows began to shower on expedition leader Fritz.

On August 28, George ("Joe") Trench appeared at a luncheon that included Fritz, Jack, the ever amiable Ken Hadow, and Hadow's successor as Kashmir secretary of the Himalayan Club, F. A. Betterton. The latter could not help noticing "definite hostilities...between him [Trench] and Fritz and Ken." As Jack deeply feared, for he wanted no part of it, the expedition's dirty linen had begun to hang out for all to see. Jack reported in his diary for August 29:

> To my regret I found that Toni and George [now that Sheldon was gone, Trench had recovered his first name] had not kept their displeasure of relationship with Fritz a secret from the general public and it was a bit awkward that he [Fritz] was not asked yesterday or today to visit their houseboat.

The local situation was no doubt exacerbated by the imminence of war, and Fritz's German origins were certainly no secret. By August 30, Trench and Tony were about to depart for Peshawar and home; unfortunately, they had both had time to post inflammatory letters addressed to Joel Ellis Fisher in New York, recently president and now treasurer of the American Alpine Club.

The precise contents of Trench's and Tony's letters are unknown. Trench's letter, at his request under pressure from the British resident, Lt. Col. D. M. Fraser, was presumably returned unopened. Tony's letter cannot be found. But American Consul Edward Miller Groth, who had the letters read to him while in the company of Lt. Col. Fraser, had this to say about both in a September 13, 1939 memorandum accompanying Calcutta Despatch 1211 from the American Consulate General in Calcutta to the U.S. Secretary of State:

> *Colonel Fraser, the Resident at Srinagar, on whom I called on Tuesday,*
> *September 5th, had just received from Mr. Cromwell copies of his and*
> *Trench's letters addressed to Mr. Joel E. Fisher, Treasurer of the Ameri-*
> *can Alpine Club in New York City. Colonel Fraser very kindly read the*
> *letters in question to me and we both came to practically the same con-*
> *clusions in our reactions to the contents of these communications. Lieut.*
> *Trench's letter was of such a superficial character as to deserve no cre-*
> *dence whatever. Mr. Cromwell's letter, on the other hand, seemed to*
> *Colonel Fraser and myself to contain numerous unwarranted accusa-*
> *tions.[2] We both felt that the final paragraphs were of such a vindictive*
> *nature that one might almost question the motives which prompted*
> *their writing. Certainly the exaggerated nature of these concluding*
> *paragraphs must largely, if not entirely, nullify any truths contained in*
> *the earlier part of the letter.*

Searching for guidance, Jack dined with Major Hadow on August 30. When the other guests left, Jack broached the expedition grievances to Hadow, mentioning most especially the disparaging letters Tony and Trench had mailed to Fisher. Hadow had already guessed the situation and was upset. As Jack wrote on August 31:

> *[Hadow] told me of his preparation [Hadow wanted to fete the party]*
> *for everyone & his disappointment when it was (rudely) not accepted.*
> *Also of Trench's rude and deplorable conduct. We both agreed some-*
> *thing must be done that no unfair injustice be done Fritz who was sort*
> *of knocked down by war & finances anyway.[3] I agreed to forget my com-*
> *plaints as the trip is over, etc. etc. . . .*

Jack kept his word. Never, in the ensuing quarrel, did he speak out against Fritz, toward whom by now his private feelings were anything but friendly. For his part, Fritz was less restrained.

THERE WERE STILL THINGS TO DO. Fritz and Jack spent the next morning revising the expedition report, then stayed up until 3:30 A.M. the following day rewriting the whole thing once more and discussing the expedition troubles. In the course of their labors, Jack told Fritz about Tony's and Trench's letters to Fisher.

Meanwhile, at a convenient moment during one of their many meetings, Ken Hadow had drawn Jack aside for a few moments. He informed Jack that their discussion about the letters had so bothered him that he had gone to the resident, Lt. Col. Fraser. Hadow was particularly concerned with Trench's letter, which, he told Jack, "necessarily had an official stamp to it and which should never have been sent without the resident's and the Himalayan Club's consent." As a result, the resident had telegraphed for Trench to return to Srinagar; but the orders were canceled after Fritz discovered the trip would cost the expedition 200 rupees, which they either didn't have or which would become another bone of contention with the treasurer. Instead Trench was instructed to cable Fisher asking that on its receipt the letter be returned to the sender unopened. Whether Trench complied is not known.[4]

Fritz and Jack had meanwhile accepted an invitation to spend the weekend at Ken Hadow's place in Gullmarg, above Srinagar and below the Killmarg ski area, with the Staniers family, who had rented the property. But first there was some business Friday morning, September 1: a visit with the Himalayan Club's incoming secretary, F. A. Betterton, who approved Fritz's reports and invited him to join the Himalayan Club; then to Lt. Col. Fraser to obtain a death certificate for Dudley. The same afternoon Jack rode by horse to Gullmarg, followed the next day by Fritz and Ken Hadow.

The sojourn proved an idyllic one, disturbed only by the news of Great Britain and France's declaration of war on Germany on Sunday, September 3, and the equally bad news that Fritz's and Jack's ship, scheduled to sail on September 13, had been canceled. This last action put the two expedition members in what Jack termed a "perplexing situation." "God knows how I shall get home," Jack wrote in his diary on that date.

Fortunately, official advice was near at hand. On reaching Srinagar on Monday morning, September 4, Jack and Fritz found notes inviting them to lunch with American Consul Edward Miller Groth, who was on his way back to his post in Calcutta following a local leave during which he had visited Leh in then remote Ladakh. Groth also invited Hadow, but the latter was already engaged.

Jack described the meeting with Groth in diary entries of September 4 and 5:

> *Found note that Consul Groth had us invited to Wedon's for lunch. Changed to shorts [the weather was intensely hot] and proceeded [word illegible]. Consul Groth very handsome, well spoken gentleman fussy about his bread and water. He had just returned from a trip back over the Zoji-La from Leh. After lunch where our plight as "stranded" citizens had been the topic we withdrew to the drawing room & related our mtn. experiences which Groth was anxious to hear officially & personally. He had engaged our Sherpas & knew several very well. Then as Groth had been asked by the Residency to interview Fritz & me regards the affair with Trench's & Cromwell's letters to Fisher we told him our stories separately—I spared nothing short of the truth. After an hour's private conversation with Groth regarding the unpleasant happenings of our expedition, I went to hear a record of Pres. Roosevelt's speech over the wireless.*

Durrance's diary entry for September 4

For his part Consul Groth, in his memorandum accompanying unclassified Calcutta Despatch 1211 from the American Consulate General, Calcutta, of September 13 to the Secretary of State, writes of this luncheon as follows:

> *I returned to Srinagar from Leh on the morning of September 4th and immediately got in touch with Major Kenneth Hadow [who for business reasons had returned from Gullmarg to Srinagar the 3rd] by telephone. He informed me that Wiessner was in Gullmarg but that he expected him back by noon. I invited Hadow, Wiessner and Durrance for lunch, but Hadow was unable to accept. Wiessner and Durrance arrived at the appointed hour and for almost seven hours thereafter they related to me the details leading up to and subsequent to the tragic accident which took place on K-2 and resulted in the death of Dudley Wolfe and three Sherpas.*
>
> *The aforementioned details, which are of a very complicated character, are clearly set out in the report submitted to the American Alpine Club by Mr. Wiessner, the leader, a copy of which is appended hereto, and therefore no attempt will be made to give this information as it would merely be a repetition of the report and would be based on the original.*[5]

As a final gesture to try to calm troubled waters, Jack wrote Tony Cromwell to take it easy and cabled the following advice to George Sheldon: "Withhold all expedition comment." George obeyed. Tony did not. As for Jack, if he had anything to say, it was discreetly private.

By September 18, Italian ships once more plied their way from India to Suez, thence across the Mediterranean and the Atlantic to America. Fritz, however, traveled by air to Cairo, had a short stay with General Archibald Wavell, and then continued home by ship. Jack debated a return by way of the Pacific. Aside from breaks on K2, he had been in Fritz's company since March 29, almost six months, a rather extended exposure to a heavy personality. "I have been together with Fritz about long enough," he told Ken Hadow in search of advice. Hadow agreed.

The adventure had come to an end, the youthful illusions dissipated. On September 20, at last, Fritz and Jack separated. Rather than return with Fritz, Jack stayed in India until October 25 and did not reach home until close to the end of the year.

"Fritz & I part ways," Jack noted tersely in his diary on September 20. To which he then added: "thank God."

THE CARNIVAL STARTED AT THE PIER when Tony Cromwell arrived at Weehawken, New Jersey. Tony had an advantage, being the first person to arrive who had firsthand knowledge of the events, and he baldly iterated the absurd charge that Fritz had murdered Dudley. His advantage was to become greatly enhanced when Fritz, after his arrival, told reporters for the *New York Times*, in his heavy German accent, that on big mountains, as in war, one must expect casualties, a statement that played not at all well to contemporary national sentiments.

As in a Shakespearean tragedy, on K2 normal men had been thrown together amid extraordinary events with which most of them were unprepared to cope, and they reacted accordingly. Once the catastrophe happened, bitterness followed.

George Sheldon and Chappell Cranmer kept to the sidelines; besides, they had been in no way involved with the final scenes of the drama. Jack, too, aside from a brief discussion with Charlie Houston, stayed out of it; with more knowledge and grievances than anyone, he wanted no part of the controversy. During the months that followed, it was Tony and Fritz who held center stage.

Fritz's expedition to K2 was the first American overseas mountaineering effort in which lives were lost: twelve men who had set foot on the mountain had been casualties, of which four were deaths—all this in the short space of seven weeks. The expedition had the sponsorship of the American Alpine Club. Its officials and members asked questions.[6] The survivors, they soon learned, quarreled over the causes of the tragedy.

People took sides, and the controversy became increasingly bitter. Fritz's supporters, quite rightly, described his efforts as a mountaineering tour de force. They maintained that in spite of his efforts and example, lukewarm, irresponsible, and incompetent companions had let him down.[7] At the other extreme were those who, while acknowledging Fritz's superb climbing, believed he had shown poor judgment and leadership by failing to take into account his companions' weaknesses.

Rather than cooling off and being forgotten, the quarrel over the expedition's conduct grew increasingly acute. It threatened to break up the American Alpine Club. Those on the expedition with low visibility in the AAC managed to stay in hiding—for a while. But both Fritz and Tony had reputations at stake. They had to defend themselves.

On October 27, 1939, the Club appointed a committee of inquiry to look into the expedition's conduct. Four of its members—Joel Ellis Fisher, Bill House, Terris Moore, and Bestor Robinson—could be counted on as understanding of Fritz. The chairman, geographer Walter Wood, was unknown in his leanings.

After months of investigation, the committee completed its report. Not wishing to add fuel to a raging fire, it decided by unanimous vote to adopt a middle-of-the-road position. It left any account of the expedition in the hands of the participants with the statement: "It was obvious that members of the expedition could best tell the story themselves."

Although Fritz objected to some passages in an early draft version, the report did have the desired effect. Things simmered down.

When the debate calmed, in early 1941, Fritz quietly resigned from the Club. Tony, for a time at least, did likewise. But Fritz's and Tony's resignations did not end the matter. Many times in the following years mountaineering "historians," often after inadequate research, have tried to revive the story.

A quarter of a century later, in 1966, friends of Fritz Wiessner in the American Alpine Club, headed by the authors of this book, persuaded him to rejoin the organization. Immediately thereafter, though not without considerable discussion, the Club's board of directors conferred on him honorary membership in recognition not of what he had done on K2, but for his many contributions to American and international mountaineering over prior and subsequent decades. For another twenty years Fritz served the AAC faithfully and with distinction. Most notably, he helped transform it from a purely national organization into a globally respected institution.

For his part, Fritz did well in later years. He made a fine marriage, raised two splendid children, prospered, traveled throughout the world, and continued to climb. When he died in 1988 he was still one of the most respected alpinists in America, if not in the world.

Over those many years Fritz Wiessner had also transferred his hostility toward Tony Cromwell to Jack Durrance–and somehow, and for some unexplained motive, managed to persuade most people, on the flimsiest of evidence, that if there had been a villain in his party, it had to have been that last-minute interloper.

The evidence points elsewhere.

15

THE UNANSWERED QUESTIONS

O N THE FIRST PAGE of his memorandum submitted to the U.S. Secretary of State as an enclosure with Calcutta Despatch 1211 of September 13, 1939, Consul Edward Miller Groth asserts that the details of the 1939 American Karakoram Expedition to K2 were of "a very complicated character." True enough, but even more puzzling, both then and later, have been certain questions that, until now, have remained unanswered.

Among them, the one given the most attention has been what can only be described as a "phantom note" that Fritz Wiessner says he picked up in a tent at Camp II during his descent from Camp VII on July 23, 1939, and whose author he believed to have been Jack Durrance. References to this note do not begin to appear until years after the event, and only in Fritz's accounts. To Fritz and several of his chroniclers, however, the significance of the note, assuming it ever existed, was that, based on the evidence available and in combination with Fritz's other allegations, it could be read to shift responsibility for events leading to the disaster from Fritz's shoulders onto those of Jack Durrance.

The problem with the story of the note has been that no one except Fritz, who could benefit from it, ever claimed to have seen the document; that Fritz was never able to supply the original nor even a copy; and that Jack has steadfastly disclaimed any such authorship. There is no mention of any note in the expedition report completed at Srinagar a few weeks later. So, from the outset, the evidence of the note's existence is skimpy. And today, with the revelation in Jack's diary that deputy expedition leader Tony Cromwell was the motivating force behind removal of the sleeping bags at Camps IV and II, the story of the note has, if any significance at all, a vastly different one from that which Fritz chose for years to ascribe to the outcome of the 1939 K2 expedition.

Still, a few people will always be interested in the tale of the "phantom note," partly because it makes good copy and partly because it has been exploited all too vigorously by those who have viewed Fritz Wiessner as the unfairly abused hero of the 1939 undertaking. Accordingly, Appendix H of this book presents the authors' conjectures regarding this elusive piece of paper.

IT WOULD BE ABSURD for the contents of an ephemeral–perhaps imaginary–note to serve as the major, if not the sole, explanation for the catastrophe that overtook an expedition so complicated in its fate as the 1939 American Karakoram Expedition to K2. Far more important are certain factual events that occurred sometimes for reasons not well established and that had a major impact on the outcome of the undertaking. To be sure, the removal of the sleeping bags was a significant factor, but it was by no means the most important thing that went wrong on K2.

The first of these events goes back to the United States and relates to the often discussed composition of the party, which, except for Jack Durrance, had been hand-picked by Fritz Wiessner. Of this Groth, in his memorandum, wrote as follows:

> . . . I should be inclined to reach the conclusion that the unfortunate accident was due to a combination of circumstances over which Wiessner did not have entire control nor for which he could be held solely responsible. I am under the impression that Wiessner's responsibility may possibly lie in another direction, viz., that he should have exercised far greater care in selecting the members of his party and in studying their temperaments.[1]

What Groth probably did not know was that Fritz's original party, with Alfred Lindley and Bestor Robinson, would in all likelihood have been equal to the challenge. What he did know, as everyone else knew in retrospect, was that Fritz chose to proceed with a weak and unbalanced team, about which Charlie Houston had expressed his reservations at Joel Ellis Fisher's farewell dinner for Jack Durrance. Ability to finance the venture seems to have represented to Fritz something as important as climbing skill or suitable temperament. Cranmer, Cromwell, and Wolfe– half the team, were either independently rich or belonged to rich families. Of the three, only Cromwell could lay claim to real mountaineering experience, and then mostly under the tutelage of professional guides, and his climbing record, aside from length, had in it nothing of distinction or difficulty. So who would provide the climbing ability needed to get to the top? Who if not Fritz alone? So on the one hand the party had a strong, dedicated leader, and on the other hand it had insufficiently skilled or experienced troops. This was something Jack later described as a "drastically unequal party regards to age, position and ability combined with experience."[2]

Was this the way to set off on the first ascent of the world's second-highest mountain? By July 2, in his diary entry for that day, Jack had supplied one part of the answer: "we move only as puppets, it is definitely a one man's trip."

In addition to the expedition's unbalanced nature, there existed a potential for trouble on which Consul Groth put his finger in the early paragraphs of his memorandum:

After the protracted conversations with Wiessner and Durrance I retained the impression that at the very outset the composition of the expedition provided potential elements of a clash of temperaments before the end of the tour. Confidentially, I believe that one of the primary factors precipitating the dissension which finally arose was the inescapable fact that, although on paper and by law, Wiessner is an American citizen, he is still in many respects largely German in his outlook and actions. This is not unnatural in view of the circumstance that he became an American citizen but a few months ago [Wiessner claimed he became a citizen in 1935]. With his German background, also owing to the fact that he possesses a large share of German bluntness (a national characteristic which was apparently unknown to all but one of his colleagues and fellow expedition members) it is not remarkable that there should have been a clash of temperaments. Wiessner is undoubtedly an excellent climber and a good leader, but, like every German [Groth might better have used the words "many Germans"], he is very forceful in giving commands and totally unaware that the abrupt, blunt manner in which the order may have been given might have wounded the feelings of his associates, who in this instance, being Americans, naturally had a different attitude and outlook in matters of this sort.

Although I recognize the aforementioned German characteristics and can easily understand the reaction which they caused among the other members of the expedition, I received the impression that the latter made comparatively little effort to analyze or understand Wiessner's temperament. Had this been done, they would probably have realized at an early date that Wiessner's bite was not as bad as his bark. It may also be that the other members of the expedition had never previously been in a position where it was necessary to accept and carry out the orders of so imperative a leader.

Until recent years, expeditions composed of climbers of different nationalities have not fared well. Exceptions exist, to be sure, notably in

Anglo-American parties, whose participants share a common language and, in some respects, a common culture. But on K2 there is no question that Fritz Wiessner had a very different attitude, at least toward mountaineering, from that of most of his comrades, few of whom ever tried to analyze his thinking. By 1939, Consul Groth had served in consular or diplomatic posts in seven countries (including Germany) on three continents and had no difficulty in appreciating the ethnic differences that separated Wiessner from his American companions.

FRITZ NO DOUBT HAD HIS REASONS for sailing from New York with an inferior team–he wanted to climb the mountain. But some people have questioned his judgment at the next point of no return. This was at Camp IV on July 11, when he reached his personal decision to make an attempt on the summit. By then almost all of his companions were against it–all save Dudley. And Fritz knew it, for in his official report to the American Alpine Club he stated: "Most of the members and porters were physically tired out (some low in spirits as well)." Two American expeditionaries, Sheldon and Cranmer, were out of the running; another, Cromwell, demoralized, had suffered a bad fall; the British transport officer, Trench, had proven himself incompetent; Durrance, though requested by Fritz to join the assault party, was in low spirits; and one Sherpa, Sonam, had been injured. On top of this was clear evidence from events of the previous weeks that any support team might be unwilling or unable to provide the back-up Fritz considered necessary, or at least desirable. Should Fritz have persisted at this point?

Despite the risks, the decision Fritz made was not unreasonable, even if debatable. He and two Sherpas had already carried loads almost to Camp VII. Additional supplies were in place at Camps IV and V. The weather, as Fritz noted in his report to the American Alpine Club (Appendix F), had now taken a real turn for the better. There was adequate time remaining. And he could count on seven Sherpas, Dudley, and, in his opinion, Jack. So there was a good case for allowing the undamaged part of the team to continue upward.

The real question, however, is why Fritz selected Dudley, physically strong but a poor climber, to serve as a member of the assault team and, accordingly, to tread onto difficult mountain terrain of a hitherto unknown nature. Any climber who has seen films of Dudley Wolfe in the Alps, roped to two guides–one ahead who pulls, and the other behind who pushes, while Dudley teeters in the middle–has to label him an inept mountaineer who had no business as a member of the climbing team of a major expedition. Surely Fritz, otherwise an excellent judge of competence, must have made this observation. If he did not, there were those to remind him–notably Jack at the confrontation at Camp VI on July 13, when Jack expressed his misgivings about Fritz's decision to take Dudley to Camp VII and points beyond. Even if Dudley could continue in good weather, what might happen if conditions took a turn for the worse, as they already had earlier?

In the course of the expedition the relationship between Fritz and Dudley, always more than ordinarily friendly, had grown noticeably closer ever since Chap Cranmer's illness. The relationship reached the point where other members of the expedition began to wonder if there might not have been a pre-expedition arrangement between the two in which Fritz promised to do his best to get Dudley to the summit in exchange for expedition financing. Such was Jack's opinion. "It is," he wrote in his diary in "Medical Notes" under the date of November 25, "unfair to take a man along and use valuable time hauling him about just because he was able to finance the undertaking."

The perceptive Consul Groth hints at somewhat the same thing on pages two and three of his memorandum. And Louis Audoubert in his book *Baltoro, Montagnes de Lumière* remarks: "When Wiessner approached [Wolfe] for money to finance the K2 expedition, he agreed–on condition he be made a member of the climbing team."[3]

If the above citations are to be believed, then the primary link between Fritz and Dudley was financial.

But should not preexisting financial agreements be swept away by the rigors and demands of a perilous mountain venture? That, at least, was Groth's opinion, and although not a mountaineer of wide experience, he knew much from his interests and travels in the Himalaya and his membership in the Himalayan Club and the Colorado Mountain Club. On page two of his memorandum he wrote:

> I received the impression that the general feeling of several of the expedition members [Groth does not limit his remarks to Wolfe] was that, as they had borne their share of the expenses and had contributed liberally to the expenses of one or two members unable to pay the entire cost out of their own pockets, they were entitled to have just as much to say about the running of the expedition as the leader. This, of course, was a most unfortunate attitude, for there can be only one leader, regardless of who foots the bills.

But unlike his rich companions Cranmer and Cromwell, and although clumsy and perhaps lazy (Groth twice refers to reports of Dudley's indolence), Dudley had displayed dogged determination and great strength– "We can't get him off the mountain," George Sheldon had written in his letter of June 14 to the American Alpine Club. He and Fritz were the only two members who had not succumbed to illness or loss of faith. In retrospect Fritz might have, and probably should have, replaced Dudley with a good Sherpa; but it was a tradition of the times that, if at all possible, the summit team should consist of two or more sahibs.

Fritz's clinching argument for the inclusion of Dudley in the assault party was his retort to Jack's expressed misgivings at Camp VI. Fritz simply could not, he said, turn anyone down who could carry a load and wished to continue.[4] Once Jack fell ill, no other sahibs were available. Also, anyone who ever climbed with Fritz knows how he reveled in leading less qualified companions to places they could not reach without him. This trait of Fritz's was, of course, logical for a man like him, but in Jack's opinion also represented faulty judgment.

Aside from Dudley's value as a source of funds, his determination and physical strength, plus the general breakdown to which Fritz refers on the first page of his report, are probably the best explanation why Fritz allowed him to follow in his footsteps. In so doing the question arises: did Fritz Wiessner overestimate Dudley Wolfe's ability to deal with the perils that lay ahead, even under the best of weather conditions? Or was he even thinking about such matters?

FRITZ'S DECISION TO PROCEED to K2 with a weak team; his refusal at Camp IV on July 11 to reconsider the wisdom of continuing; his inclusion of Dudley Wolfe in the assault team at Camp VI; and other elements not subject to debate, such as his reluctance when close under the summit to compel Lama to follow him through the night, all played a role in the expedition's disastrous outcome. So, too, did the removal of the sleeping bags in which Fritz had no part. But it was the utterly untraditional act of July 23, when Fritz split his small party and left Dudley alone at Camp VII, that led directly to the ensuing catastrophe. If at that critical moment the three men had stuck together, as Fritz could have insisted, the outcome of the expedition would have been vastly different. The matter is, therefore, of capital importance in any examination of expedition events. Why, in short, did Fritz split his party?

One reason, probably not the decisive one, may have derived from a practice Fritz initiated and that later degenerated into a habit. Beginning at Camp V and continuing at Camp VIII, Fritz had left Dudley alone in a tent for several consecutive days while he and the Sherpas went ahead to equip the route for the final climb to the summit. By the time the assault team had reached Camp VII this practice had become an accepted and apparently benign procedure: Dudley's isolation had never given rise to apprehensions nor caused any trouble. But at Camp VII the situation differed markedly from earlier experience. Rather than having a party up ahead able to climb down to Dudley in case of trouble, it would thereafter be necessary to climb back up–a harder job at high altitude–to provide him assistance. On top of this, there now existed overwhelming evidence that something below was very wrong. Yet in the face of these facts, Dudley, remained at Camp VII all alone–top man, so to speak, as well as the poorest climber of the team. "Tired but well" was how Fritz described Dudley's condition on page four of his official report to the American Alpine Club.

What are the other possibilities? Did Fritz and Lama, fearing they could not handle the heavy and clumsy Dudley on the rope, simply leave him behind–after all, the previous day's near-fatal fall had been the result of Dudley's ineptness? Was Fritz suffering from altered brain function as a result of hypoxia and hypocapnia (shortage of carbon dioxide) after nine days' exertions above 25,000 feet (7620 meters), and therefore unable to think clearly? Or did Dudley, almost suicidally attracted to the summit, but always a bit lazy and for the moment tired, somehow persuade Fritz to leave him behind so that he could rest and recuperate while the others descended to pick up fresh supplies and renew the ascent?

It is almost impossible to believe, as some critics have charged, that Fritz callously meant to abandon Dudley. All those who climbed with Fritz before and since the K2 expedition know that it was never his practice deliberately to leave behind him weaker and unsupported rope companions. Indeed had not Fritz, just four days earlier, in effect sacrificed his chance for the summit because he did not wish to leave his Sherpa comrade alone? So why, assuming Dudley was in good health and ambulant, should he have reversed himself at this point unless he was not thinking properly or unless he was persuaded by Dudley to change his habits? The party's fall above Camp VII on July 22 may have shaken Fritz a bit, but Fritz had an uncanny ability not to remain shaken for long.

So it becomes necessary to look elsewhere.

There is also the possibility that the three men at Camp VII, after long exposure to extreme altitude, were not thinking as clearly as they might, and that they had fallen victim to the dullness of thought observed by high-altitude physiologists. Findings on the cost to the central nervous system of climbing to extremely high altitudes, published in the December 21, 1989, issue of the *New England Journal of Medicine*, suggest that climbers at high altitudes without supplementary oxygen sooner or later experience slight modifications in the function of the brain, and that some of these modifications, especially in people who are good acclimatizers, can be of long duration. Fritz had not only just spent nine days above 25,000 feet (7620 meters), something unheard of at that time, but had also undergone physical exertions that would have taxed any ordinary man at sea level. Fritz–and his loyally supportive family–would never admit to this possibility, but there seems to be evidence, in view of his actions and decisions, that when he reached Camp VII on July 22 his mind may not have been functioning as alertly as it usually did at lower levels. This would partly account for his fatal decision that Dudley could safely be left behind.

A further possibility, perhaps related to the preceding one, is that Dudley insisted on remaining at Camp VII, and that, after discussion, Fritz yielded, perhaps reluctantly. Such a scenario would not surprise those who knew Fritz really well. Throughout his life there existed a chink in his otherwise imperious and obstinate armor. Earlier reference was made, perhaps too briefly, when writing of Fritz's creed that he believed "the weak must perish so the strong can live" – a philosophy that all too often he shelved, particularly when family or old friends were involved.

In personal relations with him, those people Fritz considered dear and who had the courage to stand up to him could on occasion win him over. The likelihood of this taking place increased in cases when, as with Dudley, the pleader had a large bank account. Consul Groth, albeit surmising, seems to have believed something of the sort may have happened at Camp VII:

> ... if Wiessner is to be held responsible for anything, it would seem to me that the responsibility might be based on the fact that he was influenced by Wolfe's argument regarding his right, because of financial contributions, to go as high up the mountain as possible. Wolfe seems to have used the financial argument as a club over Wiessner's head and Wiessner, instead of sticking to his better judgement and insisting that Wolfe go down the mountain with him, yielded to his request to be allowed to remain in Camp VII until such time as Wiessner would return, when Wolfe expected to be rested and attempt with Wiessner to attack the summit.[5]

It is quite likely that, because of a slight loss of willpower caused by altitude and weariness and in the face of Dudley's insistence, Fritz yielded to persuasion and, at Dudley's initiative, decided it would be safe to split the team, not fully appreciating the consequences in such an uncertain environment and with such a dubious and weakened party.

Not to be forgotten is that following the exertions of several days at extreme altitude, a late-afternoon fall that almost killed the high-camp party, the unexpected sight of a deserted and plundered Camp VII, and a bitterly cold night with limited protection must have greatly taxed the expedition leader. Under such stressful circumstances, a normally rational person might well make decisions that under easier circumstances would seem irrational. To have split his party when he had indications of serious trouble ahead was no doubt a serious error on Fritz's part, but he was nonetheless in the grip of a most extreme situation, only part of which was of his own making.

Whatever the reasons, and whoever the originator, that decision was the immediate reason why catastrophe followed. Under the circumstances prevailing at Camp VII at the time – not in the light of calm and comfortable hindsight – was the action taken by Fritz Wiessner, both as expedition and rope leader, reasonable and prudent?

THERE IS A FINAL HITHERTO UNANSWERED QUESTION about the expedition: why did Jack Durrance not speak up at the time about Tony Cromwell's orders to remove the middle camps' sleeping bags, but instead withhold his diary for half a century? Based on the authors' conversations with both Jack and his brother-in-law and lifelong friend Henry Coulter, the answer would appear simple, even if it involves several factors.

Initially, when Fritz berated Tony in Base Camp on July 24, 1939, Jack felt that anything he said would merely fan the flames of what was becoming a bitter quarrel. Jack's diary entries in Kashmir on the way home clearly demonstrate his sense of pity for Fritz and his distaste for his friend Tony's insistence on creating a scandal. Then, when Jack returned to the United States, he was appalled to learn that the matter had turned into a major conflagration.

By that time Jack wanted to put the entire expedition behind him and turn his attention elsewhere. His association with Fritz had been painful and unpleasant. He decided to keep out of the action unless called upon. The American Alpine Club's committee of inquiry never approached him, and Jack volunteered nothing.

Years passed, and new issues caught public attention. Fritz and Tony both resigned from the American Alpine Club. Jack resumed skiing as a professional and climbing as a Teton guide. Then the rigorous demands of medical school held his attention, following which he moved to Denver, where he specialized in pulmonary medicine, taught, and practiced his profession. He married, raised five children, developed an intense interest in flowers, and, except for rare lectures, slowly forgot about K2. It is likely Jack never consulted his diary after 1940; rather, it remained to gather dust on a bookshelf. In short, he believed he had nailed the coffin on K2.

When Fritz's 1956 *Appalachia* article appeared and for the first time in America placed the blame directly on Jack for removal of the sleeping bags, Jack paid no attention. Besides, if he revealed the facts, the quarrel was bound to resurface and at that time would hurt people, notably Tony, who despite his failings Jack considered an old friend.

Then came the time in the late 1970s and early 1980s when American writers developed a renewed interest in K2's history – and especially in the 1939 expedition. Over the years these writers had developed enormous admiration for Fritz and accepted his version of events without question. Their approach to Jack was tactless, and, as might be expected, he reacted by refusing to answer questions. There was also an incident at the American Alpine Club's annual meeting in December 1978 in Estes Park, Colorado, where Jack had accepted an invitation to speak about K2 with the understanding that Fritz would not be there; Jack had not seen Fritz since September 1939 and had no desire to renew his acquaintance. But Fritz showed up. Unexpectedly, however, early in the day they met Durrance and several young friends in a hallway. He immediately introduced Wiessner to them as "America's foremost mountaineer." Later, a well-meaning club member urged the two and a few members of subsequent K2 expeditions to join him and his wife for cocktails in their room. At one point, while Wiessner was discussing K2 with Lou Reichardt (in 1978 one of the first Americans to scale the peak), he slightly slipped off the soft edge of the bed. In an opposite corner of the room, Durrance made the remark, "There he goes, falling off the Abruzzi Ridge!" Wiessner either didn't hear or pretended to ignore the comment. But at the evening program, when Durrance presented one of his rare slide shows on the 1939 climb, he rapidly glossed over the events up high on the peak with a comment to the effect that other people in the audience had more details on what occurred there.

In the mid-1980s it became almost impossible to persuade Jack, then in his seventies and sometimes crusty, to say anything in public about his K2 experiences. It was not until 1989 that Jack finally consented to part with his diary so that those who read it could at long last set the record straight in the interest of historical truth.

16

FAREWELL TO THE DRAMA

I NEVITABLY AFTER EVERY EXPEDITION, successful or not, there are post-mortems to determine what things went wrong or right and what steps should be taken to do better next time. On the 1939 American Karakoram Expedition to K2, so much went awry from the start that most people do not know where to begin. In the back of his diary (on the pages for October 15 through 18) Jack Durrance listed a litany of major and minor suggestions for future Himalayan expeditions, beginning with seemingly trivial items such as kitchen implements and eating bowls; the desirability for smaller, more efficient thermos bottles; and improved clothing and more of it, particularly woolens and reinforced trouser bottoms. As he progressed, his suggestions became meatier:

> 5. Some definite means of communication between camps & base camp very desirable; e.g. small wireless sets. Also a general plan of attack which participants are well acquainted with along with possible alterations due to changes in weather and climbing conditions. It is in my mind doubtful whether the selected leader should be like a "lead dog" that is always out in front and often as not quite out of touch of secondary and supporting parties – their condition & accomplishments.
> 6. Better footgear for Sherpa porters (waterproof) & plenty of cheap woolen socks – also some kind of slippers for camp wear – saves socks.
> 6.[sic] By all means one member of the party should be an M.D. – by far more important than English transport officer.
> 7. Transport officer should be for transport only – not as member of climbing party.

*8. The Himalayas is a poor place for a man to learn mountaineering,
for there everything goes to extremes, particularly everything connected
with the weather. It would be wise to know that a man had at least led
parties for several seasons elsewhere or quite capable of doing it. There
should be team work on the Himalayan giants . . .*

*. . . 11. It should be very clear and distinctly understood that success de-
pends largely on luck with the weather. Maybe the Himalayas aren't
technically as stiff or anywhere near as difficult as mountain achievements to date in the Alps and elsewhere but combined with high altitude effects upon man & high altitude weather changes they become
very difficult indeed – also quite dangerous if one becomes overconfi-
dent and oversteps caution.*

These afterthoughts of Jack's say much about the expedition, its participants, its leader, and the team's shortcomings. What Jack does not dis-
cuss in the diary is the leader's responsibility for things that go wrong.
Fritz's early critics were more vocal and echoed the view of President
Harry S Truman, who said about executive responsibility that "the buck
stops here."

But is the leader totally responsible, except in theory? Consul Groth
leaned toward charity. "I should be inclined to reach the conclusion," he
wrote on page four of his memorandum, "that the unfortunate accident
was due to a combination of circumstances over which Wiessner did not
have entire control nor for which he could be held solely responsible."

Substitute "chain" for "combination" and you get back to the series of
events mentioned at the outset of this unhappy story. In order to understand their evolution, it is first necessary to examine three elements that
influenced events: (1) the underlying weakness of the team; (2) Fritz's inability to delegate duties, the result being that he took on too many jobs;
(3) most important, poor communication.

The team that accompanied Fritz to K2 was markedly different from
the one he had envisaged earlier in New York. The best men, those on
whom he had counted most – Alfred Lindley, Bestor Robinson, and Roger
Whitney – never signed on, and the British transport officer turned out to
be a poor substitute for the more experienced McLeod. Fritz could have
canceled the expedition, but by the time he could consider this option,
money had been spent, at least one member (Wolfe) had embarked, and
expectations had been raised – on top of which there was Fritz's stubborn
temperament. The question was not so much whether the expedition
should have set sail, but whether Fritz should have considered a more
modest objective, such as Chogolisa, Gasherbrum II, or even Hidden
Peak.

To any suggestion that the expedition ought to have been postponed or
diverted, Fritz, with some justice, developed a standard reply. After all, he

would argue, he and Pasang Lama almost reached the summit. Yes, almost, but not quite – and, in any event, at what cost? Is it not a far different thing to win with a 10 percent reserve than to play 10 percent above your head and lose?

There is no question that, once on the mountain, Fritz's team provided him with considerably less support than he expected. For a climber of his stature, the men in the party represented more of a handicap than a help. Had he been a modern-day mountaineer, he would doubtless have dispensed with most of them and proceeded with a few good Sherpas. Instead he counted on Dudley Wolfe's brute strength and entrusted the job of encouraging the troops and keeping supplies moving to an insecure deputy, Tony Cromwell. The higher the party went, the more its reserves dissipated: Chap Cranmer first, in Base Camp; then George Sheldon; Cromwell through demoralization and some sort of chest injury; Jack Durrance, technically his best man, by illness; and finally Wolfe above Camp VIII; while for their part the Sherpas, left without strong guidance, drifted off on their own. The result was that, at the critical moment, there existed behind the assault party a manpower shortage that stretched all the way down the Abruzzi Ridge and on to Base Camp.

The existence of a weak party undoubtedly contributed to the second element: the necessity for Fritz to take on more tasks than he could conveniently handle. It was only with the greatest difficulty, if possible at all, that he could serve as point man, which he relished, and at the same time correct the administrative shortcomings and errors of a weak deputy – on top of which he also elected to serve as Dudley's teacher. So long as he held his team on a short leash by his physical presence, Fritz could deal satisfactorily with a multitude of jobs and at the same time encourage his companions. But the moment he was out of sight things went wrong. In short, his team included no one else who could properly carry out any of his jobs, the principal two of which were to blaze the way and to make sure that those behind, as Jack Durrance stated in his diary, were providing the proper support and protection for those ahead. As a consequence of trying to do too much he outran his reserves. By sheer willpower he ended up only 750 feet (229 meters) from K2's summit, but with nothing behind. A magnificent effort, but was it wise?

Far worse than the shortage of highly qualified men on the 1939 expedition and the necessity for Fritz to attend to every detail was the lack of satisfactory communication and understanding among the forces that formed the party. The absence of mechanical devices, such as two-way radios, which most previous climbing parties had done without, represented the least of the problem, although their presence would have helped. Far more vital in affecting the outcome of the undertaking and its bitter aftermath was the cultural and philosophical wall that separated the leader from his American companions. Fritz had a different attitude toward mountaineering from the others. The Americans played for fun, Fritz for keeps. Fritz also adhered to an authoritarian leadership model, whereas the Americans had a tradition of independence, even of rebellion. They were accustomed to reaching major decisions via general discussion and to participation by all, even under a leader's guidance; for them, no single person, however influential, could be the decisive force.

From the start, Fritz did seem to have been aware of a possible problem. As he reported to Consul Groth, he tried to deflect it–at least theoretically–as Groth noted in his memorandum (see Appendix E):

> *Wiessner explained to me several times that it had been thoroughly understood prior to their departure from the United States and in the course of the journey to India, that if at any time any of the expedition members felt that things were not being handled as they should, or if there was any dissatisfaction with the leadership of the expedition, whatever differences of opinion might arise would be immediately brought to the leader's attention and the problem in question be thoroughly thrashed out and not be brooded over by the persons involved.*

A fine arrangement indeed. But those persons, before and after K2, who have had to deal with Fritz in controversial matters would observe, "Easier said than done." Fritz's personality, as indicated earlier, could be intimidating when he disagreed with someone. Moreover, both by nature and background, Fritz did not appreciate criticism. In situations where he absolutely wanted his way, he could be difficult to handle. Groth continued:

> *Unfortunately this admitted advantageous arrangement for smoothing out difficulties seems seldom, if ever, to have been resorted to, with the result that gradually molehills grew into mountains and apparently the mountains became volcanoes, which, during most of the expedition's duration, smouldered under a quiescent surface but finally erupted in a most unfortunate fashion.*

As Consul Groth noted, and as anyone who has read the available chronicles and writings of the expedition members will acknowledge, there was never a sign of serious conflict until the participants returned from the mountain to Srinagar–at which point the bomb exploded. Nor, for that matter, is there any indication of conflict in Fritz Wiessner's carefully worded but, curiously, undated report to the American Alpine Club that he had prepared with help from Jack Durrance.

But did expedition members ever take up any serious grievances with Fritz or express misgivings about proposed courses of action? And is it possible, assuming they did not do so, that Fritz's authoritarian attitude as well as his position as the best and most experienced climber in the group raise a barrier to awe his companions into silence?

We know that on at least two occasions Jack clearly spoke up. The first time was when, from Camp II, he sent his July 1 message to Fritz at Camp IV in which he asked for instructions as well as assurances regarding protection from stonefall for climbers headed upward. The second, more dramatic, took place at Camp VI, when Jack warned Fritz about the dangers that could ensue if Dudley were allowed to climb higher. In those two cases the evidence suggests that either Fritz did not listen, or did not choose to listen, or simply disagreed.

On the other hand, there exists at least one occasion (and possibly two) when Fritz proved all too open to persuasion. He yielded with little fight to Pasang Lama's plea to descend from the high point reached on July 19, and, at least according to his account, he thought Dudley's request to remain alone at Camp VII was not unreasonable. Still, these may have been exceptions. Or perhaps Fritz gave in to Lama and Dudley because of their loyalty to him.

Differences in culture, upbringing, education, attitudes toward mountaineering, and maybe even different linguistic backgrounds (albeit Fritz had a magnificent command of written English) helped break down communication between the leader and his comrades.

In addition there existed the difficulty in exchanging information with the Sherpas, a problem common to all expeditions of those times. The best trained of the Sherpas had at most a smattering of English and could only understand rudimentary instructions.

Was it the expedition leader's job to make sure at all times that plans and orders were properly understood and obeyed? Or was it the duty of the troops to anticipate their leader's wishes and, if they did not approve of them, to complain? This takes us back to the beginning, to the concept of an unbalanced team with a giant of alpinism in command of inadequate companions, who, because they do not understand him, cannot summon the confidence to follow in his footsteps.

This book states at the outset that the 1939 K2 expedition's failure and catastrophe resulted not from a single event, as is the case in most mountain tragedies, but from a chain of circumstances that could be traced back to the undertaking's inception. Another series of events led to the acrimony that arose after the expedition's termination. As the venture progressed, these unhappy incidents accumulated and gathered strength so that, in the end, everything exploded.

The first step toward disaster occurred in New York with the last-minute loss of the team's three strongest members. Then came Sporthaus Schuster's inability to supply Jack Durrance with suitable footwear at an early date, thereby handicapping his performance during the first month on the mountain. The acquisition of inferior boots for the Sherpas hampered them at the high camps and may have been instrumental in causing Pasang Lama to refuse to climb in the cold snow through the night of July 19–20. There was the decision not to include two-way radios. Chappell Cranmer's severe illness deprived the party, as Fritz stated, of one of its strongest men, and George Sheldon's frostbitten toes and Sonam's fall in the House Chimney reduced personnel even more. Tony Cromwell's unexpected demoralization and his perpetual vacillation made for an unreliable deputy leader where a strong personality was needed. Jack's illness above Camp VI brought to an end all proper supervision of Sherpas and supply movements at the high camps. Lama's refusal to climb through the night and Fritz's reluctant acquiescence probably cost the expedition the mountain. Tse Tendrup's removal of sleeping bags at Camps VI and VII and similar action a few days earlier at Camps II and IV at Tony's initiative deprived Fritz and Lama of the little strength they had left after nine days of deterioration at extreme altitude. Above all, the last link in this chain – the decision to leave Dudley Wolfe alone and unattended at Camp VII – represented the final and critical prelude to the ensuing tragedy.

By the time a rescue could be attempted, only a feeble Jack and the Sherpas were left. Chap and George had long since departed. Tony and "Joe" Trench, unable or unwilling to assist rescue operations, marched down the Baltoro with the Askole porters to rejoin Chap and George in that village. Jack, still sick, made a valiant rescue attempt, but failed. With Fritz physically spent but still dreaming of the summit, that left the Sherpas, all other human resources having been dissipated. Three of them and Dudley Wolfe died – we will never know how.

Without a tragedy no serious recriminations would have resulted, even if, after the fact, lingering differences of opinion had later surfaced. But from the moment that Dudley and the three Sherpas were lost, the accumulated vitriol was fated sooner or later to splash on the participants. The miracle is that the poison did not leak out while the party still kept the field.

Again, the damage was cumulative. First there was the incident in Genoa, when Fritz gave Jack an icy welcome; then Fritz's abrupt admonitions to George for his caper on the Godwin-Austen Glacier; and, later, in a reverse episode when, above Camp II, Fritz left Jack in bad boots on icy slopes and galloped alone down the mountain. There was the major misunderstanding over Jack's request from Camp II to Fritz at Camp IV that he be given instructions, followed by Fritz's caustic reply addressed to both Jack and Tony. Then came the confrontation between Jack and Fritz at Camp VI over the wisdom of allowing Dudley to continue. Finally, and most important, was Fritz's understandable but ill-advised temper tantrum on his return to Base Camp from up high in which he accused Tony, in front of the other team members, of attempted murder and other egregious misconduct. By the time the last expedition members reached Srinagar, Tony, who had arrived earlier and was probably in search of revenge or of an alibi to conceal his role in the removal of the sleeping bags, had turned the tables on Fritz and thrown fat into a fire that inevitably burned out of control.

AS INDICATED AT THE OUTSET of this tale, on K2 and elsewhere Fritz Wiessner demonstrated outstanding skill as a climber. But what can be said of his leadership on the 1939 K2 expedition? If there existed elements in the chain of circumstances that led to catastrophe and venom that were beyond his control, what about those things that he could either command or at least influence? Did he, overall, exhibit good judgment and good leadership? Did he retain the trust and confidence of his subordinates? Did he treat his companions evenhandedly? Did he make allowance for the weaknesses of those less competent than himself and recognize the perils to which these weaknesses might expose the undertaking? Finally, did he overextend his human resources and, at the critical moment, rely on luck? These are but a few of the many questions that must be asked in any appraisal of his administrative qualifications.

As expedition leader, Fritz was a good organizer, a skillful mountaineer, and a reasonably good planner; but the key element for any commander to observe, ahead of all others, is to take care of his troops. Did Fritz show this quality on K2, or did he neglect the welfare and feelings of those who tried to follow in his footsteps?

American Consul Edward Miller Groth seems to have had an opinion. Though not a serious mountaineer, Groth was knowledgeable of the qualities needed in that era to conduct major Himalayan ventures, and his membership in the Colorado Mountain Club and Himalayan Club suggest a more than passing interest in alpinism. He knew the Sherpas and other mountain peoples of India, and his profession required him to develop a keen perception of human behavior.

On page two of his memorandum, Groth, reporting to the U.S. Department of State, made a statement particularly meaningful for foreign-service officers or for anyone in the Department of State who has ever prepared a subordinate's efficiency rating. Groth wrote: "Wiessner is undoubtedly an excellent climber and a good leader." Taken at face value the remark seems innocuous, even praiseworthy. But in the special language of diplomacy, such as a report by a field officer to the appropriate Department of State desk officer in Washington, the statement acquires new meaning. Damning with faint praise has long been an accepted method of expressing one's opinion without causing resentment. In the above quotation the use of the comparative–that is, "excellent climber" versus "good leader"–is especially significant: it suggests that Groth's private opinion of Wiessner after examination of the facts is to the effect that Wiessner's leadership in no way measured up to his abilities as an alpinist.

Groth's opinion is that of just one man. But unlike many others he had an opportunity to speak personally with two knowledgeable surviving members of the expedition–both together and with each man privately for several hours. These men had diametrically different interpretations of the facts, and they related them to the consul at a time when they had only just returned from their adventure and events were still fresh in their minds.

THE PURPOSE OF THIS BOOK is to lay down as accurately as possible the events of the 1939 American Karakoram Expedition to K2 and to dispel misconceptions that have grown over the years. To a large extent this has been possible because, after half a century of silence, Jack Durrance has provided access to his expedition diary, which clarifies one critical issue (who ordered the removal of sleeping bags at Camps II and IV) and offers a personal view and interpretation of expedition events as they occurred. Simultaneously, documents have been discovered, notably copies of letters from the field to Joel Ellis Fisher in New York, Edward Miller Groth's despatches and impressions, Dudley Wolfe's death certificate, and despatches from the United States Consulate in Karachi concerning the disposal of Wolfe's effects as well as problems regarding the repatriation of American-owned optical and photographic material that was promptly embargoed at the outset of World War II. There were those who believed these papers no longer existed, if indeed some ever existed at all. Above all was the discovery of a copy of the official expedition report, which is nowhere to be found in American Alpine Club archives.

The present analysis, overall, does not differ much from the old one, except for important details. But it very much shifts the heretofore accepted emphasis from a sort of glorification of Fritz Wiessner as an expedition leader (who was blameless) to the concept that, like the rest of us, he had faults, some of them serious enough to be detrimental to the smooth operation of the 1939 American K2 expedition. The story, as Consul Groth stated, turns out to have been more complicated than anyone believed. The new information shows that many forces, not one, were responsible for the tragedy; that at least one person–Jack Durrance–was wrongly blamed; that another–Tony Cromwell–only passingly suspected heretofore, may have unwittingly caused critical difficulties by ordering the removal of vital equipment; and that a third – Fritz Wiessner – may have tried to unburden his mistakes on shoulders other than his own by trying to rewrite the story according to his own beliefs.

"Once upon a time . . ." Yes, it was indeed long ago. And what became of the participants?

Fritz Wiessner, as noted earlier, married, raised two children, and returned to the mountains year after year to ski and climb until just some fifteen months before his death in 1988. Jack Durrance, too, returned to the mountains, making some of his best first ascents in the Tetons in 1940 and 1941; but, owing to the demands of medical school, his interest gradually flagged, shifting first to pulmonary medicine (he became an outstanding specialist on tuberculosis) and then to the cultivation of irises. Chappell Cranmer, ever quiet and introspective, joined the ministry. George Sheldon, after service in World War II, found the comfort and security of the peace-time army irresistible; so he made a career of the military as an intelligence officer. Tony Cromwell, never up to much, expatriated himself to Switzerland to ski and, sometimes, engage in a little climbing with his last wife, Georgia Engelhard. Both Cromwell and Sheldon died in 1987.

In 1865 the Matterhorn supplied the terrain for the nineteenth-century's most dramatic mountain story. In 1939 K2 provided the arena for one of the most gripping mountain dramas of the twentieth century. But unlike the Matterhorn venture, the events on K2 took place in what was – and in many respects still is – a remote, little visited part of the world at altitudes rarely attained by human beings and over a period of months instead of days. On K2 the very weakness of the party added force to the story – that of five ill-prepared men led by one strong, dedicated man on a mission beyond their collective abilities in a land where people do not belong.

Six Americans and their Sherpa companions were the actors. Most are gone. Three brave Sherpas – the indomitable sirdar Pasang Kikuli, with Kitar and Phinsoo – lie with Dudley Wolfe somewhere under K2's snows. Four other Sherpas, along with Lieutenant George ("Joe") Trench, have faded from sight. Pasang Lama, Fritz's companion at the highest point, died years ago; Cromwell, Wiessner, and Sheldon more recently. Soon all that is left will be a few written records and unfounded legends.

All ordinary people, Fritz Wiessner's companions did ordinary things in extraordinary surroundings. They reached their limits and could do no more. Except for Wolfe, they did not tempt fate. Were they the cause of the disaster, or was it that their leader, Fritz Wiessner, unmindful of the collapse of his support, gambled with the gods and lost?

APPENDICES
A. Biographical Sketches

THE FOLLOWING BIOGRAPHICAL SKETCHES of certain personalities whose names appear in the text is by no means complete. Only those figures of special interest to this narrative are included.

Luigi Amadeo Guisepe Maria Ferdinando Francesco, Prince of Savoia-Aosta, Duke of the Abruzzi (1873–1933), was nephew to the king of Italy and commanded the Italian Navy during much of World War I. At the time of his birth (and for a few days thereafter) his father was king of Spain. Elected to the Alpine Club of London at age twenty-one, the duke became honored around the world as one of the great international mountaineering figures of all time. He died in a small African village where he was working to improve health and living conditions for the local inhabitants.

Pierce Alain (b. 1904) was one of the outstanding amateur French climbers of the 1930s and best known for his first ascent of the North Face of the Aiguille du Dru, where he led the first Class VI passage ever to be scaled in the Alps. Later climbers have found an easier way around his crux pitch, which is no longer used. Alain participated in the 1936 French expedition that reached 22,000 feet (6705 meters) on Hidden Peak. In later years he ran a climbing-equipment store and developed several new and unique items, notably in footwear.

Sir Joseph Barcroft (1872–1947), cited in Appendix B and a leading authority in his time on human physiology, was knighted for his work by King George V and received recognition from medical societies around the world. Of his many publications, *The Respiratory Function of the Blood, Part I: Lessons from High Altitude* (1925) was the most relevant to high-altitude alpinists.

Robert Hicks Bates (b. 1911) of Exeter, New Hampshire, became one of the most popular and effective leaders in the history of American alpinism.

The story of his ascent of Mounts Lucania and Steele with Bradford Washburn and return to civilization is one of the great epics of Alaskan mountaineering. A 1933 Harvard graduate, he took part in numerous expeditions to the Himalaya and Karakoram. Well into his seventies he participated in the expedition that made the first ascent of Ulugh Mustagh (22,923 feet; 6986 meters) in northwest China. He served as president of the American Alpine Club from 1959 through 1961 and at this writing serves as its honorary president.

Thomas Graham Brown (1882–1965), one of the great British alpinists of the first half of the twentieth century and a native of Edinburgh, was a professor of physiology at the University of Wales and later became a Fellow of the Royal Society. Though his climbing career started after he was thirty, he rapidly won his laurels, first in the Alps, then in Alaska, and finally in the Himalaya. On Mont Blanc he did the first ascents of the dangerous Arête de la Poire, the Route Major, and the Red Sentinel. With Charles Houston he made the first ascent of 17,400-foot (5303-meter) Mount Foraker in 1934 and, two years later at age fifty-four, reached 23,000 feet (7010 meters) on Nanda Devi in the Garwhal Himalaya.

Richard Burdsall (1895–1953), a graduate of Swarthmore and by training an engineer, served with the American Friends Service Committee in World War I. His first serious, and most successful, climb took him to the top of 24,900-foot (7590-meter) Minya Konka (now Gonga Shan), the highest summit in China and at the time (1932) the second-highest mountain ever scaled. Though he did not do much climbing, his next venture was as a member of the 1938 K2 expedition. He died on Mount Aconcagua on the Chilean-Argentine border in 1953 during an attempt to rescue stranded climbers.

Hubert Adams Carter (b. 1915), an honorary member of the American Alpine Club, attended Harvard and at first was primarily known as a skier, then later as a climber. A teacher by profession, Carter participated in several expeditions to Alaska while an undergraduate, then joined the 1936 Anglo-American Nanda Devi expedition, during which he reached an altitude of 23,000 feet (7010 meters). He participated in numerous later ascents and explorations, many in the Andes. An excellent linguist and writer, he has for many years served as editor of the *American Alpine Journal,* transforming that publication into what is regarded as the best publication of its kind in the world.

Emilio Comici (1901–1940), an outstanding Italian alpinist, was the first to climb the North Face of the Cima Grande de Lavaredo in the Dolomites.

He was killed in a rappelling accident in 1940.

Sir William Martin Conway, Lord Conway of Allington (1856–1937), was one of the great alpine explorers of his time. An artist and antiquarian, he studied at Cambridge. An early interest in geography led him to become a member of the Royal Geographic Society. He explored glacial areas in Spitzbergen, the Himalaya, the Andes, and Tierra del Fuego. An excellent topographer, he made some of the best maps of the Karakoram. He is remembered for two books: *The Alps from End to End* and *Mountain Memories.*

Aleister Edward Alexander Crowley (1875–1947) was a brilliant but totally unpredictable figure who participated in several early Himalayan and Karakoram expeditions. In 1905, on an expedition to Kangchenjunja, he refused to leave his tent to participate in a rescue mission of some of his companions, one of whom (Alexis Pache) died, preferring instead to sip tea and complete an article he was writing for his newspaper, *The Pioneer.* In later years he became enamored of black magic and Satanism and may have been involved in more than one unsolved murder. Though he is most often remembered for his occult activities, Crowley was a far more experienced alpinist than is commonly believed.

Hans Dülfer (1893–1915) was one of the outstanding mountaineers of his time. He was born in Bavaria, Germany, and, starting at a very early age, pioneered a large number of extremely difficult routes, both for the time and by today's standards, in the Kaisergebirge and the Dolomites. He believed in the minimal use of aid and related equipment. Dülfer is best remembered for a particular rappelling technique that was long regarded as the best and the safest. It remains in many respects superior to more sophisticated systems using brake bars that can damage the rope and often serve only to add unnecessary complexity to the process. Dülfer was killed during World War I in the fighting at Arras, France.

Oscar Eckenstein (1854–1921) was a British mountaineer who had been with Sir William Martin Conway's 1892 expedition to the Karakoram but had parted company along the way. An engineer by profession, he felt more in tune with his friend Aleister Crowley, with whom he had also climbed in Mexico. Eckenstein was the inventor of a long-popular style of crampon as well as the fabricator of a kind of ice axe no longer in use.

Arthur Brewster Emmons (1910–1962) was an avid climber since early childhood and a lover of adventure; his mountaineering career began as a Harvard undergraduate when he accompanied Bradford Washburn on an unsuccessful attempt on Alaska's Mount Fairweather. He had better luck two years later on Minya Konka (now Gonga Shan), China's highest peak, where he reached 23,000 feet (7010 meters), but where his toes were badly frostbitten. In 1936 he accompanied the successful Nanda Devi expedition, returning to the United States after walking from India through Tibet and China. Thereafter he joined the foreign service and served in posts in Canada, China, Korea, Uruguay, Spain, Austria, Ireland, and finally as American minister to Malaysia.

Filippo de Fillippi (1869–1938) was the author of the accounts of the Duke of the Abruzzi's trips to Mount St. Elias, Ruwenzori, and K2, as well as other expeditionary ventures. His books have become collectors' items and are prized not only for their literary quality and scientific completeness, but for the quality of their photographs (by Vittorio Sella).

Joel Ellis Fisher (1891–1966) came from a wealthy, established New York family and was one of the American Alpine Club's most energetic presidents, as well as one of its ablest and longest-lasting treasurers. As long as he believed they had something to offer, Fisher would befriend mountaineering and scientific mavericks and eccentrics. For years he successfully ran the old and famous Melville Shoe Company. He also at one time cornered the stock on two small connecting railroads around St. Louis and Denver. These lines were vital to major trunk lines, and Fisher amused himself by setting lease terms so as to reap fine profits from companies such as the Burlington and the Rio Grande. Fritz Wiessner was often quoted as saying that if the American Alpine Club had listened to Fisher, it would have become rich.

Lieutenant Colonel Denholm de Montatt Stuart Fraser (1889–1958), British resident in Kashmir, was a graduate of Sandhurst who in 1910 joined the Central India Horse Regiment. He had a long career as a political agent in India after 1919. In 1944 he retired to Forfar, Scotland.

Edwin Rex Gibson (1892–1957), English by birth, became one of Canada's strongest mountaineers. He worked extensively on developing mountain equipment and training methods in the early 1940s, notably in cooperation with the U.S. Army's Quartermaster Corps on Mount McKinley. While serving as president of the Alpine Club of Canada, Gibson was killed in a tragic accident in the Coast Range of British Columbia, where one of his companions, Sterling Hendricks, was seriously injured.

Henry Haversham Godwin-Austin (1834–1923), explorer and geologist, was the principal assistant to then Lieutenant T. G. Montgomerie in the

1856 "Great Trigonometrical Survey" of India, when K2 was first sighted. In 1861 he explored the Baltoro Glacier and mapped the terrain above Askole.

Edward Miller Groth (1894–1977) was a foreign-service officer born in New York City who studied at Columbia University. From 1911 to 1916 he was employed in the manufacture of jewelry. During World War I Groth served in the Naval Hospital Corps. His consular and diplomatic career started with a two-year tour as vice consul in Antwerp and, later, Rotterdam. Then followed a year of embassy duty in Belgrade, followed by Beirut, Damascus, Surabaya, Copenhagen, and Capetown. He was assigned as consul in Calcutta in 1934, at age forty-one, remaining there until 1942, and then was assigned as counselor of legation in Pretoria, South Africa.

Henry Snow Hall, Jr. (1895–1987) was for fifty years an officer or director of the American Alpine Club and then its honorary president. A man of affluence, he made the support and cultivation of alpinism the primary interest of his long life. In addition to his own extensive climbing accomplishments, he became a catalyst for expeditions, encouraging and providing opportunities for countless budding alpinists to make their mark in the mountains. Quietly and unobtrusively, on repeated occasions, Hall assisted young climbers financially and came to the aid of worthy expeditions that were short of funds. He was probably the most consistent patron of alpinism the world has ever known.

Kenneth Atwood Henderson (b. 1905), a 1926 Harvard graduate and a Boston investment counselor, was author of the American Alpine Club's authoritative *Handbook of American Mountaineering* (1943), which served for a generation as the standard American textbook for novice mountaineers. Though a councilor of the American Alpine Club at the time, he took little part in the controversy over the 1939 K2 expedition, seeing no point in impugning anyone's reputation in the absence of hard evidence about matters that could not be well understood by those not present. He later served with distinction as president of the Appalachian Mountain Club and was honored with the American Alpine Club's Angelo Heilprin Citation in 1982 for his contributions to the AAC.

Sterling Brown Hendricks (1902–1981) was famed for his many first ascents in Canada's Rockies and Selkirks. He was an extremely modest, yet brilliant scientist with a fine sense of humor and received awards and recognition for his work in photoperiodism. He is remembered as a delightful companion and superb teacher on many mountaineering trips.

Elbridge Rand Herron (1902–1932) was one of the most exceptional people ever to take up alpinism. Born in Italy of expatriate American parents, he climbed much in Europe, but for only two seasons in the United States. His father was a professor, an internationalist, a socialist, and independently wealthy. His mother was Caroline Rand, of the family that founded the Rand School in New York. Professor Herron's efforts to combine socialism with Christianity were not well accepted, so the couple expatriated themselves to a lavish villa outside Florence. Herron attended school in Geneva and Florence, specializing in music and philosophy, then studied in Berlin, Vienna, Rome, Moscow, and Munich. He compiled an extensive collection of alpine photographs and partook in expeditions to Lapland, the Caucasus, and the Atlas Mountains of North Africa. In 1929 he returned to the United States, where he met Elizabeth Knowlton and Fritz Wiessner, who convinced him to join the 1932 Nanga Parbat expedition. Herron had a distinguished record of climbing in the Alps and an extensive classical education, which brought him wide acceptance. He met his death in a fall from the Great Pyramid of Khu-fu (Cheops) on his return from Nanga Parbat.

William Pendleton House (b. 1914), a 1935 Yale graduate, was regarded as one of the best rock climbers in the United States by the late 1930s and had been for some years the principal figure of the Yale Mountaineering Club. Subsequent to his Mount Waddington trip in 1936, House climbed extensively in the Tetons and became a member of the American Alpine Club's 1938 K2 expedition, on which he was responsible for forcing the notorious House Chimney at the base of the Red Rocks, one of the major technical obstacles of the Abruzzi Ridge. Now a retired forester, House lives in southern New Hampshire and is an honorary member of the American Alpine Club.

Charles Snead Houston (b. 1911), a 1935 Harvard graduate, is one of the outstanding figures in American mountaineering. He started out in the 1920s in the Alps, where he made a number of fine ascents in the company of Thomas Graham Brown and some of the era's best guides. While in college he participated in several of Bradford Washburn's trips to Alaska and in 1934 organized and led the first ascent of 17,400-foot (5303-meter) Mount Foraker in the McKinley Range. In 1936, as a member and part organizer of the Anglo-American expedition to Nanda Devi, he reached a point only 1000 feet (300 meters) below the summit and would have been a member of the summit team had he not suffered food poisoning the night before the final attempt. Fourteen years later, he led the expedition to Everest that discovered the now standard route up that mountain. In 1953, he once more led an expedition to K2. Houston's interest in alpinism and his training as a physician led him to the study of high-altitude physiology, in which he is one of the world's outstanding experts. He lives in Burlington, Vermont.

Elizabeth Knowlton (1895–1989) was, in her time, one of American's most distinguished women mountaineers. Daughter of Marcus Perrin Knowlton, chief justice of the Massachusetts Supreme Judicial Court, she spent her undergraduate years at Vassar and received her master's degree from Radcliffe in 1917. After 1918 she climbed extensively in the Canadian Rockies and the Alps and made many demanding climbs in the Penines, French Alps, and Dolomites, as a result of which she was elected to the prestigious Groupe de Haute Montagne. She was the only woman (and one of two Americans) to participate in the 1932 Nanga Parbat expedition, where she reached an altitude of almost 21,000 feet (6400 meters). Later she climbed in Colombia and Mexico, where she made a number of first ascents. As a journalist she wrote an excellent book on the Nanga Parbat adventure entitled *The Naked Mountain.*

Alfred Damon Lindley (1904–1951) started mountaineering at age sixteen in the Alps and continued, along with a·wide variety of other sports, until his death in an airplane crash. In 1924 he stroked the Yale crew that won that year's Olympic races in Paris. In 1936 he participated in Olympic ski competition. He was an excellent sailor, competed successfully in Golden Gloves tournaments, was an able horseman and polo player, and was active in tennis, squash, and hockey. A magna cum laude graduate of Yale, he married Grace Carter, another avid skier, in 1937. Lindley was a lawyer; he became interested in politics and for years championed Harold Stassen and himself ran for various offices. In World War II he served four years in the U.S. Navy, where he attained the rank of commander.

Willi Merkl (1900–1934) was a German railway executive and one of the outstanding mountaineers that Germany produced in the years of the Weimar Republic. With companions such as Willi Weltzenbach, he made numerous new routes in the French Alps and led expeditions to the Caucasus, then still relatively unknown and unexplored. He was selected over Fritz Wiessner to serve as leader of the 1932 Nanga Parbat expedition. Despite a gruff exterior, Merkl proved to be a competent leader: on a first try at the world's ninth-highest peak, and despite many setbacks, his party reached 23,000 feet (7010 meters). He was less fortunate two years later when he died on Nanga Parbat in a storm that killed nine.

Noel Ewart Odell (1890–1987), a climber and geologist honored by alpine clubs around the world for his climbing achievements, was famous as having been perhaps the last person to have sighted George Leigh Mallory and Andrew Irvine on Everest in 1924. Odell, a remarkably good acclimatizer, had made his way up from a lower camp to over 27,000 feet (8229 meters) when he presumably spotted the pair. In 1936 he was one of two to reach the summit of Nanda Devi.

Bestor Robinson (1898–1987) was a skier of note and one of the earliest persons to develop modern rock climbing in California, specializing in direct aid and "rock engineering." He organized and led many Sierra Club expeditions during which significant ascents were made. During World War II Robinson served in the U.S. Army's Quartermaster Corps, where he developed climbing equipment for the mountain troops; among the items for which he received much credit was the "Tent, Mountain, M 1942."

James Grafton Rogers (1883–1971) served as president of the American Alpine Club. Born and raised in Colorado, he graduated from Saint Paul's School in Concord, New Hampshire, attended Yale, and in 1908 received his law degree from the University of Denver Law School, where he later taught. He maintained his own practice in Denver and later taught at Yale. In retirement, Rogers served as mayor of Georgetown, Colorado.

Hjalmar Horace Greeley Schacht (1877–1970) was a German financier of the first half of the twentieth century. He is credited with having twice rescued Germany from bankruptcy, once by curing the inflation of the early twenties and some years later by assisting the National Socialists in creating a sound financial base. He later parted company with Hitler because of his objection to the Nazi arms race. Any reader interested in Schacht should consult the *Encyclopaedia Britannica,* which contains more details.

Vittorio Sella (1859–1943), mountain photographer without peer, was an honorary member of the American Alpine Club and several other mountaineering clubs. His uncle, Quintino, was a founder of the Club Alpino Italiano and initiated him into alpinism. Among other achievements, he made the first winter ascents of the Matterhorn (1882) and Monte Rosa (1884). The quality of his mountain photographs was ensured by his practice of exposing plates that measured thirty by forty centimeters (approximately twelve by sixteen inches).

Robert Lindley Murray Underhill (1889–1983) and *Miriam Elliott O'Brien Underhill* (1899–1976) were, for a generation, the foremost husband-and-wife mountaineering team in the United States and in the forefront of technical progress in alpinism. Robert was an instructor and tutor at Harvard, and Miriam served with distinction as editor of *Appalachia*. The pair were the first, with Chamonix guide Armand Charlet, to make the traverse of the famous Aiguilles du Diable on the south flanks of Mont Blanc du Tacul in the Chamonix Alps. Miriam wrote an autobiography entitled *Give Me the Hills*.

Henry Bradford Washburn, Jr. (b. 1910) is a Yankee institution. After Vittorio Sella, and with a different style, he is known as the world's finest mountain photographer. He organized and led countless expeditions into the ranges of Alaska and became the leading authority on the area, being honored by alpine societies around the world. He also served with distinction for more than forty years as director of Boston's famous Museum of Science. The precision of some of his mapping projects is legendary.

Walter Abbot Wood, Jr. (b. 1907), a distinguished geographer, served as president of the American Alpine Club, became president of the American Geographical Society, and was a founder of the Arctic Institute of North America, which he also served as president. His mother, Dorothy Eustis, established a dog-breeding farm in Vevey, Switzerland, and specialized in high-quality working dogs for the Red Cross and Swiss Army and police. This led to the founding in 1929 of the Seeing Eye Society, of which Wood continued to be a substantial supporter. His first wife, Foresta, also an alpinist, disappeared on an aircraft flight while the couple was engaged in a mountaineering trip in the St. Elias Range of Alaska in 1947.

William Hunter Workman (1847–1937) was born in Worcester, Massachusetts, and graduated from Yale in 1869 and Harvard Medical School in 1873. After taking advanced courses in Vienna, Heidelberg, and Munich, he practiced medicine in Worcester until 1889, when forced by ill health to retire. Illness, however, did not impede him in 1892, when he and his wife, Fanny Bullock Workman (1859–1925), embarked on a bicycle journey that took them across Europe, into North Africa, Palestine, Turkey, and finally, with intermediate breaks, to Ceylon, Java, and across the breadth of India. In 1899 they made an expedition to the Biafo Glacier in the Karakoram and in 1902–3 a trip to the Chomo Lungma Glacier, where William ascended Pyramid Peak. In 1906 on Nun Kun, Fanny reached a record elevation (for a woman) of 21,000 feet (6492 meters). In 1908 the couple went up the Hispar Glacier, across the Hispar Pass, and down the Biafo, a total ice journey of 74 miles at altitude. In 1911–12 they were twice on the Siachen Glacier, the largest known icefield in the Himalaya-Karakoram.

Edward Wyss-Dunant (1897–1983), a radiologist and physiologist, was a resident of Geneva who climbed mostly in the Oberland. In time he served as president of the Swiss Alpine Club and later of the Union Internationale des Associations d'Alpinisme (UIAA). In 1952 he led the Swiss expedition that confirmed the 1950 Houston expedition's suggestion about the practicality of a South Col approach to Everest through the Khumbu Icefall. He was elected an honorary member of the Alpine Club (London) in 1963.

Sir Francis Younghusband (1863–1942) was one of Great Britain's great explorers and adventurers. In 1906, some years after his extraordinary journey from Peking to Rawalpindi, he led a military expedition to Lhasa, the outcome of which was to establish trade agreements between British India and Tibet.

B. Peril in High Places

WHAT FOLLOWS IS A LAY PERSON'S description of the major medical and physiological problems encountered at high altitude. The material presented has been checked for accuracy by two outstanding high-altitude physiologists in the United States and Great Britain and by a number of physicians specializing in pulmonary and circulatory disorders. It represents, however, no more than a working summary of high-altitude physiology and afflictions.

Since the 1939 American Karakoram Expedition to K2, enormous progress has been made in the field of high-altitude medicine. Fritz Wiessner's party knew most of the conventional mountaineering medicine of the times – much of it good and basic, though primitive by our standards, and some of it, in the light of later discovery, wrong. Today's mountaineers face a far different situation from that faced by a group of nonmedical lay people two generations ago. Many critically important concepts were unknown then, even to experts, or had been published in obscure, long-forgotten journals.

One thing known then, as now, is that the ability to acclimatize to higher elevations varies, sometimes dramatically, from person to person and sometimes from year to year. Fritz Wiessner, for example, was clearly an excellent acclimatizer, while Jack Durrance appears not to have been – at least in 1939. But even the strongest persons succumb to deterioration if they remain too long at high altitude. Taking advantage of this knowledge, modern alpine-style climbers try never to spend more than a single night above 23,000 feet (7010 meters), even when fully acclimatized.

What the 1939 expedition to K2 understood was that, hard or easy, great mountains are dangerous. There are the obvious objective risks, such as avalanche, rockfall, and collapsing snow bridges, and, of course, the ever-present subjective peril that someone may fall. In lower-altitude mountains, such as the Alps, excursions into the risk zone normally last no more than a day or two; but on a big peak in the Himalaya, climbers are exposed to such dangers for weeks on end before they return to lower terrain.[1] Storms, sometimes accompanied by deadly electrical discharges, come on suddenly and can last for days. There are technical problems whose resolutions demand extreme exertion, superior skill, and unending caution and resourcefulness–as well as the complication of logistics and the constant need to supervise poorly experienced and trained, albeit sure-footed, high-altitude porters unfamiliar with Western languages.

Movement to high altitudes involves considerable physiological dangers. These dangers, in ascending order of importance, are: hypoglycemia (lack of nourishment), hypohydration (dehydration, or lack of water intake), hypothermia (exposure to cold), and hypoxia (insufficient oxygen). Individually, and within limits, each of these risks can be controlled, but working synergistically, in combination, they create a dangerous situation–one, in fact, that has been appreciated by physiologists only in very recent years.[2]

Fritz Wiessner and his companions were familiar with the individual effects of lack of food and water and exposure to cold. They knew that on high mountains people tend to lose interest in eating and that frostbite is an ever present peril.

What was not so well understood in 1939 was the effect of oxygen shortage on the human body. Climbers had managed to reach 28,000 feet (about 8500 meters) on Mount Everest and continue to function without supplementary oxygen. They had *appeared* to function in a normal manner (and by their testimony considered themselves normal) and returned with no sign of impairment. Accordingly, the accepted wisdom of the time was that the human body could adapt to extreme altitude by slowly moving to ever higher elevations, with intermediate rests, without need of descending until an objective had been reached. The concept that humans might deteriorate, rather than acclimatize, above a certain altitude, had neither been observed nor publicly theorized.

In recent years it has been scientifically demonstrated that while humans can definitely acclimatize by slow stages to high altitudes, above a certain level there comes a point where, no matter what a person does, except descend for rest, the person's stamina deteriorates. The critical altitude, with *important* individual variations, appears to be around 22,000 feet (6700 meters). Above that level deterioration increases in direct relation to altitude, and that area has been named, somewhat inaccurately, by noted Swiss physiologist and mountaineer Dr. Edward Wyss-Dunant as the "Death Zone." It is believed that at Everest's summit not even the best trained and acclimatized alpinist could survive for long, for that altitude seems beyond the limit of human adaptability. Among other things, body heat is lost faster than it can be maintained, even with the best protective clothing. A person can get there without oxygen and can remain there briefly, possibly overnight, but eventually the person will die unless he or she descends. These facts were not known to climbers in 1939.

Another fact, appreciated by a few, was generally unknown. The body suffers far more from altitude during sleep than during waking hours, since low metabolism depresses breathing. Thus modern alpinists, in contrast to those of earlier decades, have adopted the practice of climbing (or carrying cargo) high during the day and then returning to as low an altitude as convenient to pass the night, preferably below 23,000 feet (7010 meters).

In the 1930s it was generally known, as had been observed for centuries, that at high altitudes people could develop mild illnesses–defined today as acute mountain sickness, or AMS–caused by problems related to oxygen shortage in thin air, of which the symptoms were headache, loss of appetite, nausea, shortness of breath, general lassitude, and sometimes vomiting. Entirely unidentified were two illnesses, probably related to AMS, both extremely lethal. Although they had been described in medical journals even before the twentieth century, they were not generally recognized or labeled as specific illnesses until after 1950. These are high-altitude cerebral edema (HACE) and high-altitude pulmonary edema (HAPE).

As with any serious threat to the central nervous system, HACE is often a deadly affliction, involving edema of the brain. It rarely occurs below 11,500 feet (3500 meters) but can become lethal higher up. Dr. Charles Clarke, of the Union Internationale des Associations d'Alpinisme (UIAA) Mountain Medicine Center and consulting neurologist at London's Saint Bartholomew's Hospital, has this to say about its onset:

> *The patient... usually has some symptoms of AMS for several days before developing a severe headache with many features suggestive of an intercranial origin–it is worse on coughing, stooping and straining. Psychological changes may occur in the early stages, varying from irritable behavior to obvious delusions, hallucination and confusion. Clouding of consciousness with somnolence, stupor and coma follows. Early clinical features are ataxia [inability to coordinate voluntary muscular movements], particularly truncal, a staggering gait; there is slurring of speech and double vision. Irregular periodic respiration is usually present... The development of [the] clinical condition may be acute, over several hours, or gradual, over several days.*[3]

Then Dr. Clarke adds: "There have been numerous fatalities..."

Though Dr. Clarke does not say so, there have been many reported cases of HACE in which the victim, moderately rather than severely affected, has retained the power of locomotion even though suffering from partial and sometimes total amnesia and being completely irrational.

One famous such instance occurred in 1980 on Makalu II, where, during the recovery stages, the victim had to be restrained forcibly by his companions and, while regaining his senses over a period of days, managed to carry out numerous irrational actions, not one of which he recalls to this day. Similar incidents on the tourist path to Everest Base Camp have been described in *Appalachia*.[4]

Certain drugs, plus oxygen perhaps, may help in a case of HACE, but the surest therapy is to get the victim down several thousand feet as soon as possible.

There is a possibility that the 1939 K2 expedition experienced at least one undiagnosed case of HACE – specifically, that Jack Durrance's illness was, in fact, an early case of HACE rather than HAPE. Jack survived probably because he instinctively felt that he must go lower. He was ill for several days and retained only the vaguest recollection of what he did or said, certainly during the early stages of the disease.

More prevalent and almost as deadly as its cerebral counterpart is high-altitude pulmonary edema (HAPE). It is, as physiologist and mountaineer Charles Houston defines it, "a temporary, potentially lethal derangement caused by rapid exposure to high altitude and relieved by descent." HAPE has killed more people than HACE because it occurs at lower altitudes. Most of its victims have been young and healthy; they include not only mountaineers, but also tourists and other visitors to high places, such as the Andean plateau or Colorado ski resorts, who over-exert themselves without allowing time for acclimatization. HAPE has been known to occur as low as 8000 feet (2436 meters); some say there have been cases as low as 6500 feet (1981 meters).

Dr. Jean Coudert, of the Laboratoire de Physiologie, Medical School Staff, Clermont-Ferrand, France, describes HAPE as follows:

> *The first stages are usually gradual, and are associated with one or more of the symptoms characteristic of AMS: headache, insomnia, anorexia [loss of appetite], nausea, vomiting, dizziness, polypnea [hyperventilation], marked lassitude and uncoordination. Respiratory troubles progressively worsen and soon dominate the clinical picture: increasingly marked dyspnea [difficulty breathing] with coughing, first dry and later accompanied by foamy and sometimes blood-laden expectorate. Cyanosis [bluish discoloration of the skin] is always seen, mainly in the face and extremities (especially the nail beds). The pulse is rapid. Except for tachycardia [rapid heartbeat] and frequent loud sounds in the pulmonary area, cardiac auscultation is normal . . . The patients are usually feverish, [but] no signs of infection are generally evident . . . In the absence of treatment, or even in spite of, death may ensue. In some cases, HAPE may be accompanied by HACE [which] may dominate the clinical picture and lead to coma.[5]*

Understated, if anything, by Dr. Coudert is the real risk of death (27 percent), for an untreated person has only a fair chance of recovery.[6] Mentioned less dramatically by Coudert than it merits is that ominous bubbling sounds (rales) in the patient's chest are often audible both to the patient and those nearby, so that, to one climber who watched a companion die mere hours after the disease's onset, it seemed as if the victim "were drowning in his own juices"–an apt lay person's description.

The best remedy, frequently difficult to carry out on high peaks, is to move the victim promptly to much lower levels. Oxygen, if available, may help, but it must be administered continuously until the patient is brought to lower altitudes. Except for extremely lightweight pressure chambers, only recently introduced and still experimental, there is no substitute for descent.

At the time of the 1939 K2 expedition, HAPE, because of insufficient knowledge, was usually diagnosed as a form of pneumonia. But in contrast to pneumonia, HAPE is of physiologic, not infectious, origin. There was at least one very serious case of HAPE on the 1939 expedition– Chappell Cranmer. While it was not recognized as such, because the illness had not yet been identified, it was fortuitously treated as properly as it could have been under the circumstances.

There exists a third high-altitude condition, still not too well understood, that affects the actions and decisions of climbers and their ability to reason promptly and logically. This is the impact of hypoxia (and sometimes other forces, such as hypothermia, dehydration, and hypocapnia) on the brain and its reasoning process.

When not distorted, reasoning, like other bodily functions, is much slowed at high altitudes. A person can generally think straight, but cannot reason quickly. Charles Houston, while conducting two long-range pressure-chamber experiments (once in 1946 and again in 1985), observed in his volunteers a definite "dulling of thought" and made the following comment:

> . . . *Sea level men were able to study acclimatized men at very high altitudes and to note beyond all doubt that, although the men themselves felt well and considered themselves in good shape, they were, in fact, far from normal. Contrary to earlier observations, the men were definitely blue from lack of oxygen, not from cold: there were undeniable signs of dulling of thought.*[7]

Writing about men's behavior at high (though not nearly so extreme) altitudes two decades before Houston's first experiment, Joseph Barcroft, in his time the world's outstanding high-altitude physiologist, had said much the same and compared the mental effects of thin air with those of drunkenness:

Alcohol affects different persons in different ways: so on my journeyings in high altitude, I have seen most of the symptoms of alcoholism repro- duced. I have seen men vomit, I have seen them quarrel, I have seen them become reckless, I have seen them become garrulous, I have seen them become morose. I have seen one of the most disciplined of men fling his arms about the edge of a crevasse to the great embarrassment of the guide. I have seen the most loyal companion become ill-tempered and abusive to the point at which I feared international complications would arise . . . [8]

In 1939 the K2 expedition members had no way to know what would be discovered in later years and had little reason to study Barcroft, for his work was hardly known, even in the medical profession. Yet Barcroft's observations apply to events that took place in 1939 on K2 that, without our modern knowledge of high-altitude physiology, are hard to analyze.

In 1939 there was already enough known about altitude for the K2 party to give thought to the possibility of including a supply of oxygen in its equipment. Oxygen for mountaineering was, at the time, a controver- sial subject. It had been a cause for debate ever since the physiologist George Ingle Finch first tried it on Everest in 1922. Its value on that mountain in 1922 and 1924 was unproven,[9] and most subsequent Hima- layan expeditions until 1939 either did not take it at all or included it only for medical purposes. Meanwhile alpinists on Kamet (25,443 feet; 7755 meters), and on Minya Konka (Gonga Shan) (24,981 feet; 7585 meters), and on Nanda Devi (25,645 feet; 7816 meters) were proving that great peaks could be scaled without it. In fact, H. W. Tilman, one of the two men who in 1936 reached the summit of Nanda Devi, was known as a notoriously poor acclimatizer throughout his distinguished Himalayan career, while his companion, Noel Odell, was among the best. Yet the summit record he set stood for fourteen years.

Oxygen came into vogue for a generation after 1953. This was because of a general and probably accurate belief that without it Sir Edmund Hil- lary and Tenzing Norkay, under the conditions then prevailing, would never have scaled Everest. The British used it again, albeit sparingly, to ascend Kangchenjunga in 1954. That same year the Italians on K2, who had counted on it, had a terrible struggle to reach the top after their equipment malfunctioned. In 1955 the French, with equipment sophisti- cated for that time and developed on the basis of conversations with Aqua-Lung inventor Jacques Cousteau, literally romped up Makalu (27,825 feet; 8481 meters). The following year the Swiss, with the same French gear, had little trouble placing four men on top of Everest and two more on its hitherto unclimbed neighbor, Lhotse (27,923 feet; 8511 me- ters).

Then for a time oxygen was used on the lesser 8000-meter peaks, such as Manaslu and Hidden Peak, and on even lower ones, including Chogolisa and Masherbrum, although its value on those summits was considered marginal – and, because of the weight of the gear, perhaps counterproductive.

But attitudes and trends change. In 1978, Rheinhold Messner and Peter Habeler became the first persons to climb Everest without oxygen, thus demonstrating the validity of the findings of Operation Everest (Charles Houston's laboratory experiment of 1946). Since then a substantial number of other climbers have done the same, though some, weak and in a mental haze, have tumbled off near the top (notably Sherpas in 1983), never to be seen again. Today the trend is to eliminate oxygen, except for medical emergencies, and substitute pharmaceuticals, such as Diamox (acetazolamide).[10] But on very high peaks most climbers still use oxygen, if only for reasons of safety, clear thinking, and comfort.

Arguments on the propriety of oxygen use are both ethical and practical. Most alpinists are amateurs who view climbing as a sport, and all sports have ethical principles and unwritten codes – some universally accepted and some controversial. The mountaineering philosophy to which Fritz Wiessner adhered rejected the use of artificial aids for climbing except when employed for protection or in rescue operations. That oxygen equipment can be considered "artificial" is open to debate, but many of the most prominent alpinists think so, despite the fact that oxygen is as necessary to body functioning as food and water. Wiessner, his heart in the purist camp, was opposed to oxygen: if a climber could possibly reach the top without it, why use it?

On the practical side, the strongest argument for carrying oxygen is its proven value in medical emergencies. It also supplies a passive advantage by providing summit climbers with a good night's rest before the final push. Used in climbing, it definitely assists in keeping the mind clear. In effect, it simulates oxygen conditions prevalent at lower elevations: the atmosphere on an 8000-meter peak feels like that on a 6000er. But there is – or until recently was – a trade-off. Until a few years ago the equipment was heavy and cumbersome, even the gear developed by the French that had been so useful on Makalu. Climbing at 8000 meters with a twenty-pound load is probably not much more strenuous than climbing at 6000 meters carrying fifty pounds. But reverse the situation because of thirty pounds of oxygen equipment, and then add deep snow, and it is debatable whether a climber would not be better off simply jettisoning the oxygen. This is precisely what Lou Reichardt did on his final drive to the summit of K2 in 1978.

On the 1939 K2 expedition, Fritz Wiessner had only past experience and his personal philosophy to guide him. Oxygen gear in his time was extremely heavy and expensive, and its benefits were unproven. Furthermore, it would have had to have been carried for 300 miles from Srinagar, not to mention the journey from Europe. So the 1939 party took no oxygen. Instead, it followed in the footsteps of its 1938 predecessor, two of whose members, Charlie Houston and Paul Petzoldt, had reached 26,000 feet (7925 meters), just 2250 feet (685 meters) below K2's summit, without oxygen and returned believing that had the necessary time, supplies (notably fuel and matches) and, above all, reliable weather–been available, they could have gone to the top. As for Fritz's ethical standards, these had been a part of his make-up ever since boyhood climbing days in Saxon Switzerland.

The presence of oxygen on K2 in 1939 would probably have done little to change the expedition's outcome, just as its use seemed of questionable value on other summits in those years. What really counted were the known and, at that time, unknown dangers encountered on high mountains and sometimes elsewhere: on the one hand, the objective dangers–avalanches, loose stones, bad weather, and falls–and, on the other, the subjective dangers–attrition, cold, exposure, frostbite, lack of fluids, inadequate consumption of food, acute mountain sickness, impaired reasoning and memory, and high-altitude pulmonary and cerebral edema. These last are the very things so greatly stressed by Charles Houston based on his studies of people who climb high in the thin mountain atmosphere and which he summarizes as the synergetic effects of hypoglycemia, hypohydration, hypothermia, and, above all, hypoxia– and one more factor, derived from the others: loss of determination and morale, a condition that ultimately afflicted every member of the party except for its leader and a few of its Sherpas.

C. Movements of Personnel on K2 During the 1939 Expedition

CHART I RECORDS THE MOVEMENTS of the American expedition members (except Chappel Cranmer) on K2 during the party's stay on the mountain in the summer of 1939. This data was prepared by Fritz Wiessner on the basis of his records and other data available to him and was submitted to the American Alpine Club's committee of inquiry, and others, following the return of the expedition.

Chart II, which records Sherpa movements, was prepared by the authors on the basis of the same information, but only for the critical period from July 12 through August 8, 1939.

Not included are the movements and locations of the British transport officer, Lieutenant George ("Joe") Trench, who climbed briefly to a point just above the House Chimney, and the Indian interpreter, Chandra, who made at least one trip to Camp II.

The record of movements supplied by Wiessner is corroborated quite closely by the notations found in Jack Durrance's diary.

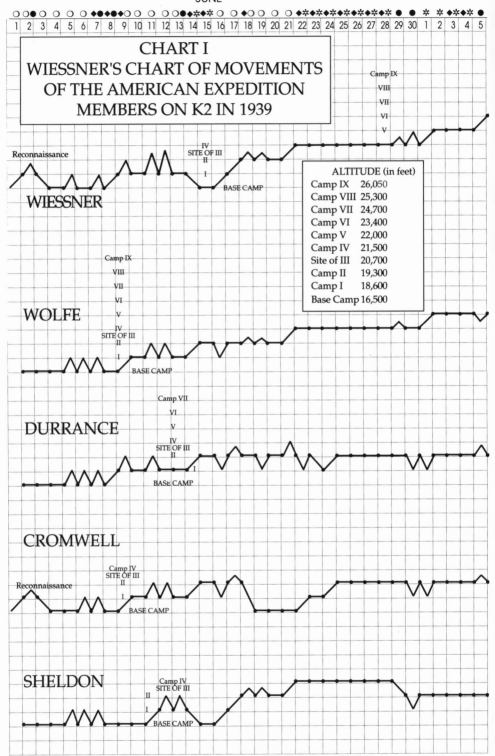

JUNE

CHART I
WIESSNER'S CHART OF MOVEMENTS
OF THE AMERICAN EXPEDITION
MEMBERS ON K2 IN 1939

WIESSNER

WOLFE

DURRANCE

CROMWELL

SHELDON

ALTITUDE (in feet)	
Camp IX	26,050
Camp VIII	25,300
Camp VII	24,700
Camp VI	23,400
Camp V	22,000
Camp IV	21,500
Site of III	20,700
Camp II	19,300
Camp I	18,600
Base Camp	16,500

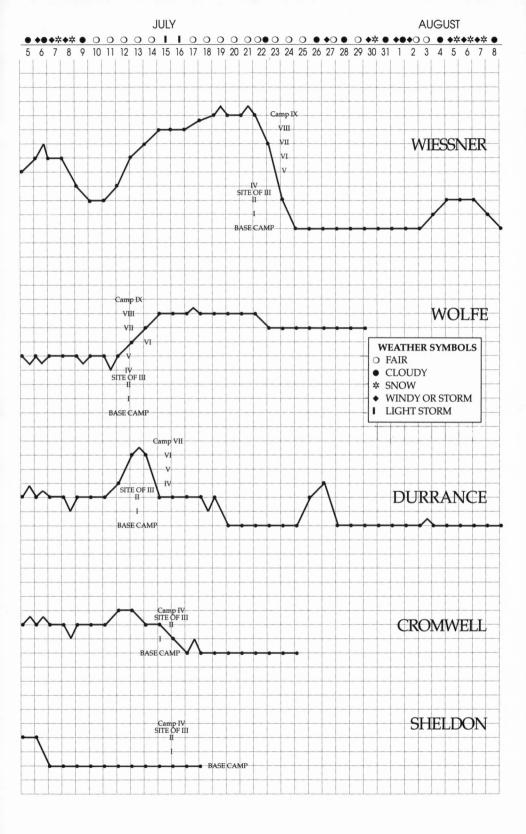

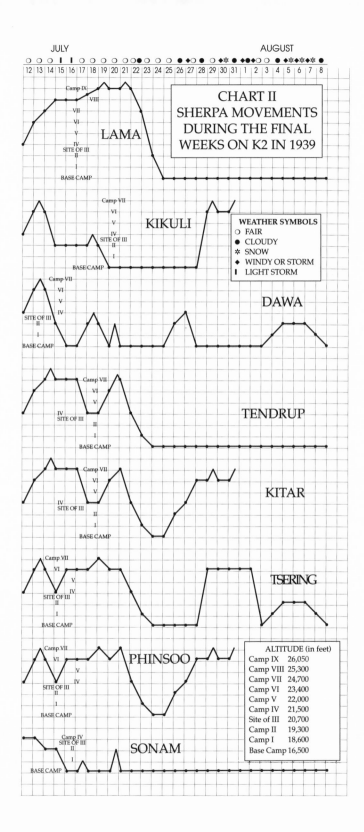

D. Sources

FOLLOWING ARE THE SOURCES, both published and personal, used in the creation of this narrative. They range from primary, such as Jack Durrance's diary, to tertiary, such as the comments of Louis Audoubert. Some sources, such as various letters from expedition members to Joel Ellis Fisher and to the American Alpine Club, are copies, the originals not having been found. Much of the written material supplied to the authors by Fritz Wiessner, such as quotations from his diary, was taken from typewritten copies, but is believed to be accurate as to facts.

American Alpine Club. "Committee of Inquiry Report on the 1939 American Alpine Club Karakoram Expedition." July 10, 1940.

Audoubert, Louis. *Baltoro, Montagnes de Lumière*. Paris: Arthaud, 1983, pp. 100ff.

Bates, Robert H., and Charles S. Houston. *Five Miles High*. New York: Dodd, Mead, 1939.

Cranmer, Chappell, and Fritz H. Wiessner. "The Second American Expedition to K2." *American Alpine Journal*, 1940, vol. 4, no. 1, pp. 9–19.

Cromwell, Eaton O. "Obituaries, Dudley Francis Wolfe." *American Alpine Journal*, 1940, vol. 4, pp. 121–23.

Cromwell, Eaton O. "Spring Skiing in the Vale of Kashmir." *Appalachia*, vol. 23 (December 1940), pp. 163–67.

Cromwell, Eaton O. Letter to Joel Ellis Fisher, 14 May 1939.

Durrance, John R. Handwritten diary covering the period of March 20 through September 20, 1939, with various addenda and comments, a major source for this narrative.

Durrance, John R. Note to Fritz H. Wiessner, of 1 July 1939; photocopy identified as being in Durrance's handwriting.

Durrance, John R. Letter to Eaton O. Cromwell of 3 August 1939; supplied in photocopy by Wiessner.

Durrance, John R. Notes by Andrew J. Kauffman of one interview in Denver, Colorado, on 7 December 1986 and two in Washington, D. C., in February 1987.

Groth, Edward Miller. Calcutta Despatch 1211 of 13 September 1939 to Secretary of State, Washington, D. C., with enclosure of an undated copy of Fritz Wiessner's expedition report to the American Alpine Club and Groth's memorandum giving a summary of impressions of the expedition following a seven-hour interview in Srinagar, Kashmir, on 4 September 1939 with Fritz H. Wiessner and John R. Durrance.

Henderson, Kenneth A. Interview with William L. Putnam, spring 1984.

House, William P. Interview with William L. Putnam, spring 1984.

Macy, C. E. Karachi Despatch 193 of 13 September 1939, enclosing Foreign Service Form 192 (Report of Death of American Citizen) and affidavit of death, signed in Srinagar, Kashmir, by Fritz H. Wiessner and John R. Durrance before Resident Lt. Col. D. M. Fraser.

Maraini, Fosco. *Karakoram: The Ascent of Gasherbrum IV.* London: Hutchinson, 1961, pp. 160–61.

Rochester, Dudley (nephew of Dudley Wolfe). Interview with Andrew J. Kauffman, February 1987, concerning Wolfe's family background.

Sheldon, George. Copies of circular letters to friends in American Alpine Club dated 6 May, 4 June, 14 June, and 8 July, 1939.

Sheldon, George. "Lost Behind the Ranges." *Saturday Evening Post,* 16 and 23 March 1940.

Wiessner, Fritz H. Copies of letters of 14 April and 8 May 1939 to Joel Ellis Fisher.

Wiessner, Fritz H. "Report of the 1939 American Alpine Club Second Karakoram Expedition" (undated), copy submitted by Edward Miller Groth, American Consul, Calcutta, and transmitted to Secretary of State, Washington, D. C., as an enclosure to Calcutta Despatch 1211 of 13 September 1939. A copy of this report was also transmitted to the Secretary of State as an enclosure to Karachi Despatch 193 of 13 September 1939.

Wiessner, Fritz H. *K2—Victory and Tragedy on the Second-Highest Mountain on Earth* (in German). Munich: Bergverlag Rudolf Rother, 1955, but presumably written in 1952. Quotations in this narrative are from a typewritten English-language translation of the book supplied to the authors by Wiessner.

Wiessner, Fritz H. Typed excerpts from what Wiessner told the authors was his diary covering the period of July 19 through August 7, 1939; also various quotations from Wiessner's diary supplied by Wiessner's son, Andrew Wiessner.

Wiessner, Fritz H. "The K2 Expedition of 1939." *Appalachia,* vol. 31 (June 1956), pp. 60–77.

Wiessner, Fritz H. Nine hours of taped interviews with William L. Putnam, conducted in Wiessner's home in Stowe, Vermont, on January 2, 1984, and later dates and at Rustler Lodge, Utah.

Wilson, Lt. Gen. Sir Roger, president of the Himalayan Club. Statement of 26 September 1939, enclosed with Calcutta Despatch 1240 from American consul Edward Miller Groth to the Secretary of State, Washington, D. C., 30 September 1939.

Wolfe, Dudley F. Letter to American Alpine Club, dated 13 May 1939, but mailed later.

Wolfe, Dudley F. Color motion picture of the 1939 American Karakoram Expedition to K2 from departure in Genoa on 29 March 1939 to near the establishment of Camp IV on K2, 21 June 1939.

Various letters or copies of letters by Henry Kingman, Alfred Lindley, and Robert L. M. Underhill; copies of letters by Lawrence Coveney; and copies of Jack Durrance's letter to Tony Cromwell of August 3, 1939, and his note to Fritz Wiessner of July 1, 1939. All copies supplied to the authors by Fritz Wiessner.

Numerous conversations at various times by the authors with Robert H. Bates, Robert W. Craig, Charles S. Houston, Dee Molenaar, Louis Reichart, and Peter K. Schoening about K2 and the nature of the Abruzzi Ridge.

E. The Groth Report

AUTHORS' NOTE: Neither this despatch nor the accompanying "Memorandum" was communicated by Consul Groth to the American Alpine Club, as indicated in the last line of the formal despatch. Indeed, the language suggests that the memorandum should be treated by the Department of State as an internal document, albeit unclassified, that might later be furnished to the AAC upon request on a "need to know" basis.

American Consulate General
Calcutta, India, September 13, 1939

Subject: American Alpine Club Expedition.

The Honorable
    The Secretary of State,
        Washington.

Sir:
    I have the honor to refer to the Department's several instructions concerning the 1939 Expedition of the American Alpine Club to the Karakoram, and to report that in returning from local leave recently I met Mr. F. H. Wiessner, leader of the ill-fated American Alpine Club Expedition to the Karakoram, in Srinagar (Kashmir). This gave me an opportunity to learn at first hand the details of the events leading up, and subsequent, to the tragedy which occurred on K-2. Mr. Jack Durrance, one of the members of the Expedition, also happened to be in Srinagar, and through him I learned additional facts in regard to the Expedition and its experiences.
    Mr. Wiessner furnished me with a copy of his report to the American Alpine Club. A copy thereof is enclosed as is a memorandum I have prepared on the basis of my conversations with Messrs Wiessner and Durrance as well as with Colonel Fraser, His Majesty's Resident in Kashmir. It is thought that the Department may wish to have this material in its files

should further inquiries be received from the American Alpine Club, which has not been furnished with a copy of my memorandum.

Respectfully yours,
Edward M. Groth
American Consul

Enclosure:
Copy of Mr. F. H. Wiessner's report to the American Alpine Club.

Memorandum

Summary of impressions received by Edward M. Groth, American Consul, Calcutta, from conversations at Srinagar, Kashmir, with F. H. Wiessner (leader) and Jack Durrance (member) of the American Alpine Club Second Karakoram Expedition.

I returned to Srinagar from Leh on the morning of September 4th and immediately got in touch with Major Kenneth Hadow[1] by telephone. He informed me that Wiessner was in Gullmarg but that he expected him back by noon. I invited Hadow, Wiessner and Durrance for lunch, but Hadow was unable to accept. Wiessner and Durrance arrived at the appointed hour and for almost seven hours thereafter they related to me the details leading up to and subsequent to the tragic accident which took place on K-2 and resulted in the death of Dudley Wolfe and three Sherpas.

The aforementioned details, which are of a very complicated character, are clearly set out in the report submitted to the American Alpine Club by Mr. Wiessner, the leader, a copy of which is appended hereto, and therefore no attempt will be made to give this information as it would merely be a repetition of the report and would have to be based on the original.

After the protracted conversations with Wiessner and Durrance I retained the impression that at the very outset the composition of the expedition provided the potential elements of a clash of temperaments before the end of the tour. Confidentially, I believe that one of the primary factors precipitating the dissension which finally arose was the inescapable

---

1. *Note:* Major Hadow is well known to all mountaineering expeditions visiting Kashmir. He is a well-known figure in Srinagar, where he operates a large factory for the manufacture of fine hand-made carpets. Married to an American, he has been especially kind to American mountaineers.

fact that, although on paper and by law, Wiessner is an American citizen, he is still in many respects largely German in his outlook and actions. This is not unnatural in view of the circumstance that he became an American citizen but a few months ago. With his German background, also owing to the fact that he possesses a large share of German bluntness (a national characteristic which was apparently unknown to all but one of his colleagues and fellow-expedition-members) it is not remarkable that there should have been a clash of temperaments. Wiessner is undoubtedly an excellent climber and a good leader, but, like every German, he is very forceful in giving commands and totally unaware that the abrupt, blunt manner in which the order may have been given might have wounded the feelings of his associates, who in this instance, being Americans, naturally had a different attitude and outlook in matters of this sort.

Although I recognize the aforementioned German characteristics and can easily understand the reactions which they caused among the other members of the expedition, I received the impression that the latter made comparatively little effort to analyse or understand Wiessner's temperament. Had this been done, they would probably have realized at an early date that Wiessner's bite was not as bad as his bark. It may also be that the other members of the expedition had never previously been in a position where it was necessary for them to accept and carry out orders of so imperative a leader. I received the impression that the general feeling of several of the expedition members was that, as they had borne their share of the expenses and had contributed liberally to the expenses of one or two members unable to pay the entire cost out of their own pockets, they were entitled to have just as much to say about the running of the expedition as the leader. This, of course, was a most unfortunate attitude, for there can be only one leader, regardless of who foots the bills.

Wiessner explained to me several times that it had been thoroughly understood prior to their departure from the United States and in the course of the journey to India, that if at any time any of the expedition members felt that things were not being handled as they should, or if there was any dissatisfaction with the leadership of the expedition, whatever differences of opinion might arise would be immediately brought to the leader's attention and the problem in question be thoroughly thrashed out and not be brooded over by the persons involved. Unfortunately this admitted advantageous arrangement for smoothing out difficulties seems seldom, if ever, to have been resorted to, with the result that gradually molehills grew into mountains and apparently the mountains became volcanoes, which, during most of the expedition's duration, smouldered under a quiescent surface but finally erupted in a most unfortunate fashion. Wiessner said he could not understand how Cromwell could, on numerous occasions, have praised his (Wiessner's) organizing ability, energy, etc., and at the same time be working against him under the surface.

The ultimate upheaval appears to have taken place before Wiessner and Durrance (who were the last to leave the mountain) returned to Srinagar and assumed the form of letters written by Lieut. Trench (the Liaison Officer) and Mr. Cromwell, both of whom proceeded to the capital of Kashmir about a fortnight in advance of Messrs Wiessner and Durrance, and in company with Messrs Cranmer and Sheldon.

Colonel Fraser, the Resident at Srinagar, on whom I called on Tuesday, September 5th, had just received from Mr. Cromwell copies of his and Trench's letters addressed to Mr. Joel E. Fisher, Treasurer of the American Alpine Club in New York City. Colonel Fraser very kindly read the letters in question to me and we both came to practically the same conclusion in our reactions to the contents of these communications. Lieut. Trench's letter was of such a superficial character as to deserve no credence whatever. Mr. Cromwell's letter, on the other hand, seemed to Colonel Fraser and myself to contain numerous unwarranted accusations. [These accusations were probably the same ones that Cromwell made later to Henry Hall, Jr., and other officials of the American Alpine Club to the effect that Wiessner had murdered Wolfe.] We both felt that the final paragraphs were of such a vindictive nature that one might almost question the motives which prompted their writing. Certainly the exaggerated nature of these concluding paragraphs must largely, if not entirely, nullify any truths contained in the earlier part of the letter.

It is not for me to pass judgement in this unfortunate case or to place the responsibility for the accident, but on the basis of Wiessner's written report, as well as the protracted conversations I had personally with him and Durrance (both together and singly) I should be inclined to reach the conclusion that the unfortunate accident was due to a combination of circumstances over which Wiessner did not have entire control nor for which he could be held solely responsible. I am under the impression that Wiessner's responsibility may possibly lie in another direction, viz., that he should have exercised far greater care in selecting the members of his party and in studying their temperaments. The management of an expedition of this sort and its composition may be likened to that of an Opera company. The leader must be an impressario [sic], a person of great tact and patience, but also firmness. The difference between an Opera company and a mountaineering expedition lies, however, in the fact that while, if there is a clash of temperaments in an Opera Company, the impressario [sic] is in a position to change the cast, or the Opera; in the management of a mountaineering expedition the leader is neither able to change the cast nor the Opera. He has to put up with the singers and if these happen to have particularly delicate temperaments, his touch must also be delicate – but firm.

I gathered that, although Wiessner was firm enough in the issuance of instructions, when the supreme test came, he faltered. That test arose on the mountain in connection with Wolfe. It appears that Wolfe, although enjoying an excellent reputation as a mountaineer, was not as sure of himself as might have been expected. It also appears that he had a definite tendency to be lazy. Physically, he seems to have been in better condition than any member of the expedition save possibly Wiessner. So far as I was able to learn, practically all members of the expedition, except Wolfe and Wiessner, had succumbed to various physical disabilities. As the time of the crisis approached, Wolfe, either as a result of the debilitating effect of the altitude, or through sheer laziness, expressed a desire to rest a few days at Camp VII.

It seems that once or twice prior to the time that Wolfe reached Camp VII, some allusions were made as to whether it was wise for him to attempt to reach higher altitudes. Wolfe apparently resented this imputation and gave Wiessner to understand that, as he had contributed substantially to the financing of the expedition, and as he was in better physical condition than any of the other members, except Wiessner, he had every right to go as high as he desired, so long as he did not hinder the progress of the expedition. Despite his apparent laziness and his slowness of movement and action, both Wiessner and Durrance admitted to me that actually Wolfe had really not retarded the expedition's progress at any time before he reached Camp VII. Under these circumstances, Wolfe's contention was undoubtedly correct. On the other hand, the altitude was unquestionably beginning to affect Wolfe, and if Wiessner is to be held responsible for anything, it would seem to me that the responsibility might be based on the fact that he was influenced by Wolfe's argument regarding his right, because of financial contributions, to go as high up the mountain as possible. Wolfe seems to have used the financial argument as a club over Wiessner's head and Wiessner, instead of sticking to his better judgement and insisting that Wolfe go down the mountain with him, yielded to his request to be allowed to remain in Camp VII until such time as Wiessner would return, when Wolfe expected to be rested and attempt with Wiessner to attack the summit.

If Wolfe had accompanied Wiessner on the downward trip, he would have had to continue to Base Camp, as Wiessner did, because of the evacuation by the Sherpas of all the camps below Camp VII. Of course, Wolfe never knew that the lower camps had been evacuated, nor the state of affairs that existed in them, nor did he know the poor physical condition of his fellow-expedition-members at base camp, so by the time the relief party returned to Camp VII, he seems already to have been in

bad physical condition and slightly unbalanced mentally; partially perhaps by the altitude and also no doubt due to a growing feeling (when
Wiessner did not return two or three days after his departure) that he had
been deserted by his fellows. This is the only way to account for his alleged action toward the Sherpas when they returned to rescue him. It is
possible, of course, that by that time (that was almost a week after
Wiessner had left Wolfe) his physical condition had deteriorated to such
an extent that he was no longer able to make the descent.

The criticism made by Cromwell to the effect that the Sherpas should
not have been sent up alone to rescue Wolfe might be justified were it not
for the circumstances which prevailed in the base camp where none of
the expedition members were physically able to re-climb the mountain
and aid in Wolfe's rescue. The physical condition of all members at the
base camp had so deteriorated that any immediate re-climb of the mountain by them seems to have been entirely out of the question. The three
Sherpas were the only ones physically able to reach Wolfe, and it was
their splendid attitude, their feeling of responsibility toward their employers, and their desire to bring Wolfe safely down, which alone made the
attempt to do so possible. Wiessner should not be held responsible for
the Sherpas independent re-ascent of the mountain. Had the time factor
not been so important, it seems unlikely that Wiessner would have ordered (actually, I think, they all volunteered to return to Camp VII) the
porters to proceed to the rescue of Wolfe without an expedition member
accompanying them, but it was known that the supplies available to
Wolfe were limited and therefore it was imperative that someone go to
his rescue without delay. Had three or four days rest been possible it
seems he would have recovered sufficiently from the effects of the altitude and the tremendous strain under which he had labored as a result of
descending (without a break) from Camp VII to base camp, to have led
the rescue party himself. I have no doubt but that he would have done so,
for Wiessner does not impress one as being the type of individual to shift
his own responsibilities to the shoulders of another. For this reason I feel
that Cromwell's accusations against Wiessner are unfounded and unjust,
and that to the recommendations made in his letter, credence should not
be given.

In the course of listening to the accounts of Wiessner and Durrance, the
question arose in my mind as to why Trench and Cromwell left Base
Camp before Wiessner and Durrance. It was known that Cranmer and
Sheldon would have to proceed in advance of the rest of the party, in fact,
this was, I believe, understood before their departure from the United
States as they had to return in time for their University work. In so far as
Cromwell and Trench were concerned, the time factor was of relatively
minor importance. Trench's time, it is true, was limited, but Cromwell

was in no way bound to return before Wiessner, and in my opinion should not have done so, especially in view of the fact that Wolfe was still on the mountain; because his fate and that of the Sherpas was unknown and also because at the time he left both Wiessner and Durrance were still indisposed. (Note: in this connection it should also be mentioned that either in their letters to Mr. Fisher or possibly in conversation with Durrance – I cannot recall which – both Cromwell and Trench stated that they had felt a premonition that Wolfe would not return). Cromwell offered the excuse that he felt obliged to accompany Cranmer and Sheldon because of their youth (both being 21 years of age). Actually, this flimsy excuse seems only to have been offered to provide a means of escape for Cromwell from what he considered to be an intolerable situation, and is concerned, primarily, with his relationship with Wiessner, who, as already mentioned, informed me that at no time during the expedition were frank open statements of dissatisfaction made. Wiessner felt that if, in accordance with the original agreement, such statements had been made, most of the misunderstandings which apparently arose would have been obviated. There was of course no reason why Cranmer and Sheldon could not proceed to Bombay without an escort. Even if Cromwell felt that it was necessary for him to leave Base Camp, Trench, it would seem, in view of his position as Liaison and Transport Officer, should have remained at Base Camp until the last member of the expedition left that point.

According to the reports of Wiessner and Durrance, Trench proved to be not only unreliable, but entirely unsuited for and inefficient in the work he had been employed to do.

One final point in the matter of responsibility might be made and that is the part played by the Sherpa [Tendrup] who gave the false report that Wiessner and Wolfe and one Sherpa must have perished, as he received no reply to his call near Camp VIII. It was on the basis of this totally false assumption that this man and his two companions evacuated as much equipment as possible from all the camps below Camp VII. It seems incredible that those at Base Camp who received this word should, without considerable questioning, have believed the Sherpa's story, viz., that those remaining on the mountain had perished. The alacrity with which this tale seems to have been believed would seem to point to two things, viz:

1. That Cromwell, who in Wiessner's absence, was in charge of the affairs of the expedition at Base Camp, being apparently unaware of the Asiatic tendency to exaggerate and to give credence to rumor, accepted without thorough investigation the report brought down by the Sherpas.

2. That Cromwell was unable to conduct such an investigation because of his lack of knowledge of Hindustani, the lingua franca of the Sherpas.

If the last point was the cause of superficial questioning and investigation, then it would appear that Trench failed signally in the performance of his duty, as he, of all present, was best fitted to act as interpreter in such an examination.

Edward M. Groth
American Consul

Calcutta, India.
September 13, 1939.
EMG-dmt.

F. Report of the American Alpine Club Second Karakoram Expedition

630 Fifth Avenue, New York City.

AUTHORS' NOTE: There are two versions of this report, but with only minor differences. We believe the Srinagar version to have been the original developed by Wiessner and Durrance. A similar version emanated from the office of Consul Groth in Calcutta and was typed by Dolly M. Taylor, a long-term consulate employee. Where the latter version contains words not in the Srinagar version, we include them in [brackets]; where the obverse is true, we show the Srinagar words in (parentheses). We have also modified the punctuation slightly to add clarity.

> *The expedition suffered under very poor weather conditions during the first 6 weeks and, when after July 16th an 8-day period of good weather set in, most of the members [and porters] were physically tired out (some low in spirits as well). One of the stronger members fell sick on the day the party arrived at Base Camp, he nearly died and could not risk to go high afterwards. Before June 14th the weather allowed the party to establish and provision Camps I, altitude 18,500 ft. and II, altitude 19,300 ft. In the higher regions storm reigned most of the time. On June 15th and 16th heavy snow storms blew as low as Base Camp. Five days of changeable weather followed during which a cache at 20,700 ft. altitude and Camp 4, 21,500 ft. were established. Then eight days of severe storms suffocated all climbing activities. The following days of changeable weather made it possible for Wolfe, Wiessner and 3 Sherpas to establish Camp 5, altitude 22,000 ft. on July 6th. Three more days of heavy storm followed, then two days of fine weather during which Wiessner and two Sherpas established Camp 6, altitude 23,400 ft. and prepared the route to Camp 7, altitude 24,700 ft. (Wolfe stayed at Camp 5 during that time). Again a two days storm held up progress, Wiessner descended to Camp II where the other members had passed the stormy periods. The weather by that time seemed to have turned for the better and preparations were made for a quick push to Camp (7) [VIII]. on July 11th Cromwell, Durrance, Transport Officer Lt. Trench, Wiessner and the rest of the Sherpas went up to Camp 4. One member, Sheldon, had to return to Base Camp because of frost bitten toes acquired while weathering the stormy days with Wolfe and Wiessner at Camp 4. Cromwell, who had not planned to go very high, and Trans-*

port Officer Lt. Trench, were to stay at Camp 4 or below to keep up proper connections with the party above. Durrance, Wolfe, Wiessner and Sherpas (with the exception of Sonam who had had an accident on the previous day) went to Camp 6, altitude 23,400 Ft., the following day. On the 13th the whole party at Camp 6 continued to Camp 7. Durrance had to turn back above Camp 6 on account of mountain sickness. Wiessner, Wolfe and three of the Sherpas remained at Camp 7 while the others returned to Camp 6 with instructions about their future movements. They were to bring more supplies to Camp 7 and also Durrance hoped to be able to follow later. The next day Wolfe, Wiessner and the 3 Sherpas continued and established Camp 8, altitude 25,300 ft. Two of the Sherpas, Tendrup and Pasang Kitar, went back to Camp 7 that afternoon with the understanding to bring more supplies to Camp 8 the next day. On July 15th and 16th storm confined everyone to their tents. On the 17th of July, Passang Lama and Wiessner went up to the shoulder on the S.E. Ridge with heavy loads. A bergschwund [sic], 3 rope lengths above Camp 8, [altitude 25,300 ft] whose lower lip consisted of bottomless fine powder snow, nearly stopped them, from here Wolfe returned to Camp 8, Wiessner and Passang Lama were left to try the summit. They camped on the shoulder of the mountain approximately at 25,500 feet altitude. They had planned to lay their camps higher but the negotiation of the Bergschurund had taken a long time. They were still too far from the summit to make an attempt, and needed another camp which was established the following day (at an altitude of approximately 26,000 feet).

On the 19th of July they made an attempt for the summit, their route led up along the S.E. ridge to the base of the vertical step on the summit [cone]. The latter was overcome on its west flank. A point 27,450 feet high, 800 feet below the summit, was reached (here). A 60 feet traverse was all that separated them from a short snow field which led on to the gentle summit ridge. By this time it was six o'clock in the afternoon and they decided to return to Camp. The weather was settled and they were convinced that they could reach the summit two days later. They arrived back in Camp at 2:30 A.M. and spent the rest of the day there.

The next morning they left early. As the rock route, west of the ridge, had proven long and difficult, they were attracted by the shorter and apparently easier route between the S.E. ridge and the great ice cliff east of it. From the first, this route seemed the logical route but it appeared to be exposed to ice fall from the great ice cliff. However, during the previous days no ice had fallen and from all appearances they felt justified to examine its possibilities. They followed the S.E. ridge again to the vertical step, here they traversed to the East to the top of a snow (couloir) [conton] which ends about 90 feet below the western end of the ice wall. The 400 feet snow gully between the ice wall and the ridge was hard and icy. Step cutting over the 400 feet would have taken too long and, though crampons would have solved the problem, the party had to re-

turn because the crampons had been lost on their descent two nights before. After they regained the ridge they found it too late to use the other route and they descended to Camp. Provisions were running very short so it was necessary to make a round trip to Camp 8 for more and at the same time bring up the necessary crampons. On the morning of July 22nd, they went down for Camp 8, only Wolfe was there, and he told them that, since the 17th, no one had come from Camp 7. His supplies also were getting short, and all three continued to Camp 7 where they expected to find the porters and supplies. A large supply of food, fuel and sleeping bags had been left there on the 14th. However, they found only two tents in great disorder with one of them torn. Some food and a stove were left but no sleeping bags or air mattresses. The late hour forced them to spend the night at Camp 7. They had only one sleeping bag and air mattress between them, as another sleeping bag which they had taken from Camp 8 had been lost when the party had a fall above Camp 7. The next day, Wiessner and Passang continued to Camp 6 hoping to find the party there. Wolfe, who was tired but well, wanted to remain at Camp 7 and wait until the others had returned from Camp 6 with supplies for another summit attack. They found Camp 6 also cleared with the exception of two tents which had been folded up and some food, the same was true of Camp 5. Camp 4 had also been cleared of sleeping bags; Camp 3 had served only as a dump throughout the climb. At Camp 2 two tents were found pitched but sleeping bags and air mattresses had also been removed. They spent another cold night using one of the tents for cover. The next morning they continued to Base where they found the party. On the way down they met a searching party led by Cromwell who had looked for signs of an accident on the glacier below the route.

After Durrance had returned to Camp 6 on July 13th, he fell ill, and with difficulty descended the next day to Camp 2 with Dawa and Passang Kikuli. The Sherpas remaining at Camp 6 had received instructions about their future movements. Tendrup and Passang Kitar had stayed at Camp 7 (after returning from Camp 8 on the evening of July 14th) over the 15th and 16th of July while the weather was cloudy and windy. On the 17th a fine day, they descended to Camp 4 instead of returning to Camp 8 with loads. Passang Kikuli, who on the 18th arrived in Camp 4, found Tendrup and Kitar there; he immediately ordered the two to go up and bring supplies to Camp 8 and asked the two to tell Phinsoo and Tsering at Camp 6 to make transports between Camp 6 and 7. Tendrup and Kitar went to Camp 6 the next day. They say that on the following day they went to Camp 7 taking Pinsoo with them and that on the same afternoon they went half way to Camp 8. They shouted to the upper camp but as there was no response they felt certain that the 2 sahibs and Pasang Lama had fallen off. When Tendrup returned to the lower camp and the Base Camp with Phinsoo and Passang Kitar, he reported that Wolfe and Pasang Lama [oddly, Wiessner *fails to name himself as one of those allegedly killed] had been killed high up on the mountain. The other Sherpas, convinced of this report of the death of the advanced Party, now cleared, together with him, the camps of as much equipment as possible. None of the members (excepting the advance party) were on the mountain during that time, each having a reason for being at Base Camp.*

On the 25th of July, after Cromwell and Trench had left Base Camp with 22 coolies, Durrance started for Camp 7 with Dawa, Phinsoo and Passang Kitar, so that Wolfe could descend. Also, there was the tentative plan that Wiessner, Pasang Lama and another Sherpa might follow two days later in order to make another summit attempt with Durrance, providing the former had sufficiently recovered.

Durrance and the three Sherpas reached Camp 2 the evening of July 25. On July 26 they continued to Camp 4. Here Durrance had another attack of mountain sickness, also one of the porters, Dawa, could not go higher as he had lost his voice during the ascent and had become very ill. On the morning of the 27th the weather had changed, high wind and light storm prevailed at Camp 4. Durrance, due to his and Dawa's condition, decided to return immediately to Base Camp and call for assistance. Passang Kitar and Phinsoo continued to Camp 6 the same day where they remained until the next party arrived. As Wiessner's and Pasang Lama's conditions had not improved and the weather as aforementioned had taken a turn for worse, they were forced to give up any hopes for a second summit attempt. Durrance and Dawa reached Base Camp in the evening of July 27th. After a consultation during which Passang Kikuli (who by this time had recovered from frost bite and was in excellent condition) insisted that he and Tsering could go to Camp 6 in one day. On the following day he proposed to continue to Camp 7 with Phinsoo and Passang Kitar and to return with Wolfe the same day. This proposal was accepted as the best plan because Durrance and Wiessner were in poor health(s) and would not have been able to make the trip to Camp 7 at that time. Also Passang Kikuli's performance throughout the climb left no doubt as to his ability and good judgment to lead safely and successfully in any situation. Likewise, the other two Sherpas had won the admiration of the party for the safe manner in which they had climbed. Naturally, Durrance and Wiessner began to feel some anxiety regarding Wolfe who, by the time Passang Kikuli would arrive at Camp 7, would have been alone for 6 days. Wolfe had been somewhat tired on the day when Wiessner and Pasang Lama left him, but was otherwise in good condition. The weather had been good on an average since that day. Fuel, a good assortment of food for at least 10 days, two tents, one sleeping bag with air mattress and good personal equipment seemed to limit any reasonable grounds for anxiety. However, it was agreed that Passang Kikuli would give fire signals in case anything was wrong. Passang Kikuli when he left with Tsering, had also expressed hope that Phinsoo and Passang Kitar would have already gone up to Camp 7 and returned with Wolfe before Kikuli would reach Camp 6.

On the morning of the 28th, Passang Kikuli and Tsering left Base Camp at sunrise. The weather had improved. On the morning of the 29th, the party at Base Camp observed through powerful glasses 3 men climbing from Camp 6 to Camp 7. As Tsering related later, they were Passang Kikuli, Passang Kitar, and Phinsoo. Passang Kikuli and Tsering actually had ascended from Base Camp to Camp 6 the previous day – an extraordinary feat. Late in the afternoon of the same day only 3 men could be observed returning along the route from Camp 7 to Camp 6. Darkness was anxiously awaited at Base Camp that evening but there was no fire signal. The 30th was cloudy until late afternoon and no action between Camp 6 and 7 could be observed from Base Camp, after it had cleared the tent at Camp 6 was visible, but again no fire signal that night. On the 31st the cloud veil again prevented the party at Base Camp from observing the actions above, only occasionally the tent at Camp 6 could be seen. Again no fire signal was given from above. On the 1st of August the weather improved and the route between Camp 6 and Camp 7 was visible, but nobody was climbing between the two Camps and there were no fire signals that evening. The tent at Camp 6 was still standing. On the morning of August 2 a person was observed moving along the tent at Camp 6 and fresh tracks could be seen on the snow slope between Camp 5 and 6, but the tent at Camp 6 was still pitched. After one P.M., Tsering arrived at Base Camp, having been the person observed early in the day at Camp 6. He reported: Passang Kiluli and Tsering had reached Camp 6 on July 28th. The following day, Passang Kiluli had continued to Camp 7 with Phinsoo and Passang Kitar. They had found Wolfe in a sad condition. He apparently had not eaten for several days [and all the food in his tent was spoiled.] (nor had he even been out of the tent. All the food was spoiled.) He also complained that he had no more matches to light the stove. The Sherpas insisted on taking him down but, as he staggered when he was taken out of the tent and requested to be left at Camp 7 for another day before descending with them, the Sherpas let him remain there. They cleaned his tent, prepared tea and descended to Camp 6, for they had not brought any equipment or food for the night.

The next day, July 30th, the weather was stormy and the Sherpas had to remain, by necessity, at Camp 6. On July 31st, although the weather showed little improvement, they had left early for Camp 7 and had instructed Tsering to have tea and food ready in the afternoon for they would return in any event. If, contrary to their expectations, they should not be able to persuade Wolfe to descend with them, they would carry him down by force, and if they should also fail in that they would demand a note from Wolfe confirming that they had done everything within their powers to aid him. [Tsering] (They) waited, in vain, for them at Camp 6 that night and the following day August 1st. On the morning of August 2nd, he had decided to return to the Base Camp as he was convinced that an accident must have occurred. He reasoned that it would have been impossible for the 3 Sherpas to have spent two nights at Camp 7 without sleeping bags and food. Besides Passang Kikuli had assured him that he would return without fail on July 31st. In case that Wolfe could not have been moved that day and would have needed the attendance of another person, one of the Sherpas could have stayed with him while the other 2 could have gone to Camp 6 and return with sleeping bags and food.

After Tsering's report it was decided that Wiessner, Dawa and Tsering (in spite of the fact that the first two were suffering from acute sore throat and Wiessner also from frost bite) would leave the next day as a rescue party if, in the meantime, no action was observed at Camp 6. Durrance was in no condition to go back on the mountain and Pasang Lama was still completely unfit, and they had to remain at Base Camp. Dawa and Tsering were sent ahead early in the morning to search the glacier below Camp 7 for any signs of accident, while Durrance and Wiessner observed the route for [any] signs of the four men above. Later in the day, Wiessner joined the two Sherpas and they continued to Camp I. The weather was perfect on that day. A list of signals was prearranged between Wiessner and Durrance so that the former could be informed as to any movements above observed by (Dawa) [Durrance] from the Base Camp. The next day the rescue party reached Camp 2 in good weather, they could not continue to Camp 4 on that day due to their poor condition, and the loads they had to carry. There were no fire signals given at Base Camp on that day or the previous evening. As Camp 2 and Camp 6 were within hearing distance and no replies came to Tsering's frequent and loud calls, the rescue party felt the greatest anxiety. The next morning the party woke up finding a snow storm in progress, it was impossible to continue in such conditions. It cleared at Camp 2 in the afternoon but the heavy storm was raging above Camp 3. The following night, of August 5, it snowed and stormed heavily, more than a foot of new snow had fallen during the past 2 nights. The storm continued on August 6 until afternoon at Camp 2, but, as on the preceding day, it still snowed and stormed above. The temperature had fallen considerably during these days and with alarm it was observed that the afternoon sun did not melt the new snow as it had done earlier in the season and winter had set in above 19,000 feet altitude. During these days, the route above Camp 3 had been continuously under clouds. More snow fell during the night of August 6th and low temperature continued so that it became absolutely impossible for the rescue party to go [any] higher. At this point, the hope for any life above was given up and the safety of the remainder of the rescue party demanded their retreat. 1 1/2 feet of snow were then lying on the rocks at Camp 2. They left Camp 2 at noon of August 7 and arrived that evening at Base Camp, having weathered the heavy snow storm on their descent.

On August 8th the party with Durrance searched again the glacier but with no result. The weather was still cold and stormy. During the last 3 days it had snowed as far down as the Base Camp. Considering that the four missing men on August 9 had been above Camp 6 without food and camping equipments for 10 days, of which the last 5 days had brought most severe storms, any hope for their lives or the recovery of their bodies this season had to be given up. The group at Base Camp were running dangerously low on provisions and fuel, was forced to leave and could not await the arrival of the Askole coolies due at Base Camp on August 11. They departed on August 9, leaving part of their loads at Base Camp, which were called for on August 11 by the Askole coolies.

Durrance(,) [and] Wiessner (and the porters Dawa, Pasang Lama and Phinsoo) arrived at Shigar on August 18th.

Cranmer, Cromwell, Sheldon and Trench joined forces in Askole and continued together at Shigar, arriving at Shigar on August 4, this party continued towards Srinagar on August 6th.

F. H. Wiessner. [Signature]

G. The Wilson Analysis

SIR ROGER COCHRANE WILSON (1882–1966) was a 1901 Sandhurst graduate who joined the Indian Army in 1904 and thereafter spent most of his life on the subcontinent. He served in Mesopotamia in World War I and then on India's troublesome northwest frontier until becoming adjutant general of India in 1937. As an alpinist he was active in the Alps, joining the Alpine Club in 1927 after two years of explorations among the Himalayan peaks and glaciers; he was president of the Himalayan Club in 1939 and, following his retirement at the close of World War II, became president of the Mountain Club of South Africa.

Writing on the letterhead of the Himalayan Club, under the date of September 26, 1939, Wilson addressed the following statement to Consul Groth, who noted that Wilson was "setting forth what appear to him to have been the causes of the K-2 disaster, and I am enclosing copy of that report for the Department's perusal and so that its files on the subject may be complete." (This letter, or a copy thereof, was attached as an enclosure to Calcutta Despatch 1240 of September 30, 1939, to the Secretary of State in Washington, D.C.)

> *1. I have read the Report of the American Alpine Club second Karakoram Expedition, and the Summary by Mr. E. M. Groth of his conversation with two of the members of the Expedition. I have not seen the letters of others nor have I met any of the members of the Expedition which was mainly remarkable for the antagonism which developed between the members. Squabbles within parties are not unknown, indeed they are incidental to a prolonged stay at high altitudes, but nothing like this one in intensity has ever come to notice. It divided the expedition into two hostile factions and even endured after the tragedy, for which, incidentally, it was mainly responsible.*

> *2. To this feud must be ascribed the lack of organization among the climbers, the absence of support to those at the high camps, and the fact that porters were so often alone on the mountain. The unfortunate clearing of equipment from the intermediate camps and the departure of four members of the expedition from the Base at a critical moment, were due to the same cause.*

3. On July 23rd Wolfe was left alone at Camp 7; he was suffering from the effects of altitude and the longer he stayed the worse he was going to get. It is not certain what food he had but the intention was to rejoin him next day from Camp 6. When the retiring party found Camp 6 evacuated, this policy became impossible and Wolfe's best chance of getting down, was for somebody to have gone back and spent the night with him and to have brought him down next day.

4. On July 29th when the three Sherpas returned to Camp 7, they found Wolfe very weak, but had a climber been with them to compel him to come down, he might still have been saved.

5. It is still uncertain how Wolfe and the three Sherpas died. If they fell near Camp 6 on July 31st it would probably have been heard or seen by Tsering at Camp 6, and it is unlikely that all three died of exposure; the most likely theory is that the party fell whilst helping Wolfe down.

6. The conduct of the Sherpas was magnificent.

[Signature]

H. The Phantom Letter

THE STORY OF THE NOTE that has so often been used to exonerate Fritz Wiessner and blame Jack Durrance for the 1939 K2 expedition's failure is both intriguing and mysterious. It is, from the outset, significant that Fritz never mentions it anywhere in his notations at the time of the expedition nor in his report to the American Alpine Club. Nor is there any evidence he discussed the note until he referred to it in his book *K2–Victory and Tragedy on the Second-Highest Mountain on Earth.*[1] The German-language edition of this book was published in Munich in 1955, sixteen years after the expedition. Jack Durrance, the alleged author of the note, has no recollection that he ever wrote it, and no one, except Fritz, has ever admitted to having seen it. But the note merits attention because of the role it has played in what may well have been an ex post facto reconstruction of history.

Fritz has provided two written versions of the incident, the first in the aforementioned book and the second in an article that appeared in the June 1956 issue of *Appalachia,* the official publication of the Appalachian Mountain Club. Since both versions are identical in substance, cited here is only the one from *Appalachia:*

> *. . . After my recovery in a New York hospital I came upon a slip of paper that enlightened me. This had been left by Durrance for Wolfe and me in Camp 2 on July 19. I had at that time put it in my expedition papers, but in my then condition not paid any attention to it. He began by congratulating us on having attained the summit. He then went on to write that on the day before (July 18) he had had all the sleeping bags carried down from camp 4 by Kikuli and Dawa and that they all would now descend with these bags and those from camp 2, thirteen in all, to base camp. Thus, he said, there were no longer any sleeping bags on the mountain from Camp 4 on down; he was expecting us to bring bags with us from higher up.*[2]

Years later, Fritz alleged that he had turned the note over to a member (specifically named by him to one of the authors) of the American Alpine Club's committee of inquiry, along with other expedition records. Eventually he got everything back–except the note. It had vanished, he said. And, when asked, no one on the committee of inquiry or in the American Alpine Club ever recalled having seen it. Fritz said he never made a copy. Years later, the best he could do was to produce a paraphrase based on his recollection and on the chart of expedition-member movements (see Appendix C).

Thus the story of the note, which, if true, supported Fritz's case against Jack, seems at best based on the flimsiest of evidence and depends entirely on whether Fritz's unsupported story is to be believed. There was no one else who could ever corroborate his testimony. Yet at least four respected commentators on the 1939 expedition have, without any expressed misgivings, cited the story in order to discredit a member of the expedition who, we now know, never issued the instructions that resulted in removal of the sleeping bags.

On serious examination there seem to be only three possibilities: (1) that Jack did indeed write the letter and that it was then lost or destroyed, as Fritz charged, when in the hands of the American Alpine Club's committee of inquiry; (2) that Fritz, unable over the years to provide written evidence that might shift responsibility onto shoulders other than his own, decided to fabricate the story; (3) that Fritz somehow confused Tony Cromwell's handwriting for Jack Durrance's and picked up, as addressed to him and Dudley Wolfe, the note Tony had sent up by Dawa to Jack on July 17 that directed removal of the sleeping bags.

The above possibilities are all conjectural, but they must be examined.

Regarding the first possibility, Jack Durrance has steadfastly maintained that he never wrote the note, or, if he did, has no recollection of having done so. It is, of course, possible he did; he was still a very sick man at Camp II when he reached it on July 14, and lapses of memory are not uncommon for people who have suffered symptoms of HAPE or HACE. But neither the content nor the handwriting of Jack's diary shows any sign of mental impairment in the period of July 15 through 19, although he admitted to little recollection of July 14, when he descended from Camp VI. Throughout the period his handwriting remains pretty much the same, and in general his observations are those of a man in full control of his senses. But, assuming he wrote a note, whether he remembered it or not, why did he not send it up with Dawa and Kikuli on July 18 to Camp IV? There, as he knew, it would have served an informative and cautionary purpose for a descending party. Left at Camp II, the note merely iterated in words what was already self-evident on the premises had it not become clear elsewhere en route. At Camp II the note served no purpose; why even write it?

Fritz's paraphrase of the alleged letter had to have been made long after the events of 1939–1940, when it was either in his possession (assuming it existed) or in what he considered to be the safe hands of the American Alpine Club. Only in 1955 does the story first pop up. So the paraphrase must have been made a long time after Fritz had last laid eyes on the original. The paraphrase therefore depended entirely on Fritz's memory and to a bit of refreshing thereof through consultation of the personnel movement charts. That paraphrase, whether the one published in Fritz's book or the *Appalachia* article, seems strangely out of character for anything authored by Jack. As a complete reading of his diary indicates, Jack was a meticulous and careful thinker who always wanted to be sure of his facts before conferring either praise or criticism. Why then would he congratulate Fritz and Dudley for a successful ascent when he had no evidence of what had happened above except that Camp VIII had been established on July 14, still 3000 feet (nearly 1000 meters) short of the top? More to the point, why include Dudley as a summiter when, as everyone knew, Jack considered Dudley not only inept, but a menace to the other participants? The congratulations sound more like Tony Cromwell, who, while he considered Dudley a poor climber, later described him in his *American Alpine Journal* obituary as at least physically the strongest man on the expedition.[3]

It has been observed that nobody except Fritz ever reported having seen the note or a facsimile. Yet the members of the committee of inquiry – Walter Wood, Joel Ellis Fisher, Bill House, Terris Moore, and Bestor Robinson – were all responsible individuals, with nothing to gain from any chicanery regarding the note. It is entirely possible that one of them picked up a dirty sheet of paper, considered it unimportant, and tossed it in the trash. But it is almost unthinkable that the men who composed the committee should have deliberately destroyed or suppressed important evidence as Fritz pointedly intimated to one of the authors.

As for the possibility that Fritz deliberately invented the story, this also seems unlikely. When in pursuit of an objective Fritz could bend the truth here and there, but he was not known to invent lies. Surely he wanted to clear his name, and men are known to do strange things for honor. But the scheme he would have had to create so long after the event was far too crude for as clever a mind as Fritz's. Besides, the story of the note served only to confirm long-established facts and perhaps embellish them. For, as Fritz's writings reveal, he was well aware of what had happened at Camp II. Pasang Kikuli, with Chandra as interpreter, told him about Jack's instructions at Camp II, though of course he might have been unaware that Jack was acting under Tony's orders. "Pasang tells me," Fritz wrote in his diary on July 26, "that he should never have been taken away from 6 by Doctor Sahib [Durrance] . . . At Camp 2 Doctor Sahib told him to go to 4 with Dawa and bring loads down. The next day Doctor Sahib wanted him to go with him to Base Camp."

So Fritz knew all along that Jack played a role in the removal of the sleeping bags from Camp IV down. What he didn't know and never learned was *why* Jack acted as he did. But since he had Kikuli's word, why should he fabricate a story and risk getting caught in a lie? If there was to be any lie at all, why not emulate Dr. Frederick Cook and claim conquest of the mountain?

Fritz may at times have wandered a bit from reality in his personal versions of the truth, but he was not a fabricator. Therefore, he would appear to have seen something that he either misunderstood or failed to study with care. This leads to the third possibility–that, indeed, there existed a note, but that Jack was not its author.

Regarding this third possibility, remember that "Dawa danced up" (to use Jack's phrase) to Camp II on the afternoon of July 17 with two notes, one from Chap Cranmer and the other–the important one–from Tony Cromwell. Chap's note, probably consisting of words of farewell from a college chum, may be disregarded. Not so Tony's, the deputy leader. This Jack must have had in front of him when he took out "pencil and paper to figure out loads and weights...," as he noted in his diary on July 18, to carry out Tony's orders, something Jack was by no means sure he could accomplish with his limited manpower. Tony's note could then easily have fallen to the floor after use, where it picked up dirt to look like trash. This could be an added reason why the exhausted Fritz, discovering it on July 23, should have considered it unimportant at the time. Later Fritz erroneously believed the note had been written for him by Jack. On expeditions, chits frequently consist of a folded sheet of paper with a message on the inside and the addressee's name on the outside, often without salutation or signature, the identities of sender and recipient being obvious.

Something like the following, for example, may have been written:

On the outside of the folded sheet, one word: Jack.

Inside, a message running more or less as Fritz much later paraphrased: "Congratulations to Fritz and Dudley on their success in climbing K2! Send Dawa and Kikuli to IV to bring down as many sleeping bags as they can carry as well as other valuable equipment; do the same at II before descending. This will leave no bags below VI, but the others have plenty and will bring down their own."

No salutation.

No signature.

No dates, which would have been entered into Fritz's paraphrase much later, following consultation of personnel movement chart.

Should something like the above have been the case, Fritz might easily have picked up Tony's note from the tent floor and stuck it away, as he said, as being of no consequence. In the hospital, where Fritz presumably discovered the letter and its importance, and where medication sometimes confuses patients, he could have mistaken Tony's handwriting for Jack's. He might also have mistaken the name "Jack" on the outside as referring to the sender rather than the recipient of the note. What took place thereafter in the American Alpine Club – the fate of a rumpled, dirty note with no salutation nor formal signature on the message – is anyone's guess, but almost anything could have happened to cause it to vanish.

That Jack wrote a note, or that Fritz fabricated a story, or, more likely, that a note existed, but that Tony was its author, was never crucial despite the efforts of various writers to make a mountain out of this molehill. But if, at one time, it may have had some significance, that significance vanished forever with the revelation that Tony Cromwell, not Jack Durrance, bore the responsibility for the stripping of the intermediate camps. Jack merely did what, as a subordinate, he was instructed to do.

In the final analysis of the events that took place on K2 in 1939, the matter of the note, therefore, merits little attention. American Consul Edward Miller Groth wisely indicated that the story of the 1939 expedition was of a very complicated nature. Far too many verifiable aspects of the adventure deserve serious attention for any analysis to be sidetracked by the tale of an ultimately inconsequential and ephemeral piece of paper.

NOTES

INTRODUCTION

1. Maraini, Fosco. *Karakoram: The Ascent of Gasherbrum IV* (London: Hutchinson, 1961), p. 160.

CHAPTER 1

1. The term "coolie," from the Hindu word *kuli,* means an unskilled laborer, carrier, or porter hired for subsistence wages. A better description of the Sherpas would have been "high-altitude porters," to distinguish them from load carriers. The word "coolie" is still in current use in South Asia, as it has been for many centuries.

2. *American Alpine Journal,* 1939, vol. 3, p. 372.

3. The easiest route on K2 is certainly more difficult than its Everest counterpart. On K2 the greatest dangers lie above 24,000 feet (7317 meters), whereas on Everest's South Col Route they are far lower, in the Khumbu Icefall. As a counterbalance, the last 800 feet on Everest are more exhausting than on K2.

4. In addition there was a high incidence of goiter and cretinism due to lack of iodine. Modern climbers tend to shrug off infectious diseases and reach for antibiotics, but in 1939 Alexander Fleming's discovery of penicillin as a germicide had yet to gain medical acceptance.

5. K1, the first summit in the survey, is Masherbrum, a remarkable 25,668-foot (7828 meter) peak on the Baltoro. Tony Cromwell, in his article "Spring Skiing in the Vale of Kashmir" (*Appalachia,* vol. 23, pp. 163–67), says Montgomerie's survey was made from the shoulder of Mount Haramukh, near the vale. The distance is more than 200 miles (322 kilometers), at the limit for the tools at Montgomerie's disposal.

6. The duke's expedition to Mount St. Elias took place in 1897. A second expedition achieved a "farthest north" in 1900, while his trip to Ruwenzori's Mountains of the Moon was carried out in 1906.

7. De Filippi was party to several books on the area: *Karakoram and the Western Himalaya* (1912), a narrative of the duke's trip; the report of the Survey of India detachment with the 1914 De Filippi Scientific Expedition; *Himalaya-Caracorum* (1923); and *An Account of Tibet,* on the travels of Ippolito Desideri, SJ, of Pistoia, in the years 1712 to 1727.

8. There were three separate expeditions to Everest in the 1920s. In 1921, the visit was clearly labeled a reconnaissance; in 1922, some members of the party reached a height of almost 27,000 feet (8230 meters); and 1924 is the year in which George Leigh Mallory and Andrew Irvine disappeared while on a bid for the summit. There are many volumes on this subject.

9. In 1929 and 1931 Bavarian parties under Paul Bauer attempted the mountain by its difficult and dangerous Northeast Spur. The second of these expeditions, after the loss of two lives, reached 26,000 feet (7924 meters), only to be turned back by dangerous avalanche conditions. In 1930, an international expedition under Professor G. O. Dyhrenfurth attempted the mountain from the north and northeast, only to be turned back by a similar threat.

10. In the 1930s, Nanga Parbat was the scene of unparalleled catastrophes. In 1934, three climbers—Willi Merkl, Willi Weltzenbach, and Uli Wieland—together with six Sherpas, perished in a storm; Alfred Drexel had earlier succumbed to "edema of the lungs," an early diagnosis of what is now called high-altitude pulmonary edema (HAPE). In 1937, an entire climbing party of sixteen was wiped out in one disastrous avalanche.

11. Hettie Dyhrenfurth, the only woman on the expedition, set an altitude record for women even though she only climbed Sia Kangri's lower West Peak.

12. The main summit of Sia Kangri was reached by Hans Ertl and Anders Höchst.

13. In this reconnaissance, which they almost transformed into an outright attempt on the summit, Hans Ertl and André Roch climbed to 20,300 feet (6190 meters) on the southeast rib, later known as the IHE Spur (for International Himalayan Expedition). The ground covered was not very difficult, but Roch, a specialist on the subject, judged the area subject to avalanche risk. It was by this line that Hidden Peak was first ascended in 1958 by an American party.

14. The French had originally planned to follow the route reconnoitered by Roch and Ertl two years previously, but they mistook the south ridge for that of the southeast. By the time their error was recognized, several camps had been established and it was too late to change. As for the monsoon, there is some question as to whether it reaches the Karakoram more than rarely; but the range is quite capable of fomenting its own weather problems.

15. One of the iciest mountains on Earth, Denali defied several attempts following its sighting by Europeans in the late nineteenth century. On one occasion, Belmore Brown reached a point barely 300 feet (100 meters) below the higher south summit. The first ascent was made in 1913 by Archdeacon Hudson Stuck. The imposter was Dr. Frederick Cook, who claimed to have climbed the mountain in two days but was soon exposed for his fraud.

16. In July 1958, this bay, on whose shores Washburn's parties had often camped in earlier years, was literally overwhelmed by a tidal wave, which, according to subsequent studies must have washed close to 1800 feet (548 meters) above sea level. The bay was uninhabited, but a number of fishing vessels present were lost with their crews.

17. A little-known facet of this venture is that, according to Terris Moore in conversation with Andrew Kauffman, the party set out at the enticement of a mysterious gentleman who promised to lead its members to "a mountain higher than Everest." Once the team was in China, the stranger disappeared with the expedition funds. Most members, then broke, had to head home. Emmons, Moore, Burdsall, and Young managed to cope despite great adversity.

18. Under British policy, large parts of India remained under the rule of local rajahs and nawabs on a protectorate basis, with the colonial government, in theory at least, responsible only for their security. A British "resident," usually a member of the famous Indian Civil Service (ICS), was always present to "advise." Kashmir was such a state, ruled by a Hindu maharajah despite the presence of a Moslem majority.

19. "Various Notes," *American Alpine Journal,* 1938, vol. 3, p. 225.

20. A valued member of the team, Streatfield later drowned during the evacuation from Dunkirk in June 1940.

21. The American Alpine Club had traditionally been blessed by a series of anonymous "angels." Among them, during these years, were Henry Hall, Jr., Joel Ellis Fisher, and Dr. William Ladd.

22. All altitude figures given in this text are those used by the various American expeditions to K2. Professor Ardito Desio uses slightly different altitudes; but the differences are minor, and the need for consistency mandates using the Americans' numbers.

23. Bates later observed in a conversation with Andrew Kauffman in 1990: "We spent four hours climbing the chimney because I first tried to lead a route on the snow, passing the chimney on the left. It proved too steep for climbing with loads and we returned to the chimney, where I belayed Bill. Much of the time was taken trying to find a belay stance. We never did find a good one. If Bill had fallen from near the top of the chimney, we certainly would have both gone down."

24. Burdsall, in addition to Houston, had also climbed in Asia, but he was at that moment down on the glacier doing cartography.

25. The decision to retreat conformed to the mountaineering philosophy of the era that safety considerations invariably prevail. Forty-eight years later, in the same place and season, the philosophy had changed, and, as a result, many lives were needlessly lost. Moreover, in 1938 the weather had shown signs of deterioration.

26. Petzoldt opted to remain in India, where he joined a cult that allegedly tried to detain him. In an altercation, he struck one of its leaders, who, as he fell, struck his head and died. Petzoldt was accused of murder. Through American government intervention and money from his friends, he was released but ordered never to return to India.

27. André Roch, the most notable Swiss alpinist of the first part of the twentieth century, and one of the world's greatest, had this to say about Houston's expedition on page 181 of his book *Karakoram Himalaya* (published, under the auspices of the Swiss Foundation for Alpine Research, by Victor Attinger, Paris, 1945): "This expedition was certainly one of the best run ventures of any that ever entered this region."

CHAPTER 2

1. Frank Smythe, *Over Tyrolese Hills* (London: Hodder, Stoughton, 1936), p. 234.

2. Wiessner's cousin Otto was killed in an unroped fall from one of the Saxon Swiss pinnacles in 1924. Fritz's safety consciousness must be described as tactical rather than strategic. He was meticulous in his observance of safe climbing techniques during the hours and minutes of each climbing day;

but it was difficult for him to contemplate changes in an overall plan, especially when the evidence suggested a need for major modifications, including possible abandonment of a project. Nor did he care to listen to the advice of his companions and lieutenants and too often failed to communicate his own plans to them.

3. Fleischbank, Totenkirchl, and Predigstuhl are among the many summits of the Kaisers. The routes cited here were, in their day, among the hardest in the area and pioneered by the best climbers of the era.

4. We do not know precisely when Wiessner became an American citizen. He indicated it as stated herein, but Edward M. Groth, American Consul in Calcutta, wrote in a despatch of late-summer 1939 that he had been an American citizen for "a few months." The discrepancy is of no consequence.

5. Nanga Parbat, the most solitary of the Himalayan summits, is also the highest peak on Earth from its base at about 3000 feet (914 meters) to its summit 16 miles away and 23,500 feet (7163 meters) higher. It is also known as the deadliest.

6. Wiessner did make the critical move, however, in what has become the standard route on this spectacular peak. A year later, the Wiessner Traverse was used by Raffi Bedayn and Jack Arnold to gain access to the five-acre snowpatch and thence to the summit.

7. Mount Robson, highest of the Canadian Rockies, is also one of the most elusive of ascent. Its altitude of 12,972 feet (3954 meters) is but 150 feet (46 meters) less than that of Mount Waddington in the Coast Range. Several early attempts on it had failed. In 1913 it was first ascended by a party of three, led by the Austrian-born guide Conrad Kain, but in order to descend, the party had to traverse the mountain. Until recent years it was not often climbed, and because of summit rime conditions, in some years it cannot be climbed at all.

8. From page 19 of the unpublished English-language translation of Fritz Wiessner's book *K2 – Victory and Tragedy on the Second-Highest Mountain on Earth,* published in German by Rudolf Rother, Munich, 1955.

CHAPTER 3

1. Eaton O. Cromwell, "Obituaries, Dudley Francis Wolfe," *American Alpine Journal,* 1940, vol. 4, p. 123.

2. Significantly, Wiessner had also planned on making that ascent.

3. See Jim Curran's excellent book *K2, Triumph and Tragedy* (Seattle: The Mountaineers, 1987).

CHAPTER 4

1. All research sources are listed in Appendix D.

2. Durrance diary, under the date of January 1, 1939, but actually written on April 16 in Srinagar.

3. Durrance diary, under the date of January 6, but written later in Srinagar.

4. American Alpine Club, "Committee of Inquiry Report on the 1939 American Alpine Club Karakoram Expedition."

5. The Sherpa bags were made by Ome Daiber; but most of those for the sahibs were made by Woods, and some were obtained in Europe.

6. Later that summer, Ogi's cousin, Hermann Ogi, widely regarded as a top climber, began field-testing Vitale Bramani's experimental cleated rubber soles. Herman climbed extensively in the Swiss Alps with H. A. Carter, who later brought the idea to the materiel needs of the U.S. Army's mountain troops.

7. "General Impressions of My Atlantic Journey," written in the front part of the Durrance diary under the dates of January 20–22, 1939.

8. Ibid., under January 22, 1939, but written in Srinagar on April 16.

9. This letter was datelined Srinagar, April 24, but was obviously written by Wiessner while on a ski outing at Killmarg, outside the city.

10. Among Dudley Wolfe's effects, later listed by the American Consulate in Karachi, was an unmailed letter from Wolfe to Mrs. Dunn.

11. Wiessner's close association with Schacht did not go unnoticed. On the expedition's return and after war had started, a number of Britishers in India suspected Wiessner of being a German agent despite his American citizenship.

12. Sheldon also commented on a resemblance to the diligence then popularly associated with America's Works Progress Administration.

CHAPTER 5

1. Elizabeth Knowlton, *The Naked Mountain* (New York: G. P. Putnam Sons, 1934), p. 34.

2. Sometimes appelled Killenmarg.

3. Some of Houston's subsequent bitterness toward Wiessner understandably stemmed from personal feelings of loyalty to his friend Pasang Kikuli.

4. This was a missionary school for South Asian students. No attempt was made to proselytize, but rather to provide a sound education with English as the key language. This is outlined in Fritz Wiessner's letter of May 8, 1939, to Joel Ellis Fisher from Kargil.

CHAPTER 6

1. Marco Polo passed almost the entire year of 1273 in this vicinity.

2. A minor coin equivalent to one-sixteenth of a rupee. Its purchasing power was then roughly equivalent to one U.S. cent.

3. These films came out well and may still be viewed.

4. A more credible legend is that the barge had been built by a deceased local rajah, who held the equivalent name to Alexander – in Balti.

5. Wolfe's account indicated 29 goat skins.

6. These were written in the diary pages starting with the "Memo" before November 1 and continuing through November 29. Included are medical notations of the expedition up to August 9, 1939.

CHAPTER 7

1. This was Bride Peak to the Duke of the Abruzzi.

2. From the authors' conversations with Wiessner; also a note on page 22 of the unpublished English-language translation of Wiessner's book *K2 – Victory and Tragedy on the Second-Highest Mountain on Earth.*

3. This event is well documented by Dudley Wolfe's moving pictures.

4. This name was borrowed from a place with a similar configuration located south of the Jungfrau on the much smaller Aletsch Glacier of the Bernese Oberland.

5. This quotation is from Wiessner's original diary—not the typescript—and was supplied by his son, Andrew Wiessner.

CHAPTER 8

1. Though the article, "Lost Behind the Ranges," appeared in two segments, this citation is from the first, published in the *Saturday Evening Post* on March 16, 1940.

2. A still famous sporting-goods firm in Munich.

3. The Sherpas who performed these feats anticipated the modern techniques of alpine-style climbing in the Himalaya.

4. From a taped interview with William Putnam.

5. Quoted on page 23 of the unpublished English-language translation of Wiessner's book *K2—Victory and Tragedy on the Second-Highest Mountain on Earth.*

CHAPTER 9

1. The Sherpas are a generally friendly people, always willing to laugh, and very easily, at themselves. But the other side of this coin is often a never-ending casualness about business affairs and important duties.

2. Sheldon's article in the *Saturday Evening Post* describes this event with graphic poignancy.

3. In fact, however, Durrance spent much time in Rome before his return to the United States.

4. Durrance's spelling of Tony's nickname.

5. A photocopy of this note, containing latter-day commentary thereon by Wiessner, was given to the authors by Wiessner. The text is clearly in Durrance's handwriting.

6. One of the authors had considerable experience with two-way radios during World War II, after the pressure of military urgency had spurred their development. They were still cumbersome and heavy. Solid-state technology was yet another generation away.

7. Cromwell may have broken some ribs in this fall. If so, the resulting pain and inconvenience could help to explain some of his subsequent reluctance to go higher than Camp IV—but not his failure to exercise his responsibilities as deputy leader.

CHAPTER 10

1. From page 26 of the unpublished English-language translation of Wiessner's book *K2—Victory and Tragedy on the Second-Highest Mountain on Earth.*

2. From a conversation between Robert H. Bates and Andrew Kauffman.

3. According to Robert H. Bates of the 1938 expedition, it was more likely only a few dozen feet.

4. Excerpted from original Wiessner diary in a written comment by Andrew Wiessner to William Putnam.

5. Though Durrance does not so indicate, he took Kikuli with him because the Sherpa sirdar needed to recover from his frostbite.

CHAPTER 11

1. The reasons for Durrance's silence, which are in no way mysterious, are discussed at the end of Chapter 15.

2. This passage may be more fully understood following a reading of Appendix B.

3. Durrance diary, "Medical Notes," entered on pages dated November 19 through November 25.

4. All sources agree that this information was supplied to expedition members by the Sherpas involved, but some days later, when events had deteriorated even more.

CHAPTER 12

1. This part of the narrative is based on statements made by the Sherpas involved and, while probably accurate, cannot be otherwise verified.

2. Hornbein, Townes, Schoene, Sutton, and Houston, "The Cost to the Central Nervous System of Climbing to Extremely High Altitude," *New England Journal of Medicine,* vol. 321, no. 25 (December 21, 1989), pp. 1714ff.

3. This passage and subsequent quotations are from the typed copy of Wiessner's diary. The only source for all information about what happened high on the mountain between July 14 and July 22 is Wiessner, either from his diary, his other writings, or personal conversations years later. While his opinions may be questioned, there is no reason to challenge his statements of fact.

4. The late start is hard to understand. Most summit parties get going early to take advantage of all possible daylight. Wiessner may have wanted the sun to warm the ice-covered rocks, but he never said so. In any case, this delay contributed to the failure to reach the summit.

5. In his book *K2–Victory and Tragedy on the Second-Highest Mountain on Earth,* Wiessner says 8 meters [25 feet]; in his and Chappell Cranmer's article in the 1940 *American Alpine Journal* he says 50 feet. No one will ever know which figure, if either, is correct. If not affected by altitude, Wiessner was certainly sufficiently weary to have misjudged distances.

6. Night climbing on 8000-meter peaks had not been done before; but it has become quite common in more recent years, particularly among Americans attempting K2.

7. While Fritz says in this diary entry that he and Pasang Lama were not exhausted, there is no doubt that by this time both were very tired.

8. The crampons, a hindrance on rock, were almost essential on ice slopes, unless one resorted to the laborious job of cutting steps.

9. This was a vastly more sensible departure hour for a summit bid than when they had left the same camp two days earlier.

10. A climber generally feels more comfortable when facing into the slope on the descent, but his or her movements are much slower.

11. These allegations came from persons–notably Kenneth Mason, Charlie Houston, and others–who had no on-the-spot knowledge of the situation.

12. On pages 38 and 39 of the unpublished English-language translation of *K2–Victory and Tragedy on the Second-Highest Mountain on Earth,* Wiessner writes: "Then began the night...three men at a height of over 7,400 meters, *without air mattresses* [authors' emphasis], with only Pasang Lama's sleeping bag..." Sixteen years earlier, in his diary typescript for July 22, 1939, Wiessner had written of this night at Camp VII: "It was miserable and cold–three men crowding *on air mattress* [authors' emphasis] partly covered by a narrow sleeping bag awaiting the morning." This is one of many inconsistencies and apparent memory lapses that may be found in the different versions, written and oral, of Wiessner's account of the 1939 expedition. As the years passed, and as happens to all of us, the number of inconsistencies grew, so that taped conversations with Wiessner when he was in his early eighties are often in conflict with the written records of 1939.

13. Consul Groth (see Appendix E) suggested that "although Wiessner was firm enough in the issuance of instructions, when the supreme test came, he faltered" because Wolfe held some financial club over Wiessner's head, and he yielded to the latter's request to stay high.

14. This was not the first time Fritz had left Dudley alone, but on the other occasions there had been no sign of trouble elsewhere on the mountain.

CHAPTER 13

1. This diary excerpt and all subsequent Wiessner diary excerpts in this chapter are from the diary typescript submitted to the authors.

2. From page 45 of the unpublished English-language translation of Wiessner's book *K2–Victory and Tragedy on the Second-Highest Mountain on Earth.*

3. A severe sore throat frequently develops after prolonged exposure to high altitude and often lingers on even after descent.

4. This is the version given on page six of Wiessner's official expedition report to the American Alpine Club. Other versions have it that Kitar and Phinsoo were picked up in Camp IV by Kikuli and that the four continued together to Camp VI. Whatever the truth, the only source was Tsering (Norbu), the one survivor of the team, who may very well have garbled his report.

CHAPTER 14

1. Wiessner's final report is given in full as Appendix F. It seems factual and objective, with nothing in it that should have disturbed Cromwell.

2. Hinted at, but not specified by Groth, was Cromwell's absurd allegation that Wiessner had murdered Wolfe.

3. Everyone knew that war had become inevitable as a result of the Hitler/Stalin Pact of August 23, 1939. Hitler invaded Poland nine days later, and Great Britain and France declared war on Germany on September 3.

4. In any case, Cromwell's letter has never surfaced from any files, those of the American Alpine Club, Wiessner, or Durrance.

5. Wiessner's report, as reproduced in this book, came not from the files of the American Alpine Club, but from the National Archives in association with Consul Edward Miller Groth's despatches.

6. Cromwell had publicly and repeatedly accused Wiessner of murdering Wolfe – a preposterous charge. This accusation, because of its seriousness, made mandatory an official AAC investigation. Without Cromwell's charges, it is likely the 1939 K2 controversy would never have assumed large-scale proportions.

7. The most vocal and influential among Wiessner's supporters were the distinguished couple Robert and Miriam Underhill, the greatest husband-and-wife team on the American mountaineering scene.

CHAPTER 15

1. See Appendix E for the complete text.

2. Durrance diary, "Medical Notes," under the date of November 24, 1939, to which he could have added another word – money.

3. Louis Audoubert, *Baltoro, Montagnes de Lumière* (Paris: Arthaud, 1983), p. 100.

4. Durrance diary, under the date of October 28, but clearly written as of July 13 or thereabouts.

5. See Appendix E for the complete text.

APPENDIX B

1. This is yet another reason why many people have resorted to alpine-style climbing when at extreme altitude – to reduce the time of exposure to serious risk.

2. For more complete studies of high-altitude physiology and illnesses, see Cerretelli, Rivalier, Flory, and Segantini, editors, *High Altitude Deterioration* (Zurich: UIAA, 1985); John B. West and Sukhamay Lahiri, *High Altitude and Man* (Bethesda, Md.: American Physiological Society, 1984); and Charles Houston, *Going Higher* (Boston: Little, Brown and Company, 1987).

3. Charles Clarke, "High Altitude Cerebral Edema," in *High Altitude Deterioration.*

4. James A. Wilkerson, "The Namche Hill – High Altitude Cerebral Edema in Nepal," *Appalachia,* vol. 46, no. 2 (1986–1987), pp. 83–85.

5. Jean Coudert, "High Altitude Pulmonary Edema," in *High Altitude Deterioration.*

6. It is about 27 percent. Most of the fatalities occur in persons under thirty-five years of age.

7. Charles Houston, "Operation Everest," *American Alpine Journal,* 1947, pp. 311–15. See also West and Lahiri, *High Altitude and Man.*

8. Joseph Barcroft, *The Respiratory Function of the Blood, Part I: Lessons from High Altitude* (Cambridge: Cambridge University Press, 1925).

9. In fact, in 1922 Finch's apparatus was defective, and we don't know how well it worked for Mallory and Irvine in 1924.

10. Diamox is a carbonic anhydrase inhibitor, helps prevent acute mountain sickness (AMS), and may prevent development of HAPE and HACE. A few rare individuals develop side effects and must not take the drug.

APPENDIX H

1. The note is discussed on page 43 of the typewritten English-language translation of the book supplied to the authors.

2. Fritz Wiessner, "The K2 Expedition of 1939," *Appalachia,* vol. 31 (June 1956), pp. 70–71. The editors of *Appalachia,* at that time the leading mountaineering journal of North America, were the distinguished couple Robert and Miriam Underhill, friends and climbing companions of Wiessner.

3. Eaton O. Cromwell, "Obituaries, Dudley Francis Wolfe," *American Alpine Journal,* 1940, vol. 1., no. 4, p. 123.

INDEX

About the Authors

Andrew J. Kauffman was a member of the Harvard team that made the first ascent from the south (and second ascent of the peak) of Alaska's Mount St. Elias in 1946. He was one of two Americans who made the first ascent of 26,470-foot Hidden Peak in the Karakoram Himalaya. Mr. Kauffman worked for the United States Department of State and the Foreign Service for many years. Co-author with William L. Putnam of *The Guiding Spirit,* and author and editor of many articles and books on mountaineering, he is a former director and vice president of the American Alpine Club. He lives in Washington, D.C.

William L. Putnam has climbed extensively in North America and has made over 70 first ascents (most of them in Canada). A past president of the American Alpine Club, he is an honorary member of the Alpine Club of Canada, the Appalachian Mountain Club, and the Association of Canadian Mountain Guides. Mr. Putnam is the author of several books, among them *Great Glacier and Its House, The Guiding Spirit, Place Names of the Canadian Alps,* and *The Worst Weather on Earth.* He resides in Springfield, Massachusetts.

BALTORO GLACIER
AREA